For Cardinals Fans Only

By Rich Wolfe

Printed in the United States

Published by Lone Wolfe Press

ISBN: 0-9729249-4-9

Cover Photo presented and photographed by Don Marquess, Marquess Gallery, St. Louis, Missouri
Cover Design: The Flag of the Cardinal Nation conceived by Dick Fox based on a concept and photograph of Mr. Don Marquess
Photo Editor: Dick Fox
Cover Copywriter: Dick Fox
Some chapter photos from the Marquess Gallery in St. Louis.
Interior Design: The Printed Page, Phoenix, AZ

www.marquessgallery.com
www.baseballfineart.com

The author, Rich Wolfe, can be reached at 602-738-5889 or at www.fandemonium.net.

DEDICATION

To

Pat Solon and Dan Stamatelos,

*two good friends who graduated life with honors
and no regrets*

ACKNOWLEDGMENTS

What a blast it has been doing this book. Wonderful people helped make it a reality, starting with Ellen Brewer, my indispensable side-kick of many years, in Edmond, Oklahoma; ditto to Barbara Jane Bookman on Cape Cod, Barry Friedland for Lone Wolfe Press and the good guys at Wolfegang Marketing Systems, Ltd.—But Not Very, Linda Frech and Tina Wright in Columbia, Missouri; Curt Smith and the nice folks at AOL Time Warner and Garrett Mathews in Evansville, Indiana.

A big thanks to the wonderful Bobbi Chackelson and Charlie Meegan at Busch Stadium, Dave Barry at the Miami Herald, Dave Morris, the brain of Smithton, Illinois; Ron Parsons, Whitey Herzog's double in Hannibal; the beautiful Maureen Kelly Hoener in St. Charles and wonder woman Lisa Liddy at the Printed Page in Phoenix. How about Grady Jim Robinson, Andy Strasberg and don't forget David Craft and Tom Owens, great Cardinal fans revisited in Des Moines and Marshalltown.

The author would like to sincerely thank the following authors, sub-jects, and/or publishers for their kind permission to cite, reprint, or quote from their works: Don Marquess at the Marquess Gallery in St. Louis, Andrews-McMeel and Universal Syndicate Features in Kansas City, the University of Missouri Press, Dale Ratermann, *The Miami Herald*, Diamond Gem Publications, Bob Carpenter, Jerry Reuss, and, especially the prolific people at HCI down Florida way.

A tip of the hat to all those interviewed who missed the final cut. It was close and we'll do it again next year…but the biggest thank you, the deepest bow and the grandest salute to Marty Hendin, who went way above and beyond to try to make this a better book. He's the greatest Cardinal of them all—in my book.

PREFACE

There are three things you should know about Cubs announcer, Chip Caray. Firstly, he is nice, really a nice guy. Secondly, he is tall, very tall, 6'6" tall. Thirdly, he's a Cardinal fan, born and raised. In June, 1998, we were at Wrigley Field taking publicity pictures for a Harry Caray book. While standing next to Caray, I said, "Chip, I don't want to mislead you. I really don't like the Cubs. I'm a Cardinals fan. Your grandpa made me a Cardinals fan many years ago." Chip replied, "Don't tell anyone, but I'm a Cardinals fan too." "Didn't you grow up in Atlanta?" "No, my parents divorced. I grew up in St. Louis, went to Parkway West High School and loved the Cardinals. Don't tell anyone." I said, "I'm going to tell everyone I know." Obviously, he's a Cubs fan now, but he appreciated my bluntness.

For Cardinal Fans Only is part of an 81-book series that will be released in the next 15 months. From Green Bay to Austin, from Notre Dame to Boston, and 76 other places, loyal followers will trumpet their neatest stories about their favorite teams. As a lifelong Cardinal fan no other book in this anthology—with the possible exception of my alma mater—will mean as much to me as *For Cardinal Fans Only*.

One simple thing puts Cardinals fans above all others: Our female fans are more numerous, more knowledgeable, and more passionate than those of any other team. Only Red Sox and Kentucky Big Blue fans are in the same league. That's not to say that other teams don't have smart and fanatical distaff adherents, they just don't have as many.

My proudest moment as a Cardinal fan was not a World Series win or Jack Buck's September speech in 2001, but June of 2003, when Cardinals fans invaded Fenway Park and Yankee Stadium. It was like the scene in "Butch Cassidy," where Robert Redford kept saying, "Who are those guys?" Easterners who had innocently questioned the experts who anointed St. Louis as the best baseball city in America, got their answer when they gazed at the moving festival of a sea of Cardinal red.

For some of us, baseball recalls broken glass, broken bats and broken dreams of lingering reflections of a simpler, more innocent time.

For many of us, baseball defined our youth, still overly-impacts our adulthood and is one of the few things, that can make you feel young and old at the same time.

And for all of us, it is—most of all—a game of memories: the transistor under the pillow, sitting outside a small store feverishly opening newly purchased baseball cards, our first uniform, learning to keep score, the dew and mosquitoes, the sounds of the radio or our first big league game. Little did many of us know that baseball would be the best math and geography teacher we would ever have…and none of us knew the vibrant green of the field during our first major league game would be the lushest green, the greenest green and the most memorable green that we would ever see in our entire lifetime.

Now is a good time to answer a few questions that always arise. The most often asked is, "Why isn't your name on the book cover, like other authors?" The answer is simple: I'm not Stephen King. No one knows who I am, no one cares. My name on the cover will not sell an additional book. On the other hand, it allows for "cleaner" and more dramatic covers that the readers appreciate….and the books are more visible at the point of sale.

The second most frequent query is, "You sell tons of books. Why don't they show up on the best seller list?" Here's how the book business works: Of the next 170 completed manuscripts, 16 will eventually be published, and only one will ever return a profit. To make the *New York Times* Bestseller List, you need to sell about 30,000 copies nationally at certain stores, at big book chains, a few selected independent bookstores, etc. My last eight books have averaged well over 60,000 units sold, but less than 15,000 in bookstores. Most are sold regionally, another deterrent to national rankings. While I'm very grateful to have sold so many books to the "Big Boys," I'm a minority of one in feeling that a bookstore is the worst place to sell a book. Publishers cringe when they hear that statement. A large bookstore will stock over 150,000 different titles. That means the odds of someone buying my book are 150,000-1. Those aren't good odds; I'm not that good of a writer. For the most part, people that like Mike Ditka or Dale Earnhardt—previous book subjects of mine—don't hang around bookstores. I would rather be the only book at a hardware chain than in hundreds of bookstores.

Example: My *Remembering Dale Earnhardt* hardcover sold several hundred thousand copies, mostly at Walgreens and grocery chains; places not monitored for the "best selling" lists. I sold the paperback rights to Triumph Books, Chicago. They printed 97,000 paperbacks, all sold through traditional channels. The hardcover did not appear on any bestseller list. Triumph's paperback on Earnhardt made number one on the *New York Times* list. Go figure. Also, I never offer my books directly to Amazon.com because I can't type, I've never turned on a computer and I keep thinking that Amazon is going out of business soon. For years, the more customers they recruited, the more money they lost…so sooner or later, when the venture capital is gone, the bookkeeping shenanigans are recognized, and the stock plummets, look out. Meanwhile, maybe I should call them.

Since the age of ten, I've been a serious collector of sports books. During that time—for the sake of argument, let's call it 30 years—my favorite book style is the eavesdropping type where the subject talks in his or her own words—without the "then he said" or "the air was so thick you could cut it with a butter knife" waste of verbiage that makes it so hard to get to the meat of the matter. Books such as Lawrence Ritter's *Glory of Their Times* and Donald Honig's *Baseball When the Grass Was Real.* Thus, I adopted that style when I started compiling oral histories of the Jack Bucks and Harry Carays of the world. I'm a sports fan first and foremost—I don't even pretend to be an author. This book is designed solely for other sports fans. I really don't care what the publisher, editors or critics think. I'm only interested in Cardinals fans having an enjoyable read and getting their money's worth. Sometimes a person being interviewed will drift off the subject but if the feeling is that baseball fans would enjoy the digression, it stays in the book.

In an effort to get more material into the book, the editor decided to merge some paragraphs and omit some of the commas, which will allow for the reader to receive an additional 20,000 words, the equivalent of 50 pages. More bang for your buck…more fodder for English teachers…fewer dead trees.

As stated on the dust jacket, there have been hundreds of books written about the Cardinals but not a single one about Cardinals fans—until now. From one baseball fan to another, I sincerely wish that you enjoy this unique format.

Hopefully, the stories you are about to read will bring back wonderful memories of your youth and growing allegiance to the Cardinals. Wouldn't it be nice to have a do-over? It just seems that sometimes, as you get older, the things that you want most are the things that you once had. Right, Chip?

Go now.

> Rich Wolfe
> Falmouth, Massachusetts

Chat Rooms

Chapter One

Leading Off

A Cardinal Reader
for Cardinal Readers

STAN MUSIAL WAS JUST A REGULAR GUY WHO SOMETIMES WORE A CAPE

Patrick Thompson

Patrick Thompson lives with his wife, Geri, in Irvine, California. A graduate of Cal State-Northridge, he is a freelance speaker.

Many hot summers ago, when I was in elementary school in California, I fell in love with an idea, a game, a dream. I fell madly in love with baseball.

I soaked in baseball. I threw, hit, ran, read, felt baseball. I would throw without a ball, hit home runs in my head, be a hero, be a bum. I loved it all.

For a while, baseball was bigger than even my dad. I saw that he had a hero. How could my hero have a hero?

My dad's hero was Stan the Man, Stan Musial from Donora, Pennsylvania, who played for the Cardinals. At the time, St. Louis was the closest major-league team to Los Angeles. All major-league players were heroes in my eyes, but Dad told me that Stan was the greatest of his time.

There were others who could hit the ball harder, run faster, field better or even put on a better show than Stan the Man. But Dad said that Stan was special.

God had given Stan the tools and he used them well. But that was only a small portion of what made him great. He was all the things that my father valued. He was the embodiment of all that life stood for.

I wanted to be like Dad and I felt that Dad wanted to be like Stan Musial. I knew I couldn't go wrong trying to fit into those shoes.

This particular summer was special because my dad and I were going to the place where my father grew up—St. Louis. Just the two of us.

It was hot and humid in what seemed like a foreign land where the people were pale and talked slightly off English.

In California, everything was new. In St. Louis, everything was old. Only the people were young.

Our mission was to meet Stan the Man. I almost didn't believe it. There was a part of me that didn't really think that these idols were real people. To me, they only came to life as legend, like Paul Bunyan or Robin Hood. But the closer I came to the meeting, the more obvious it was that **MR. MUSIAL** was a real man. Newspapers said so, all my relatives said so, and most important, Dad reassured me.

Through some good fortune, I got a ball autographed by Musial. An injured rookie was at the hospital where my grandmother worked. She told him my story and he got Stan's autograph on the ball. The ball was living proof that Stan was for real.

That night the Cardinals were playing the **BROOKLYN DODGERS** and we went. I held onto my ball so tightly that I elicited an inquiry from the guy next to me.

"New ball?" he asked.
"Yep, with an autograph," I teased him.
"Who?" he prodded.
"The Man," I bragged.
"No."
"Yes."
"I don't believe you."
"Here," I handed him the ball.

> Stan Musial hit 19 home runs as a grandfather in 1962. When he retired in 1963, he had every Cardinal batting record but one—highest single-season average. That was set by Rogers Hornsby.

> In consecutive years—1950 and 1951—the Brooklyn Dodgers lost the pennant on home runs hit off their last pitch of the season.

"Wow! I'll give you $20 for it right now!" Twenty dollars to a ten-year-old boy in 1955 was a pot of gold.

"Nope, let me have it back," I demanded.

"You've got a dream in the form of a baseball," he said. "Take good care of it!"

I shoved it deep into my pocket and resolved that the ball was the most important thing in my life.

The next day was the big day. We would be meeting the Man. As Dad and I walked up the walk to the door, I was in a state of shock. "He'll be here," Dad said, knocking.

Sure enough, the door swung open, and there stood Stan the Man in his robe and slippers. My dad introduced himself, then me to Stan, and explained that the ball he had signed earlier was for me.

He was just as I had imagined him: sincere, kind, strong. He looked at me in a way that only a few adults look at kids, and we knew that we had a common bond—baseball.

He inquired about my baseball playing. I bragged. Next to Stan, I felt that it was necessary. I thought that I was some great baseball player. He understood.

Getting back to Los Angeles couldn't happen fast enough. When I told everyone about my experience in St. Louis with Stan Musial, nobody believed me. Such a reality didn't exist, my friends insisted. I knew that it had happened, though, and that the ball, the meeting, the feeling would always be mine. The older I became, the less I revealed my treasure.

The seasons paraded by. Teams won, players got traded. There were retirements, rookies, home runs, other kids and other idols. My father died. As in life, he wished to carry on in death. His last request was that in his casket there be a deck of cards, a bottle of Jack Daniels and, most important, a baseball. He knew that, wherever he was going, he ought not be ill equipped.

On the day he was buried, the whiskey and the cards were ready. The last item was a baseball. I decided it should be my twenty-year-old autographed treasure.

FOR CARDINALS FANS ONLY

Since my father had been responsible for me meeting Stan Musial, I felt it most appropriate that it should be with my dad. I would miss it, but it belonged with him. Some people thought that it was a sacrifice. I did my best to assure them that it was not. The ball was where it belonged.

Spring trainings, long hot Julys and thousands of extra innings later, my sister, Kathie, asked me to stand in for Dad at her wedding. I was flattered. I was honored to give my sister away, to stand in the shoes of my dad.

On the eve of my sister's big day, we went to an elegant French restaurant for the rehearsal dinner. As the evening went on, the impact of the occasion seemed to build to an emotional crescendo. The speeches were many. I became aware that something special was happening.

My sister is an airline stewardess and had flown with the Los Angeles Dodgers for part of the 1984 season. After dinner, she thanked my younger brother for his participation in her wedding by giving him a baseball autographed by all of the Dodgers and dedicated to him by Tommy Lasorda.

I was next for a gift.

She told all of us about flying with Lasorda, about how, on the way to spring training, she had told him the story of my Stan Musial baseball.

She said she'd had a difficult time completing the story, stopping again and again to recapture her composure. She said she had been amazed to learn that Tommy Lasorda knew exactly what she meant.

"I'll get that baseball back for you." he told her.

Later during the flight, Lasorda told my sister that he, too, had had a magical relationship with his father, and that when his father had been laid to rest, a baseball accompanied him.

Lasorda told my sister that his life in baseball, his success in baseball and his love of baseball, had all come from his father.

Being a friend of Stan Musial, Lasorda called and told him the story of the baseball. Musial responded with a new autographed baseball and sent it to Lasorda. The ball was then mailed to my sister.

I looked up to see her holding the ball. "I got you another one," she said, throwing it to me.

I was a child again, coming home. I heard the distant crack of bat on ball and the roar of a crowd. I heard that man sitting next to me in St. Louis in 1955. "New ball?" he asked.

"Yep, with an autograph," I teased him.
"Who?" he prodded.
"The Man," I bragged.
"No."
"Yes."

And then: "You've got a dream in the form of a baseball," he said. "Take good care of it!"

And so I did.
And so I will.

Part of Howard Bly's Cardinal collection.

IT'S HARD TO CHEER WITH A BROKEN HEART

Andy Strasberg

Andy Strasberg worked for the San Diego Padres for twenty-two years. Since 1997, he has owned All-Star Corporate Marketing Enterprises in San Diego.

I grew up in the shadow of Yankee Stadium and just fell in love with baseball.

When Roger Maris came to the New York Yankees from the Kansas City Athletics in 1960, I was eleven. I had been burned in a fire in August, so I was laid up for a while and followed baseball even more closely. I remember a headline that said Roger Maris *"rejuvenates"* the Yankees. I had never heard the word before, but it made me think this Roger Maris was someone special.

For me, there was something about the way he swung the bat, the way he played right field and the way he looked. I had an idol. In 1961 the entire country was wrapped up in the home run race between Maris and Mickey Mantle and Babe Ruth's ghost. I cut out every single article on Roger and told myself that when I got older and could afford it, I would have my scrapbooks professionally bound—ten years ago I had all of them bound into eleven volumes.

I usually sat in Section 31, Row 162-A, Seat 1 in Yankee Stadium. Right field. I would buy a general admission ticket, but I knew the policeman, so I would switch over to the reserved seats, and that one was frequently empty.

I'd get to the stadium about two hours before it opened. I would see Roger park his car, and I would say hello and tell him what a big fan I was. After a while, he started to notice me. One day he threw me a baseball during batting practice, and I was so stunned I couldn't lift my arms. Somebody else got the ball. So Roger spoke to Phil Linz, a utility infielder, and Linz came over, took a ball out of his pocket and said, "Put out your hand. This is from Roger Maris."

After that, my friends kept pushing me: "Why don't you ask him for one of his home run bats?" Finally, when Roger was standing by the fence, I made the request. He said, "Sure. Next time I break one." This was in 1965. The Yankees had a West Coast trip, and I was listening to their game against the Los Angeles Angels on the radio late one night, in bed, with the lights out. And Roger cracked a bat. Next morning my high school friend called me, "Did you hear Roger cracked his bat? That's your bat."

I said, "We'll see."

When the club came back to town, my friend and I went to the stadium, and during batting practice Rog walked straight over to me and said, "I've got that bat for you."

I said, "Oh, my God, I can't thank you enough."

Before the game, I went to the dugout. I stepped up to the great big policeman stationed there and poured my heart out: "You have to understand, please understand, Roger Maris told me to come here, I was supposed to pick up a bat, it's the most important thing, I wouldn't fool you, I'm not trying to pull the wool over your eyes, you gotta let me…."

"No problem. Stand over here." He knew I was telling the truth.

I waited in the box-seat area to the left of the dugout, pacing and fidgeting. Then, just before game time, I couldn't stand it anymore. I hung over the rail and looked down the dimly lit ramp to the locker room, waiting for Rog to appear. When I saw him walking up the runway with a bat in his hand, I was so excited I almost fell. I don't know what he thought, seeing a kid hanging upside down, but when he handed me the bat, it was one of the most incredible moments in my young life.

I brought the bat home, and my friends said, "Now why don't you ask him for one of his home run baseballs?"

So I asked Roger, and he said, "You're gonna have to catch one, 'cause I don't have any."

MARIS was traded to the Cardinals on December 8, 1966—a dark day for me. That year, I went off to college at the University of Akron, in Ohio. My roommate had a picture of Raquel Welch on his wall, and I had a picture of Roger Maris.

Everyone knew I was a big Maris fan. My friends said, "You say you know Roger Maris. Let's just go see." So six of us drove two and one-half hours to Pittsburgh to see the Cardinals play the **PIRATES**. It was May 9, 1967. We got to Forbes Field two hours before the game, and there was No. 9. It was the first time I had ever seen Roger Maris outside of Yankee Stadium, and I figured he wouldn't know me in this setting. I was very nervous. Extremely nervous, because I had five guys with me. I went down to the fence, and my voice quavered: "Ah,…Roger."

He turned and said, "Andy Strasberg, what the hell are you doing in Pittsburgh?"

That was the first time I knew that he knew my name. "Well, Rog, these guys from my college wanted to meet you, and I just wanted to say hello." The five of them paraded by and shook hands, and they couldn't believe it. I wished Rog good luck and he said, "Wait a minute. I want to give you an autograph on a National League ball."

Roger Maris once held the national high school record for most kick returns for a touchdown in one game— five, at Bishop Shanley High School in Fargo, North Dakota. Maris received a full scholarship to play for Bud Wilkinson at the University of Oklahoma, but quit after two weeks. Roger Maris' original name was Maras. Tired of fans deliberately mispronouncing his last name, he changed it in 1955.

The Pittsburgh Pirates was also the name of a National Hockey League team for five seasons in the 1920s.

And he went into the dugout and got a ball and signed it. I put it in my pocket and felt like a million dollars.

In 1968, I flew to St. Louis to see Roger's last regular-season game. I got very emotional watching the proceedings at the end of the game. I was sitting behind the dugout, and Rog must have seen me because he later popped his head out and winked. It touched my heart. I was interviewed by the *Sporting News,* who found out I had made that trip from New York City expressly to see Roger retire. The reporter later asked Maris about me, and Roger said, "Andy Strasberg was probably my most faithful fan."

We started exchanging Christmas cards, and the relationship grew. I graduated from college and traveled the country looking for a job in baseball. When the San Diego Padres hired me, Roger wrote me a nice note of congratulations.

I got married in 1976 at home plate at Jack Murphy Stadium in San Diego. Rog and his wife, Pat, sent us a wedding gift, and we talked on the phone once or twice a year. In 1980, Roger and Pat were in Los Angeles for the All-Star Game, and that night we went out for dinner—my wife Patti, me, my dad, Roger and Pat.

When Roger died of lymphatic cancer in December 1985, I attended the funeral in Fargo, North Dakota. After the ceremony, I went to Pat and told her how sorry I felt. She hugged me, and then turned to her six children. "I want to introduce someone really special. Kids, this is Andy Strasberg." And Roger Maris, Jr. said, "You're Dad's number-one fan."

There is a special relationship between fans—especially kids—and their heroes that can be almost mystical. Like that time my five college buddies and I traveled to Pittsburgh to see Roger play for the Cardinals. It's so real to me even today, yet back then it seemed like a dream.

I'm superstitious when it comes to baseball. That day I sat in Row 9, Seat 9, out in right field. In the sixth inning Roger came up to the plate and, moments later, connected solidly.

We all—my friends and I—reacted instantly to the crack of the bat. You could tell it was a homer from the solid, clean sound, and then we saw the ball flying in a rising arc like a shot fired from a cannon.

Suddenly everyone realized it was heading in our direction. We all leaped to our feet, screaming, jostling for position. But I saw everything as if in slow motion; the ball came towards me like a bird about to light on a branch. I reached for it, and it landed right in my hands.

It's the most amazing thing that will ever happen in my life. This was Roger's first National League home run, and I caught the ball. Tears rolled down my face. Roger came running out at the end of the inning and said, "I can't believe it." I said, "You can't? I can't!"

The chances of Number 9 hitting a home run ball to Row 9, Seat 9 in right field on May 9, the only day I ever visited the ballpark, are almost infinitely remote. I can only explain it by saying it's magic—something that happens every so often between a fan and his hero. Something wonderful.

Blaine Poland, Effingham, IL with Heather (Mrs. Matt) Morris.

THE HUNT FOR RED OCTOBER

Grady Jim Robinson

Grady Jim Robinson is a former minister and stand-up comic. The Arkansas native, 62, was inducted into the National Speakers Hall of Fame in 1994.

I told my old college friend Kenny Kaaiohelo that we had one last chance. We had just driven ten hours and 500 miles from Edmond, Oklahoma, with his two sons, Jason and Jared, to see the sixth game of the 1982 World Series.

I glanced at the Goodyear Blimp hanging above Busch Stadium. Even its drone, as it fought the strong winds, seemed to be a growl directed at me.

Jason, 12, and Jared, 10, apparently unconcerned about our lack of tickets, talked excitedly as we walked past NBC equipment trucks, souvenir vendors and calm Clydesdales, which would later steal the show by pulling Gussie Busch into the stadium on a beer wagon. Rabid fans were already streaming from the parking lot chanting, waving pennants, buzzing in anticipation of a Redbird comeback against the Brewers, who led the Series three games to two. Although tickets were hard to find, I had been able to get them for two of the home playoff games with the Atlanta Braves as well as both of the Series games already played in St. Louis. But now things looked bleak.

"Well," I said halfheartedly, not very hopeful about my last shot, "I met George Hendrick the other night." "Hendrick," Kenny snapped, "you mean *the* George Hendrick, the Cardinal right fielder?"

My one brief meeting with Silent George had occurred in a rather unusual way. On the night of the first National League playoff game in St. Louis against the Braves, I was working at the local

Playboy Club as a stand-up comedian. The crowd was sparse, and, like everyone else in St. Louis, the members of my audience seemed to be pooped from the long day of rain and game delays and, finally, cancellation. But, despite the lack of enthusiasm in the nightclub, Hendrick and his two companions apparently enjoyed the show, and later they invited me to join them at their table. We talked about baseball and comedy and laughed about the horrors of performing either athletically or comically in front of hostile crowds.

"I thought he wouldn't talk to the press," Kenny said. "I'm not the press, I'm a fan," I replied. "And he said if I got to a Series game to give him a call in the locker room, and he'd have me down to meet some of the guys." "Will he have extra tickets?" "I doubt it."

The stage was set. At exactly 5:11 p.m. we entered the Cardinal office on the street level at Busch Stadium. Determined to appear confident, I walked briskly toward the World Series temporary reception desk and immediately encountered the home run king Roger Maris and sportscaster Joe Garagiola. Pausing very briefly to catch my breath, I moved through the crowded room. Because I'd urged Kenny and the boys to drive the 500 miles and because I was the guy who hadn't been able to find a single ticket in spite of a day of frantic phone calling, I was willing to try anything. I brushed past the home run king and calmly said to the receptionist, "Call George and tell him Grady Jim is here." The woman looked up from the desk without expression, a veteran at repulsing gate-crashers and con artists. She examined my face, apparently trying to determine if I were telling the truth. "What's your name?" she said sharply. "Grady Jim," I repeated with a devil-may-care tone. "Call George Hendrick, please, he's looking for us downstairs." When in doubt, be bold. Act like you know what you are doing, right? That's what we always say. With a weary sigh, the woman picked up the phone and dialed. Dozens of busy journalists, ballplayers' friends, Anheuser-Busch big shots and other notables milled about the room waiting to be escorted inside

The late Bo Belinsky married 1965 Playboy Playmate of the Year, Jo Collins, in 1968. They were married for five years...Jimmy Connors married the 1977 Playmate of the Year, Patti McGuire in 1978.

the stadium to do whatever it is people who are lucky enough to get into the inner sanctum. "Hello, is George in the locker room?" the receptionist asked. There was a pause; it seemed a very long time while she awaited word. Was he on the field already? Would he remember our brief conversation? How many other calls just like this one had he received today? Finally, she said, "Hello, George, there's a Grady Jim here to see you, and he's got some kids with him." Perspiration popped out along my upper lip and a cold chill crawled up my rigid spine. The woman repeated my name, and I knew George had said, "Who?" "Grady Jim. He says you're looking for him." Another silence. Then she hung up the phone and looked at me, again without expression. I imagined her saying, "You jerk! Clear out!" Instead she said, "OK, sign the clipboard and follow the usher over there."

Like something out of Alice's Adventures in Wonderland, the locked door clicked and opened wide. We hurried through it behind the usher. Dignitaries and club officials rushing about with clipboards and shouting orders to go-fers ignored us as we made our way to the stairs leading downward to the Cardinal locker room. Kenny mumbled in my ear, "I can't believe this!" "Neither can I," I said. "Stay close and keep the boys near you." Through a hallway we hustled, but our usher escort disappeared in the tangle of humanity. At the bottom of the stairs we turned left. I looked for the familiar face of Silent George. Sure enough, there he was, with a huge smile, buttoning his famous long-legged, double-knit pants. "Hi, fellas," he said softly. "Stick close and we'll walk out to the dugout, and after batting practice, we'll come back to the locker room and chat awhile."

From that point, the details melt together like a Technicolor dream. Passing Tom Seaver and Tony Kubek in the tunnel, we walked with Hendrick to the dugout and looked out at the Astroturf field. Was that Whitey Herzog? Who was that NBC guy? Hundreds of media people. Crack of bat on ball. Cameras clicking. Busch Stadium empty like a vast cavern reaching upward. And, above, the ubiquitous Goodyear Blimp, now benevolently droning into the wind.

Only 12 brief hours after leaving their warm beds in Oklahoma, Little Leaguers Jason and Jared sat in the dugout of the St. Louis Cardinals. Tommy Herr walked by. Ozzie Smith sat only a few feet away. Ted Simmons, Dick Enberg, Bob Costas, Jack Buck showed up. Then it was back to the locker room with Hendrick. Players, coaches, and visitors walked in and out of the busy clubhouse, some chatting with reporters, others sitting on stools in front of their lockers patiently awaiting one of the most important events of their lives. Jim Kaat, 43 years old and in his 24th season, stood only a few feet away talking quietly with John Stuper, the 25-year-old starting pitcher. A small sandbox with a spittoon sat in the middle of the floor; it seemed out of place until I remembered that modern ballplayers are still men of great expectorations.

Hendrick sat the two boys down on his locker stool and wiped the perspiration from his face. Keith Hernandez walked hurriedly to the adjoining locker and asked George for a pen so that he could autograph some pictures. "Keith, meet Jason and Jared from Oklahoma," said Hendrick. Hernandez smiled, shook hands with the speechless boys and their daddy. Hendrick, with the game only an hour or so away, sat down and pulled two bright red World Series duffel bags from his locker. The bags were filled with all kinds of souvenirs that would go back to Oklahoma and be pawed over by the boys' school friends. A new baseball was casually tossed into each bag, which held note pads with Cardinal emblems, wristbands and batting gloves. Then, without a word, the Silent One walked into the equipment room and reappeared carrying two Louisville Sluggers, George Hendrick-autographed bats. They were the real thing. The number 25—Hendrick's—was neatly inscribed on the knobs, and three single strips of tape about one inch apart were wrapped around the handles. The bats were ready for World Series action. "Here you go, fellas, something to take home from the Series," said Hendrick. The boys were stunned. Kenny smiled and muttered many thank-yous. After handshakes all around, the delirious four left the confines of the future world champions' locker room…still without tickets. I didn't have the heart to ask Hendrick for player passes, although I was sorely tempted. I felt that he had done enough. I said, "Hit a home run for us, George." "I won't hit one if they keep pitching me low and outside," he said matter-of-factly. "I'll have to keep hitting them up the middle." The Brewers did continue to throw low and outside. Hendrick slapped two singles, one to left center field and one to right, in Game 6 and knocked in the winning run in Game 7 on a sharp single to right center.

Lugging duffel bags and bats and an autographed newspaper article on Hendrick, we made our way up the stairs. My mind raced. We could turn right at the main corridor and walk out the stadium door. I knew it was likely we would not find our way back in for the game. Because we had no tickets. That would be the honest thing to do. Or we could turn left and illegally enter the area behind the box seats. Though we would not have a place to sit, we'd be inside the stadium and could watch the game in the standing-room-only area. What should be done in front of impressionable youngsters? Well, there is a time to be honorable and to do what is right in the eyes of the law. But there is also a time to get into the World Series any way you can.

I jerked Kenny by the arm and he grabbed Jason, who nabbed Jared, and we hustled through the double doors in to the box-seat area. During Game 6 of the 1982 Series, a bedraggled group of four, carrying duffel bags filled with World Series souvenirs and two George Hendrick Model Louisville Sluggers, wandered from section to section, avoiding ushers and ticket-checkers.

Each time Hendrick was at bat, five times in all, there came, from a different location in the stadium, an extra chorus of wildly enthusiastic screaming—first from behind home plate, later, in the third inning, from somewhere down the leftfield line, and still later, in the seventh, from just above the Stadium Club.

The 1942 Cardinals had the best record ever after the All-Star Break, 63-19.

IT WAS LIKE PLAYIN' HOOKY FROM LIFE

Beverly Jaegers

St. Louis

In 1941, my family moved to the edge of St. Louis Hills, on Mardel Avenue. One of my earliest memories is walking down a sizzling-hot summertime sidewalk somewhere near that area, and listening to a Cardinals game being broadcast behind the awning-shaded screen of a small ranch house's living room window. Even though I was very little at that time I have always regarded myself as a dyed-in-the-wool Cardinal fan. Shortly after we moved to Mardel Avenue, I found that I was old enough to go down the street, barefoot, being careful not to stub my toe, and buy that most wonderful of summertime ice cream treats: a black raspberry ripple five- cent cone at Dueker's Drugs on the corner. One day I was enjoying my cone rapidly, so that it would not melt all over my hands, when I saw a large group of children buzzing around the bus stop at Watson and Mardel. Within a few moments, I discovered that they were waiting for a particular person to get off the bus. His name was Stan Musial, and he was a Cardinals ballplayer. Stan and his family lived in the second house behind Dueker's Drugs, which like most of the houses on our modern block was of red brick trimmed with white. Joining the other children, I finished my cone and waited with them to see the Cardinal players arrive. Shortly, the big red bus pulled up, stopped, and a tall, slender man in a gray summer suit got off. Seeing the children waiting for him, his tilted blue-gray eyes twinkled and a smile creased his tanned face. As he stepped to the concrete, we surrounded him and some of the bigger, bolder boys waved pieces of paper at Musial, asking for an "autograph." I did not know what an autograph was, so I just watched as he pulled out a pencil and cheerfully talked and grinned as he signed the papers.

After several minutes, he walked the few steps to his home, sur-rounded and followed by the group of laughing children, went up the sidewalk and into his house. Fascinated, my daily routine changed after that, and always included a trip to the bus stop about an hour after a day game at Sportsman's Park, to wait for Stan with the other children. We hated it and felt abandoned when the team was out of town, and would often go to the bus stop anyway, just in the hope that Stan would somehow appear.

The next year, I suffered an attack of poliomyelitis, and was not allowed to join the waiting children. I spent the whole summer inside or sitting on the porch, watching the crowd down the street and wish-ing I could be a part of it. In the third year, white-helmeted men patrolled our street at dusk, watching for any light that might reveal our homes as targets for enemy bombers, but the crowds continued to wait on that simmering corner in the hot afternoons.

It was in that same year that Dickie, Musial's son, was old enough to play with some of us and, with permission from Miss Lillian, Stan's wife, we could go inside the fenced-in Musial yard. We soon learned that there was a plentiful supply of baseballs, gloves and bats inside the house. Looking back on this today, I wonder whether some of those balls, bats and gloves were not autographed by other baseball players and perhaps very valuable. At that time, however, we had no idea that such things might be.

We could play baseball all afternoon, even when Stan was out of town, but Dickie warned us that we had to be careful not to hit a ball over the back fence and into the witch's yard. That was a fearsome place, shaded by a huge apple tree, with tomato stakes sticking up like teeth over the fence. We were certain that if we hit a ball over there we would be eaten, at the very least. One day, alas, one of us, not me, hit a ball over the fence and into *that* yard. We scattered as if those planes were overhead ready to bomb us into oblivion. None of us knew *what* to do, and we knew that ball would never be seen again. It was a full week before the lure of Miss Lillian's Kool Aid and lem-onade drew us back into the yard!

In the next summertime, when I was very old and wise—almost eight and a half—Miss Lillian one day asked me to oversee the other children while she stepped to the drugstore. My job for 20 minutes was to keep order in the Musial yard. It made me feel so grown up I almost forgot to go to the bus stop when it was time for Stan to come home. Later in the summer she asked me several times again.

It was shortly after that that a new neighbor moved in on the other side of Stan's home, and their timid daughter joined us on the corner for the first time. She became so excited when Stan stepped off the bus she jumped, and the ball of ice cream dropped off her cone onto the sidewalk. Looking down at the melting blob, she burst into tears. Seeing that, Musial looked at her for a moment, then walked grandly into the drugstore and returned with another cone for her. She was ecstatic, and he smiled a big smile as he walked down the sidewalk and home.

The very next week, I decided that it was time for me to get one of those "autographs" from Mr. Musial. I borrowed my mother's purse, put in a torn piece of homework paper, and lugged it down the street. I waved that paper and felt so big when he took it and signed it for me with a flourish. Carefully, I tucked it into the purse and walked all the way back up the street, clutching it against my blue shorts. When I got home, my little brother was playing in the yard with his friends Beano and Windy, and I put the purse down by our side door to help them pull apart a large empty box for the front of a fort.

Later, when I looked for the purse, it was gone. My mom had gone to the grocery store and taken the purse along. When she returned, I looked inside and the long-awaited autograph was gone. She had thought it was just a scrap and thrown it away. I was heartbroken, for I had lost the precious signature.

Although we lived on Mardel almost another year, I never thought to try to get another autograph. In my mind, you only got one, and I'd lost my chance. Those wonderful years remain fresh in my mind, those summers of long ago during the war, and although I'd other chances, I still don't have Stan Musial's autograph. And Dickie Musial is probably still figuring out how to get his ball from the witch's yard!

VIRGINIA IS FOR LOVERS...
OF THE CARDINALS

Warner Fusselle

Warner Fusselle is a gifted broadcaster who has hosted "This Week in Baseball" and other national network and ESPN shows. He currently resides in the New York City environs.

L et's go back to the 1950s. That's when I discovered the St. Louis Cardinals. I was six years old at the time, and I haven't been the same since. Nothing has.

You must understand that at age five I was still a cowboys fan, not the yet unborn **Dallas Cowboys**, but the kind that rode the range in the Wild West, toting six-guns and chasing outlaws. My range was Rivermont Avenue in Lynchburg, Virginia, but that wasn't the problem. My problem was that I didn't like my cowboy hat. It wasn't shaped like a real cowboy hat but more like the hats worn by the Royal Canadian Mounted Police. You know, like Sergeant Preston of the Yukon. To me it was something a cowgirl would wear. I was ready for a change.

Then I met Wallace Hawkins, an older boy who lived across the street. Wallace was seven or eight. He was even in school. Wallace knew everything, and he shared his wisdom with me. He told me all he knew about the St. Louis Cardinals and their Class B farm club in the Piedmont League, the Lynchburg Cardinals. I immediately put away my six-gun.

> When the Dallas Cowboys Cheerleaders started in 1972, each earned $15 per game—the same amount they receive today.

Soon after, I got a Cardinals uniform for Christmas. It was all spread out on the blue chair by the Christmas tree when I vaulted down the stairs. It was just about the best Christmas gift I ever got.

The Lynchburg Cardinals weren't a very good team, but I loved them and listened to all of their games on the big floor-model radio in the living room. It sure beat listening to Gabriel Heatter talking about some war way off in Korea.

Wallace was my baseball guru, and how many little boys had their own guru in the '50s? He taught me how to read the box scores and the league standings, and he introduced me to baseball cards. They didn't have bubble gum with them yet but slabs of chocolate candy.

Not many Cardinals advanced from Lynchburg to St. Louis; however, one year John Romonosky won 10 games with Lynchburg and had a sip of tea with St. Louis. No, he wasn't there long enough for a cup of coffee.

In spring training one year, the St. Louis Cardinals came to town for an exhibition game against the **Philadelphia Phillies**. Mr. McGhee, an older man from our church, invited me to go to the game. Mr. McGhee not only loved baseball, but he was rich and was the only person in the whole world that I knew who had two cars. Right in front of his house sat two 1953 Buicks.

Mr. McGhee and I went to the ballpark, and there, at age nine, I had one of the greatest thrills of my life. Sitting on the bank in right field, I witnessed Stan Musial come to bat in the first inning and promptly line a double off the green right field wall. After the game, Mr. McGhee wanted to take me down into the dugout to meet "The Man:" I was terrified, so I begged off. I wanted to meet Stan; he was my favorite player. But I just couldn't.

P.K. Wrigley and Milton Hershey were bitter business rivals. When Wrigley bought the Chicago Cubs, Hershey tried to buy the Philadelphia Phillies...and sell chocolate gum. Hershey failed in both efforts.

As happy as I was to see Stan's double that year, I was equally saddened about a year later when my father called me into his bedroom to show me something in the newspaper. He wasn't a big baseball fan, so I knew this had to be important. It was, but it was also more terrible than anything I could imagine. There on the sports page was a picture of my second favorite player, Enos Slaughter, and he was crying. Enos had just learned that he had been traded to those wretched **Yankees** in New York. I cried, too.

A year or two later, disaster struck again. I was in the fifth grade when I found out that my parents were moving to Georgia. Could I survive living in a town without a Cardinals baseball team or without Wallace, my baseball guru? I didn't think so, but I decided to go along anyway.

One night I was fiddling with the dial of my hand-me-down 1946 RCA tabletop radio when I made a great discovery. I picked up station KMOX in St. Louis and heard Harry Caray broadcasting a Cardinals game, the ST. LOUIS Cardinals. Joe Garagiola was also there, and from that night on, I would tune in KMOX every evening and listen to the Redbirds on my red-painted radio. If I couldn't get the station, I would listen to the Atlanta Crackers or other teams, but every few minutes I would once again go looking for the Cardinals. I would even listen in the winter, eager to pick up any news about the Cardinals during the basketball broadcasts of the St. Louis Hawks in the NBA or the Billikens of St. Louis University.

To improve the reception, I would connect a wire to the back of my radio and then climb out my upstairs window and extend the wire onto the roof and around the side of my house, running it down a drainpipe to the ground. This made Harry Caray louder than ever. It also made the late-night crackles and pops more noticeable, but I didn't mind as long as I could hear every pitch.

The Yankees' pin-striped uniforms were designed by owner Colonel Jacob Ruppert to make Babe Ruth look skinnier.

During the afternoons I would often listen to the "Mutual Game of the Day." One day the Cardinals were on the game and were getting beaten soundly by, I think, the Phillies. St. Louis went to its bullpen and brought in the Cardinals' newest pitcher, a bonus baby who had just been signed out of high school. His name was Von McDaniel. He had just recently turned eighteen years old, and he was the brother of Cardinal pitcher Lindy McDaniel. As I recall, Von pitched near perfect baseball for the final three-plus innings of the game. I suddenly had a new hero. I liked Lindy, too, but he was old: twenty-one. Von was young and a phenom.

Von pitched a few more games in relief and then got his chance to start. He won his first four games, and as I remember it, he even pitched a two-hit shutout against the Brooklyn Dodgers on the "Saturday Game of the Week" on TV. The McDaniels reminded Cardinal fans of the Dean brothers, Dizzy and Paul (or "Me and Paul"), who won 49 games for the Cardinals in 1934.

I wrote my new hero, Von, and his brother and requested an autograph. I then waited on the swing of the front porch every day, waiting for the mailman to deliver my mail from St. Louis. One day toward the end of July, it finally came, a picture postcard of a Cardinal with a handwritten and personalized inscription: "Best Wishes Warner." But then the disappointment. It was signed not by Von McDaniel but by Lindy. Little could I imagine at the time that Von would never win another game after that season, while Lindy would go on to a brilliant career and become one of the game's great relief pitchers.

That same year, 1957, was also the year that the Milwaukee Braves called up Hurricane Hazle who batted over .400 and led the team to its first pennant. Hurricane Hazle was a sensation, but the second-place Redbirds had Joe Cunningham who was just as hot down the stretch. When Jersey Joe was hot, no one could get him out. It seemed like he got three hits every game that summer as the Cardinals battled the Braves for the National League pennant.

The Cardinals and Crackers were my teams, and a few years later I got my ultimate wish. Atlanta became the Cardinals' Triple A team.

Now I had it all. I could even go see the young Redbirds as Crackers before they got to the major leagues.

The Crackers were great. They had players such as Tim McCarver, Ray Sadecki, Fred Whitfield, Jerry Buchek, Phil Gagliano, Johnny Joe Lewis, Mike Shannon and "Hot Foot" Harry Fanok.

One night a buddy of mine and I went to see the Crackers play at Ponce de Leon Park. After the game we saw two girls sitting in a car in the parking lot. We bravely approached and struck up a conversation. What a thrill it was to find out we were actually talking to girls who were waiting on their dates, Tim McCarver and pitcher Paul Toth. For weeks I told all of my friends that I knew the girlfriends of Tim McCarver and Paul Toth.

Two decades later in my office at Major League Baseball Productions in New York City, I would tell Tim McCarver about my great "conquest" outside the ballpark in Atlanta. Jokingly, I asked Tim if he remembered that night. He laughed and said of course he remembered that night, but what he couldn't remember was what on earth he was doing double-dating with Paul Toth.

In the 1960s my loyalty to the Cardinals grew even stronger, and in 1964 I was finally rewarded with a Cardinal pennant. It almost happened in 1963. There was a late-season spectacular surge, but Sandy Koufax, Don Drysdale, Johnny Podres, and Dick Nen proved to be too much. Dick Nen? He had only one RBI that season, but without that home run against St. Louis, the Dodgers might not have had the chance to sweep the Yankees in the World Series.

In 1964 I made my first trip to St. Louis and saw the Cardinals play the Dodgers at what Harry Caray had described to me for years as beautiful Busch Stadium. Well, on first glance it was an old ballpark, and it didn't seem to be in a very good section of town, but it was still beautiful to me. It was just different.

I can still see Bob Uecker line a shot down the left field line off Don Drysdale in a big game. The Cardinals played well but were about seven games out with a month to go when I left town. The Cardinals then got really hot. The Phillies got cold. And St. Louis, in a miracle finish, ended the year as the National League champions. They even beat the wretched Yankees in the World Series. It was the grandest moment of my life.

In 1967 while serving in the infantry of the **U.S. Army** some 10,000 miles away from home, I volunteered for guard duty at three o'clock in the morning, just so I could secretly listen to the Cardinals and the Boston Red Sox in the World Series.

By 1969 I was back in the "world" and could listen to the Redbirds at a more normal hour. I heard Steve Carlton strike out nineteen Mets one evening, but Ron Swoboda hit two home runs and New York won the game. Then there was the final game of the season. That game would become Harry Caray's final Cardinal broadcast. That night he discussed the rumors of his firing on KMOX and said that you would think that after putting in twenty-five years announcing Cardinal baseball you just might be presented with a gold watch. Instead, Harry got a pink slip. Harry promised his audience that he would be somewhere broadcasting baseball games for many years to come. I was crushed, but I still loved Harry and wanted to become a baseball announcer someday.

In the 1970s I got my chance to broadcast baseball in the minor leagues. Without the St. Louis Cardinals and KMOX, I might have chosen an entirely different field. Later I would even narrate baseball shows such as "This Week in Baseball" which aired on KMOX. What could be better than that?

In 1988 I became the host of ESPN's new weekly baseball show: "Major League Baseball Magazine." I guess I must have really been lucky, because I was able to work in the baseball broadcasting world without ever having been a catcher for the Cardinals. In 1965 alone,

The last major leaguer to lose playing time during a season due to military service was Nolan Ryan of the New York Mets.

Joe Torre was player/manager of the Mets for 18 days in 1977. Since 1962, there have been four player/managers with Pete Rose (1984-1986) being the last....In 1935, there were nine player/managers.

the three Redbird catchers were Tim McCarver, Bob Uecker, and Mike Shannon—yes, Mike Shannon. Before that was Joe Garagiola. After that came **Joe Torre**. All became big-league announcers.

Although I was never able to catch for the Cardinals, I did catch FROM the Cardinals the baseball and broadcasting bug that has lasted to this day.

It's ironic that once I became a baseball announcer and then moved to New York, I could no longer listen to my favorite baseball broadcasts. Not only was KMOX out of listening range, but in order to tune in the local Mets, I would have to prop my radio upside down across the room on the window sill. At least, I had many years of experience in knowing how to do that.

I can no longer hear those faraway sounds of the St. Louis Cardinals. But I still have my memories.

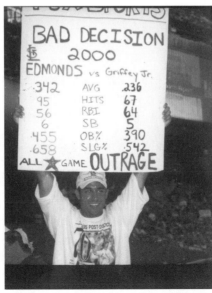

THEY PAINTED PEORIA BEIGE

Pete Vonachen

Peoria business and baseball legend, Pete Vona-chen, became one of Harry Caray's best friends. Vonachen, who owns the Cardinals single-A team in the Midwest League—the Peoria Chiefs—eulogized at Harry's funeral in 1998.

In February of 1950, Bradley University was going to play St. Louis University in basketball. Back in those days, Bradley, Cincinnati, St. Louis, those teams were all in the Top 20 in the country. Harry was doing St. Louis basketball. He'd do Cardinals baseball and then University of Missouri football and then he'd go right into St. Louis University basketball.

Back in those days, I was operating the concessions at the old Robertson Field House. That was my job. I had just graduated from Bradley in 1949. This was the first job I'd ever had. The school gave me the contract. It was a brand new field house that seated 8,000 people.

So a guy by the name of Dave Meister, who was sports information director at Bradley, came to the field house on a Friday afternoon—the game was on Saturday night—and he said, "Did you ever meet Harry Caray?" I said, "No." He said, "Do you want to meet him? I've got to go out to the airport and pick him up." Well, I listened to Harry doing the Cardinal games all the time so I thought it would be fun.

We went out and got him, and we were driving from the airport to the Pierre Marquette Hotel. Harry says, "What is there to do in this town?" I said, "We'll pick you up at 6:30 right here at the hotel."

It took us from 6:30 that night until 4:30 in the morning to show him what there was to do in Peoria. We pull up at the Pierre Marquette, and he said, "What's this?" I said, "Harry, it's after four in the morning. Everything's closed." I knew of a couple of after-hour places, but I had to work the next day.

The next day I went to work, ran the concessions and we had a jammed house. After the game I said, "I think I'll wait until Harry gets off the air, and I'll go up there and say good bye to him." He got off the air, and I went up and shook hands and said, "Harry, it's nice meeting you. Hope we can get together again sometime." And he said, "Whoa. Wait. Where are you going?" I thought, "Man, I'm beat." He said, "I've got an 8 o'clock flight in the morning. Let's you and I have a short night. Just a couple of drinks." I don't have to tell you what happened.

So that's how I met Harry Caray. Boy, we had a hell of a time.

You know, when you look at it, from a professional standpoint, he and I had nothing in common," It's just that we had the right kind of chemistry. I don't know. We just seemed to hit it off.

He was a driver's education dropout. He was absolutely the worst driver. When we would ride with Harry, do you know what we would say? "Our Father who art in heaven...." I mean this guy, if he was in the left-hand lane and wanted to go to the right-hand lane, he went. I don't care if there were sixteen semis there. He was going to go. And God always protected him.

There are two Avanti Restaurants in the Phoenix area, one on Scottsdale Road and one on Thomas. We always went to the one on Scottsdale. So one night, Harry decided we were going to go to the one on Thomas. We'd never been over there. I said I'd drive, and Harry said, "No. No. I'll drive." I said, "Okay." It's raining like a son of a gun, so we start out there, and he's bumping close to the curb, and I said, "Geez, Harry, move over." He moved over. We've got cars turning left, one right. Our friend, Don Niestrom's, hiding in the back. I'm riding in the death seat. Finally, we said, "Harry, you're driving in the turn lane." He said, "Boy. You got to watch how some guys drive around here."

Hell, I got pulled over twice with Harry, and we never got a ticket. I remember once a state trooper pulled us over and Harry said, "You stay in the car. Let me take care of this." He walked back and the trooper was coming up with his pad. I was sitting in the car, looking through the rear-view mirror. I couldn't hear, but I could see. All of a sudden, this cop looked up and got the biggest grin on his face.

Well, they shook hands and then Harry was talking to him, patting him on the shoulder. The guy got a pencil out, giving Harry his name, his son's and daughter's names. They shook hands again. The trooper got in his car. Harry came back to ours. He sat down and said, "I got to send them a shirt and a couple of autographs." He said the trooper told him, "Tell your buddy to take it easy," and that was the end of it.

More than once, he used me as a foil. There's was a place called McQuary's in St. Louis. We whizzed down there after a Cardinals game and grabbed some ribs and went right home. He said, "I was out a little late last night and Marian's not too happy with me." Marian was his second wife. It was a nice apartment. We went up there and Marian's still got a big burr under her. He brings me along because he figures she's not going to say too much. So he drags me into it.

She wasn't too happy with us. In the apartment, if you went through the bedroom window, there was a roof over the apartment below. So Harry and I crawled out on the roof and ate the ribs out there, so Marian wouldn't be giving us hell all the time. I'll never forget that night. I'll never forget Harry.

Rugged Joe Vonder Haar at Cardinal Fantasy Camp.

CARDINAL FANS CALL HIM MAD— I CALL HIM INSANE

Dave Barry

Dave Barry is a syndicated humor columnist for the Miami Herald. This story later became the subject for one of his Herald columns. His wife, Michelle, is a sportswriter in Miami.

When I was a boy, playing Little League baseball, I dreamed—as most boys did back then—of someday getting a call from the major leagues.

"Son," I dreamed the major leagues would tell me, "you stink. We're kicking you out of Little League."

I would have been grateful. I was a terrible player. I was afraid of the ball and fell down a lot, sometimes during the National Anthem. So in 1960, I hung up my Little League uniform for good—it immediately fell down—and I had no contact with organized baseball for the next forty years.

Then, I was asked to participate in the Joe DiMaggio Legends Game, which raises money for the Joe DiMaggio Children's Hospital in Hollywood, Florida. I said yes, because (a) it's a good cause, and (b) since they were asking ME to play, I figured it would be a relaxed, low-key event, like those company-picnic softball games where beer is available in the outfield and as many as six people play shortstop simultaneously.

Imagine my horror when I found myself at a real stadium, with thousands of spectators in the grandstands. Imagine my further horror when I found myself in a locker room containing several dozen former major league baseball players. Some were older guys, such as **Minnie Minoso** of the White Sox, who I believe once caught a fly ball hit by Magellan. But there were also some guys who had played big-league ball recently and still looked capable of hitting a baseball all the way through a human body.

I expressed concern about this to one of my teammates, the great Orioles third baseman Brooks Robinson, who gave me some reassuring advice.

"Don't play in the infield," he said. "You'll get killed." I was on the American League team, managed by former Yankee John Blanchard. He gave me a nice little pre-game pep talk:

Blanchard: You should see how these guys hit the ball.

Me: Hard?

Blanchard: Oh, Lord God. Are you wearing a cup?

Me: I don't own a cup.

Blanchard: Oh, Lord God.

I did pretty well for the first few innings. This is because I was not in the game. Then Blanchard sent me out to left field to replace Mickey Rivers, which is like replacing Dom Perignon with weasel spit.

I trotted out of the dugout wearing the stiff new glove I'd bought that afternoon. When I brought it home, I removed the price tag and spent a few minutes fielding grounders thrown to me by my wife, who was nine months pregnant and thus could not put a ton of mustard on the ball, which dribbled my way at the velocity of luggage on an airport conveyor belt. That was my preparation for this moment, for standing alone in deep left field, with vivid Little League memories swarming in my brain—memories of praying for the ball not to come to me, and memories of falling down when it did.

So I'm standing out there, and for almost two innings, nothing comes my way. Then it happens: George Foster, five-time All-Star slugger for the **Cincinnati Reds**, rips a ground ball between second and

> Minnie Minoso is the oldest player to get a base hit. In 1976, at age 53, he singled in eight at-bats for the White Sox. Four years later he was 0-2 for the Sox.

short. I get a good break on the ball, going to my left, running hard. Foster is rounding first, trying for a double, and the crowd is roaring, and suddenly I realize, with a sense of elation, that I'm actually going to get to the ball. Yes! I can see it clearly, and I have the angle, and I'm closing fast and I'm going to make it! I'm almost there! And now I'm there! And now OH NO! I RAN PAST THE BALL. THE BALL IS BACK OVER THERE. OH NOOOOOOO!

And of course I fall down. I've seen a video replay; I look like a man whose lower and upper body halves are being operated by two unrelated nervous systems. I make a pathetic, lunging gesture toward the ball as it zips past to the outfield wall, where center fielder Dave Henderson retrieves it. After he throws it in, he puts his arm on my shoulders and says, "You're supposed to catch the ball in your glove."

I also got to display my batting prowess. The pitcher I faced was Al "The Mad Hungarian" Hrabosky, who still looks as though he has just been kicked out of the Institute for the Criminally Insane for being a little too insane, and, and who can still throw pretty hard (by which I mean "faster than light"). He struck me out on three pitches. I was still swinging at the last one when Hrabosky was in the showers.

So it was a pretty humiliating experience. But mark my words: I'll be back next year, and that's going to be a different story. Because next time, I'll be ready to "play with the big boys." That's right: I'm going to be wearing a cup. TWO cups, in fact. Because I'm assuming you need one for each knee.

Pete Rose is enshrined in the Summit County (Ohio) Boxing Hall of Fame.

THE WRIGHT STUFF OF CARDINAL MEMORIES

Tina Wright

A Missouri native and Cardinal fan since her teens, Tina Wright is a publicist in the country music industry in Nashville.

I stumbled into Cardinal baseball at a serendipitous moment—April 1981—when the team was poised for a decade of greatness. I was 16-years old that spring, and went to spend the weekend with my grandmother, who lived in the country. The spindly antenna perched on her roof captured only one channel clearly, KSDK Channel 5, St. Louis, and that weekend Channel 5 televised three Cardinal games. After I exhausted my supply of reading material, and lamented the absence of cable, or at least another network or two, I succumbed to the "if you can't beat 'em, join 'em" mentality, and sat down next to my grandma to watch the game. At that moment, Mike Ramsey dove for a ball, leaped up and started a double play to end the inning. The Cards came to bat. Tommy Herr got a hit and promptly stole second. It was fast-paced, exciting, and I was hooked.

I'd never before watched baseball, but by Sunday I was an impassioned—dare I say obsessed—fan. I'd learned the rudiments of the game and most of the Cardinals' roster, and from that day on I followed every pitch. It seemed a cruel irony when the strike began only months after I'd discovered the Redbirds. Once glorious summer days now stretched interminably; I could no longer remember what I had done before baseball. To this day, I can't hear the name of then—Commissioner Bowie Kuhn without thinking of that "split-season," and how the Cardinals, who finished 1981 with the NL East's best overall record, were robbed. But I guess 1982 made up for that.

Several years ago I relocated from Missouri to Nashville, Tennessee. Nashville, while rich in culture and history, and steeped in the traditions of the Old South, lacks one thing: It is not a baseball town. St. Louis is synonymous with the Cardinals; when in Missouri, I'd never wanted for the smallest detail on the team. But suddenly I found myself displaced from other fans, devoid of anything more than a box score, and straining my ears to pick up KMOX's static-filled, late-night broadcasts.

I was also a big supporter of Keith Hernandez and, aside from the travesty of 1985, the saddest day for me as a fan was when we sent Hernandez to New York for Neil Allen. I cried when I heard the news. The next morning, I went into a florist's shop. The lady ahead of me was purchasing a lush, mixed bouquet, which had been spray-painted black. I remarked about the flowers, and she told me they were meant as a humorous gift for a disconsolate Hernandez fan.

Cardinal baseball has been an integral part of my life since that long-ago weekend at my grandma's. I've been witness to two truly great moments in St. Louis history: the four home games of the 1982 World Series, and Mark McGwire's 60th home run in 1998. But I treasure equally the thousands of other games I've followed when I was not at Busch Stadium, some of them pivotal victories in a championship year, others merely part of a season past. I remember autumn afternoons glued to television, and falling asleep curled up next to the radio, listening to KMOX; I remember games I've watched in other cities, while sparring with rowdy opposition fans, and the games I've followed "online," with the play-by-play transcribed to me by a friend. Baseball is best shared. This game, this team, has enriched my life immeasurably. And I am not alone.

It's also been said that baseball has been a metaphor for this country's evolution; it has mirrored our popular culture, the chasms between labor and management, our race relations. And it often has been noted that the game offers a pastoral escapism from the rigors of daily life, and continuity in the midst of change. It is a means of binding generations of families—through shared experiences playing, watching or collecting. Baseball allows us to be part of something bigger than ourselves. Whether we are in the stands, or at home with the radio or TV, we are not individuals when we follow the Cardinals; we are a collective one.

Chapter Two

Sweet Home
St. Louis

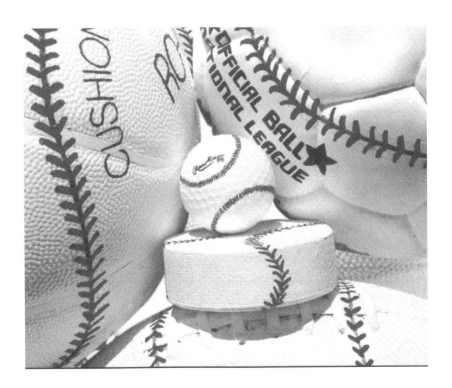

I Love Those Dear Hearts
and Gentle People

IT WAS A BALL

Philip Ozersky

In 1961, Roger Maris' 61st home run ball was caught by Yankee fan, Sal Durante. Durante sold the ball for $5000 to Sacramento restaurateur, Sam Gordon. Gordon died on September 8, 1998. On that same date, Philip Ozersky of St. Louis had a similar ball change his life forever. This is a neat story from a neat guy.

We were in a place called The Batting Cage Room which is just above the left field fence. A whole bunch of us from the lab where I work reserved the box. We thought it would be cool to go to the last game. Maybe the Cardinals might be in the playoffs, and you never know what McGwire will be doing. It was in May of '98 that we rented the room, fairly early in the season. The name of the room has since been changed to Suite 70, and updated, and they charge more money.

At the game, everybody is excited about maybe having the opportunity to see history—to see McGwire hit his last home run of the season because he had hit one the day before. It was funny how everybody talked about how cool it would be if McGwire would hit a ball into this box. The box has little picture windows, not even the size of your sliding glass doors at home. Everybody kind of had a feeling that he would hit a home run.

In the third inning, McGwire stepped to the plate. Anytime he came up to the plate, everybody stood up, and there was a huge buzz in the stadium. There was just general excitement to see what he could do next. When he came up in the third inning, he hit a shot and here it is pretty much on-line with our room, and everybody became really excited. It flew over our heads into the stands, just above our box. We were all like, "Oh my gosh! That almost looked like it was coming in here." We were just excited to see the record-setting home run.

Then McGwire came up in the seventh inning. It was tied, when he came up. The Cards had two on base. The first pitch he swings, and there's the crack of the bat. I saw it and thought, "Oh my God." I play outfield all the time so I know where the ball is going. "That ball is coming right for us." I'm saying all this to myself, but there are other people saying that out loud. Never in my wildest dreams would I imagine that I would end up with it. I'd been to hundreds of games before that game, and I'd only touched a ball that was thrown into the stands during a playoff game. That's the only time I've ever touched a ball at a serious ball game. And here the most significant ball in history, to that point, heading our way. All of a sudden, I could see—but it was like slow motion—it changed directions like it ricocheted off something and my instinct was to turn around. I realized the wall behind us was only seven to ten feet away so the momentum of the ball was so great that it wasn't going to stop at the wall so I turned the other way to be where it might bounce off. I just happened to turn, and there was nobody between me and the ball. It bounced off the back wall and it came to rest underneath this set of football bleachers.

So in this room, you can have up to a hundred people. In front of each of the picture windows, they had metal bleachers where you could view the game, or they had bar stools down toward some other windows. There's free beer and other goodies. It's like a good time gathering-type place. It's not like any luxury suite or anything real fancy.

The ball bounces underneath these bleachers. I turn around, and it's like five feet from me. I just dived—like Ozzie diving into the hole for one of his miraculous, way-out grabs. I hit the ground. My elbow hit the ground. My hand was just on top of the ball. It wasn't like a football which is an oblong ball and you bat it around and it goes everywhere. It just goes right into my hand. I pull it underneath me, and I hold on. The funny part was that underneath these stands, there are these supports and one of my friends was sticking his hand underneath and he was totally outstretched, he couldn't stretch any further, and his middle finger was rocking the ball back and forth yet he couldn't get it. I got it, and I pulled it under. People piled on top kind of like a fumble in football when they scrambled for the ball. They didn't know where the ball was, just knew it was somewhere around there and all of them were trying to find it and get it.

One of the things I was thinking—I had separated my shoulder playing flag football the week before. I was wondering how I was going to get up. Besides the excitement of having this home run ball that's like the most amazing piece of baseball history to date, like everybody had hyped it up to be. That's what it was, and I was in awe of that fact. I was also thinking, "How am I going to get up. I'm not going to put it in the hand with the bad shoulder because if somebody hits me in the shoulder, I'm going to drop the ball." I knew everybody there with me so I wasn't worried about anybody stealing the ball from me. Then people got off the pile, and everybody pulled me up. People were pouring beer on me.

As soon as I got up, there was pounding on the door. The police had run down from upstairs, but they didn't have anybody covering that area. They figured the balls were going to go into the upper area, the bleachers or upper deck. The police escorted me and my then-girlfriend, who is now my wife, to the post-game interview room. Major League baseball authenticated the ball. It had a chronological number on it, and an infrared dot on it that could be viewed under a light.

They took my name. They asked if we would like to go to Mark McGwire's press conference. They told me they might want to ask me some questions afterward, and I said that was okay. They also took me upstairs to talk to Jack Buck and Mike Shannon and Joe Buck. I did that and then we went down to the press conference. I sat on the front row for **Mark McGwire's** press conference. Then they shuttled him off, and they asked me questions.

Actually Terry Woodson, the guy who caught home run number '69,' was up there also. We fielded questions. It was like "Who are we? We just went to a baseball game and all of a sudden caught a baseball." It was just weird that all of a sudden we were thrust into this huge limelight. We were just innocent fans who went to a game to see history and saw it and came out with a piece of it. It was very surreal. It was fun, too, in a sense.

> When Mark McGwire was a high school senior, he was drafted as a pitcher by the Montreal Expos in the eighth round.

When I was laying there, with the ball in my hand, I totally was conscious of what I had in my hand. I knew that McGwire wasn't going to come up again, and this was going to be the record-setting ball. I was just happy to have that moment and share it with my friends. We got whisked away pretty quickly so not a lot of people even got to see it. It was weird. After the press conference, the Cardinals took us into some room and asked if I wanted to give it back to McGwire or not. Basically, they offered McGwire's standard thing of a bat, ball and jersey signed by him. They offered a life-time membership to go into the Hall-of-Fame anytime. I said I'd like to meet Mr. McGwire, and then decide whether to give it back or not. They said because of previous actions by people making demands, McGwire didn't want to do that. I ended up just walking out the front door with the ball. They offered to escort me home, but I thought that wasn't a big deal. Some of our friends stayed, and I went out the front door with the police and went into a van, and went home.

Everything was such a thrill. I was calling and talking to my family, trying to get hold of them, trying to get hold of my now-wife's family and my friends. A lot of people had already heard. The Rams were playing the Arizona Cardinals at the same time. My dad and my other brother and sister-in-law were all at the Rams game. The football game ended and they got out to the car right after the home run was hit. So they are getting into their car and are listening to Jack Buck trying to interview this kid who just caught the seventieth home run ball, and it was me. They were all like, "Oh my God."

It ended up that we went back to my parents' house and had a whole bunch of people come over to see the ball. The next morning I woke up to phone calls starting at five in the morning, people calling from radio stations all over the country and TV shows trying to get me to go on in live appearances. So all that was pretty incredible. I went on the Today Show, but I didn't go to New York, I stayed in St. Louis. I went on the Fox Network's morning show. I didn't do Leno because Leno was out of town, but I went to LA for the Howie Mandel Show. It was such a whirlwind at the time.

By the time I got home, people were talking about a million-dollar offer. Later, I put it on display at the Cardinal Hall-of-Fame downtown. The next day after I caught the ball, I went in to work and had everybody at work see it. I had gotten rushed out of the box so quickly that not everybody got to see it the day of the game. I wanted them to all see it because they shared the moment with me. It was important to me to have people see it. If I would have given it back to McGwire right away, nobody in St. Louis would have seen it. My friends, who were actually there when the ball came in that room, wouldn't have seen it, and also my family and a lot of other friends. I was trying to get it sold to where somebody would take it on tour or give it back to the Hall-of-Fame. It ended up that I put it to auction just because that's the way it worked out. It seemed the best way to do it. The person who I thought was going to buy it, Todd McFarlane, bought it, and he ended up taking it on tour to all the Major League stadiums and a whole bunch of minor league stadiums and in Japan. I'm really thrilled with how it all worked out, with the maximum amount of baseball fans being able to see it at no charge. Basically, McFarlane collected donations for **Lou Gehrig's Disease** and he didn't charge anybody to see it. He has a big collection, and is a big baseball fan.

The ball ended up selling for 2.7 million dollars, but with the commission the auction house got, it ended up costing MacFarlane over three million dollars.

I've invested the money. I bought a house for my parents in Florida. My dad had a stroke when I was a freshman in high school so he has paralysis on his left side. Winters in St. Louis aren't so kind to him so that was important for me to do. I've helped a lot of people. I donated seventy thousand dollars to Cardinal Care, which is the St. Louis baseball Cardinals' charitable foundation. I actually donated more than that—Cardinal Care, Leukemia Society, and American Cancer Society. I decided to donate seventy thousand dollars to the Leukemia Society because my friend, who had picked the day for us to go to the box, had a brother-in-law who died of leukemia during that time.

Jacob Javits, Charles Mingus, David Niven and Catfish Hunter have all died of ALS—Lou Gehrig's Disease.

My favorite splurge since getting the money—I was able to take my father, brother and sister-in-law to the Super Bowl when the Rams beat the Titans.

After I caught the ball, I really put a lot of thought into it and why I decided to do what I did. I even wrote a letter to McGwire about it. I was just happy with the decision I made. There was a lot of controversy on whether or not to give it back. I got uncomfortable with keeping it because they always talk about the guy who worked for the Cardinals who caught "62," and he gave it to McGwire. He ended up getting some fringe benefits but obviously I made a lot of money off of selling it. I also donated a lot of money to charities and that ball affected so many people, not only myself and my immediate family and friends, and it gave me financial security and the freedom to do what I want in life. I can spend time with my kids growing up so I don't have to work. I still choose to work, but I don't have to. I still work in the same place where I was working when I caught the ball. The lab I work in is called the Genome Sequencing Center. Basically I work on the human genome project helping make a blueprint of human DNA map. That's very loose terminology.

The guys who caught later home run balls called me to get my advice on what to do and who to deal with and who not to deal with. Their situation was different. My selling the ball for as much as I did kinda caused that, but that's not my problem.

Some people think that **Barry Bonds'** 73rd ball sold for a small amount, but if you think about how lucky I was with regard to where the economy was in 1998, and just the excitement that home run race took on, it's not that surprising that the Bonds ball sold for that much less. That auction was a season removed from Bonds actually doing it so you lose the momentum of that having just happened. Then he hit that seventy-third home run not even a month after September eleventh, and the economy had already taken a pretty hard swing down. Actually, I kidded with many a person that wouldn't it have been ironic if I had bought the

In 2002 Barry Bonds received 68 intentional walks…Eight came when no one was on base.

73rd home run ball. I sold the home run record ball for 2.7 million, and I could have bought the new home run record that I think will stand a lot longer than three years for over two million less. I thought about doing it. It was entertaining to think about and to share with other people.

McGwire captivated the nation and practically the world. Since I caught the ball, every year in December I get calls from Japanese TV stations to do interviews. The Japanese like to do, around New Years, good upbeat shows that talk about good luck. Every year they do searches on baseball and good luck, and they always come up with my name and always want to interview me. Even this past year, my wife and I went to Japan so they could interview me on a show.

I have met Todd McFarlane, the guy who bought the ball. You don't want to be on his bad side. He is a very innovative thinker. He's a very nice guy if you're on the level with him and speak honestly and be yourself and don't do any B.S. He's a good guy. I talked to him several hours. I was really, really close to selling it to him privately but just had people tell me I was better off going to auction. In a sense I was, because I probably got more concrete money out of it.

The ball sold around the middle of January in 1999 at an auction in New York held at Madison Square Garden. It was an evening event and **ESPN** came and covered it. That's when they had ESPN News and they aired it live. BBC aired it live. CNN aired it live. They would go from whatever they were doing to show excerpts of it. It was really well covered. The major networks were all there.

I met Mark McGwire at the St. Louis Baseball Writers' Dinner in January of '99. He was the centerpiece of the whole thing. At this dinner, I got a seat from the person who was in charge of Cardinal Care at the time. I only got one ticket so I went by myself and sat in the very back of that big dining room at a table with people who had no idea who I was, and I didn't really know who they were. Someone announced, "We have this caricature of Mark McGwire, and we'd

> *ESPN* debuted September 7, 1979. *ESPN2* debuted October 1, 1993. *ESPN The Magazine* made its first appearance on March 11, 1998

like to raise money for St. Louis Baseball Writers' charities and for Mark McGwire's charities. We're going to auction this off." Bob Costas was the emcee that year. He starts the bidding and the owners' wives and Larry Smith, ex-coach of Mizzou, and some other people are all bidding. I'm at the back of the room. I think somebody recognized me at the table at some point and said, "You should bid on it. It would be cool." I was considering in my head, but just didn't know. I'm in back waving our table sign trying to get them to see my bid. All of a sudden, Mark McGwire stands up, and he goes, "This is money for charity. I'll even sign this caricature. It should be worth at least what that seventieth home run ball went for because I actually touched this." The bidding kept on going, and they finally saw me in the back. I ended up bidding eleven thousand dollars and winning the bid. This was pretty unnerving—I had sold the ball, but I didn't have the money yet.

I finished the bid, came up from way in the back, and Bob Costas, who is pretty witty, goes, "Boy, that's a lot of money. One of the only people who could afford that is that guy that caught the ball." He said something like that, and he didn't know it was me. As I was coming up, the sports writers recognized me, and they said, "Hey Bob, it is." Everybody thought that was funny. I went up and everybody at the front table shook my hand. Torre was there and Jim Thome and Jordan and Lankford and Gibson and Brock were all up there. I got to shake their hands. They were all really excited to meet me because of what I just did, and I was like, "Oh, no, no, no. I'm excited to meet you."

I get to the center and Mark McGwire is standing there. We shake hands, and I am just in awe, 'cause he is huge. I'm not a small guy, but his arms are like the size of my legs. He asked, "What do you want me to write on this to sign it to you?" I said, "Show my name P-h-i-l. To Philip." He asked, "But what do you want me to say?" I said, "I don't know." He said, "I know what I'm going to say. I'm really nervous in a sense. I know how to spell, but how do you spell 'catch?'" I look at him like, "Uh, uh. I know how to spell 'catch,' too, but I couldn't tell you." One of the sportswriters said, "Catch is c-a-t-c-h." 'To Phil, or Philip,' I don't remember, 'Great Catch,' Mark McGwire, "70." That was my meeting with him.

Maybe in the short term it was very stressful deciding what to do and it got frustrating with different people involved. You are put in a place that not everyone gets a chance to be in. You've got to take that exposure to people hand-in-hand with what the reward is. The reward is the money, I guess. The money is great, but to me it meant, not buying happiness, but buying the freedom to be able to be really, really involved in raising my daughter and being home. I work at my job because I enjoy the place I work. I believe in the project I work in and how it's going to impact people. Those things are important. That's what I think the greater perspective is. I was put in a situation where people want to know the story, and they want to find out what your thoughts are. I owe it to people who are fans and people who enjoy hearing the story to tell it to them and to have fun with it. People recognize me. As weird as it is, I went to the bookstore the other day and was doing some transaction where they looked at my driver's license or credit card. The guy goes, "Ozersky? Are you the guy that caught the ball?" It's just weird that some people still remember. It's amazing that over five years later that still hits a nerve or a cord in people and brings them back to that exciting time.

Like I mentioned, I'd never gotten a ball before. But before the fateful game, we had gotten there early to watch batting practice. Ron Gant hit a home run into the box, and it bounced around and bounced right underneath this little girl's seat. I walked over and picked it up. She was looking for it, but it was so directly underneath her chair that wherever she moved, unless she would have got up, she wouldn't have seen it. I picked it up and gave it to her. I said, "Well, you should have gotten it anyway." I was thinking, "Here I could have had my first ball from a ballpark, and I gave it away." Then, later on, here I got the record ball. I kind of got rewarded for that, but I ended up not keeping that either.

RACECAR SPELLED BACKWARD IS RACECAR

Kenny Wallace

If there's a trophy for great smiles, Kenny Wallace is the leader in the clubhouse. He is the youngest of the famous NASCAR Wallace Family, following in the footsteps of older brothers, Mike and Rusty Wallace.

When I was growing up, right out of high school, about eighteen years old, my uncle, Gary Wallace, owned a company called "OK Vacuum." I worked there, and I used to listen to KMOX radio all the time. I couldn't wait for the twelve-thirty Cardinal games. I was repairing vacuum cleaners all the time. I was always racing, but I had to work at the vacuum place to make a living. It was very early in my career.

The highlight of my days always used to be those twelve-thirty-five starting games on KMOX. It's true that when you listen to radio, you draw on your own imagination. You know what the stadium looks like. If Jack Buck or Mike Shannon would say, "It's in the gap down right field," you knew where it was going. So that was my first start at really listening to a lot of radio. I grew up on St. Louis Cardinal baseball and KMOX—and those imaginations—listening to the games at my dad's place and at my uncle's. Then when we got in with the Brewers in '82, those were exciting times.

Then in '83 and '84, on the flop side, I'm in Kansas City, Missouri, racing with my brother, Mike, and we were running a race at I-70 Speedway. The race was over, and I was on highway I-70 when Don Denkinger blew that call at first base that cost us the World Series. That practically tore my gut out. I thought I was part of the team.

When you're a kid, you go to a stadium, and I can still remember my first time walking into Busch Stadium. I couldn't believe how bright the lights were. At that time, we had Astroturf, and it was so green. It was just incredible to me. I was really impressed as a kid. I was just awed. It was just like me going to Daytona for the first time, walking into Daytona International Speedway. At that time I was probably watching the slowest car on the racetrack, but in my view, he was running two hundred miles an hour.

When you first walk into a major stadium or raceway, the lights are bright, and the field is so beautiful. Everything is manicured. It really gets your attention.

When I grew to eighteen-nineteen years old, the big thing was to go downtown and drink some beer and eat some peanuts. Everybody knows about St. Louis—the top team in all of Major League baseball. The Cardinals are known and St. Louis is known as a sports city. Our number one sport is baseball, whether we're winning or losing. If we're over five hundred, we're getting thirty thousand people, usually. I'm proud of Cardinal baseball just because St. Louis is known as "Baseball City."

My brother Rusty was always really focused on cars from the very beginning. Because I'm seven years younger than he, I just kind of came into baseball. I played left field in Khoury League when I was a kid. I could always run real well. But I just really liked racing. It caught my fascination building racecars. I started driving kind of late—began at twenty-two.

During these last five years, when I go to Busch Stadium, it's kind of like a time warp. I was a fan for so many years and then come back fifteen years later, and I come to the stadium, and I'm a guest with KMOX. Three or four years ago, I was asked to come in to the KMOX booth and help promote the racing at St. Louis Gateway International Raceway. I walked in and there they were—Jack Buck and Mike Shannon, the two guys I grew up listening to. Here people think I'm somebody, and I've always been very humble, and there I was. Jack Buck stood right up, at his older age, and said, "Sit down, young man." I said, "No way, Mr. Buck. I'm not going to sit in your seat." He demanded I sit in his seat because Mike Shannon was doing the interview. I will never forget that. His health was failing, and I was watching all of his characteristics. He was chewing on a piece of candy very hard. While he was announcing the game, he was opening up all of his fan club mail. "A hit to right center," and while he's saying that, he's opening up a piece of fan club mail.

Nobody could believe that Kenny Wallace would come to the ballpark in his Cardinal hat and Cardinal uniform. I have known some of the most famous people in the world. I knew Dale Earnhardt so good that he and I rode to South Carolina in a car together, just me and him. You know, at the time of his passing, he owned one-third of the Kannapolis Intimidators of the Class A Carolina League. I have met very famous people, and one thing I can tell that is one of the biggest misperceptions in the whole world is that when people become famous, most people think that they think they're somebody. In reality, so many famous people look at another person and said, "Oh man, did you see that guy?" or "Did you see that girl?" Good athletes are very respectful for other things they grew up seeing. It always catches me off guard people wanting my autograph.

This had been my dream. We didn't have a sponsor for this race. I wanted to go back home to St. Louis and run the race. So, we put together a die-cast deal. "Let's ask Major League baseball if they will let us put the Cardinals on the car." The people at Anheuser-Busch were great. A guy named Tim Schuler, Vice-President of Sports Marketing at the time, helped me get in touch with people in Major League baseball. We got the money to run the race through selling all the die-casts. It had the Redbirds on the hood. It was "car 99" St. Louis Cardinals. We're selling thousands of them right now. From all the money we make, we use that to run the race.

I'm a huge Cardinal fan, but I hardly ever get to watch them. I race Friday, Saturday, Sunday, and I do a lot of autograph sessions, and I'm real busy. Whenever I can get to watch a Cardinal game, I would have to say that I'm the biggest fan they have that can't get to go to the games because of my lifestyle.

THE LESS YOU BET, THE MORE YOU LOSE WHEN YOU WIN

Don Marquess

Don Marquess is a tower of power in the St. Louis business community. His Marquess Gallery in Union Station has become the foremost baseball art gallery in the country, frequented by thousands of Cardinal fans and dozens of players.

The most exciting time I ever had at Busch Stadium was the day that Mark McGwire signed his contract with the Cardinals. It was in September, 1997. Everybody thought that when we got Mark McGwire the last day of July in '97 that it was a rent-a-player deal… that he was going to go to bigger things because his contract was up that year. He was going to sign with one of the major market teams. We poor little St. Louisans would be thrilled for that time, but he was going to go on for bigger things. After a short period of time, we realized that Mark McGwire really seemed to like St. Louis. There was talk about him signing a contract with the Cardinals rather than waiting to be a free agent at the end of his contract.

In September, there was a meaningless game between the Dodgers and the Cardinals because the Cardinals were already out of it, and the Dodgers weren't in contention either. There is a press conference. After Walt Jocketty announced that they had signed a contract with Mark McGwire, McGwire gives his acceptance speech. I listened to him talk on my radio and everything he said was something I'd wanted ballplayers to say for a long, long time. He said, "A lot of people said that I should hold out, not sign, become a free agent, and sign with the highest bidder at the end of the season. Let me tell you, I know a lot of ballplayers who have done that, and they're not very happy right now. I can tell you right now that I am very, very happy in St. Louis. I love the city and the fans are great, and I'm happy to play here." Then he says, "It doesn't make any sense to me for a player to bleed his team to get the most money he can because then that team will be unable to sign other quality players, thereby weakening the team and having a team that's not in contention." Once again, I thought this is common sense that this guy is talking. Then he said that he was going to donate a million dollars of his contract to an abused children fund.

Well, at the end of press conference, I am so charged up and really excited about going to the game and really happy that we had signed McGwire, but I had given my tickets away. I've got six full season tickets in two different locations, but had given them away that night. I call my wife, Susan, and said I really wanted to go to the game. She said she had just heard the press conference, and wanted to go also. So we went down to Busch Stadium, even though we had no tickets, bought tickets from a hawker off the street. I was just so excited about the game that I wanted to go. I thought we could go into the section where our seats are because I know the **usher**, and if I don't have tickets, I'm sure he'll find seats for me where somebody doesn't show up. I got into the ballpark and Susan and I went down to our section. Sure enough there were a couple of seats open and the usher let us sit there. I looked around, and I saw a few other people who are usually there at the game, but they were not in their regular seats. Apparently we weren't the only people that did that.

This was a game that would normally have had seventeen, eighteen thousand people at that time. There were almost thirty thousand people in the stadium that night and I felt that probably ten thousand or more came just because of the press conference. It was incredible. There was just kind of a pulse in the stadium. Everybody was really thrilled about the signing of Mark McGwire, and this was an exciting moment.

McGwire was the third batter in the lineup. The first two guys make outs. They announce Mark McGwire and also say that he had just

The most famous usher currently is Ed Hoffman, "The Singing Usher" at Edison Field in Anaheim, CA. His son, Glenn, managed the Dodgers and another son, Trevor, holds the record for most saves with one team.

signed his contract for three years with the Cardinals. Everybody stands and applauds. Of course, they already knew it, but were thanking him for doing it. He comes up to bat, and usually when somebody gets a standing ovation, after the first pitch is thrown, everybody sits down, and the excitement kind of wanes. Well, the first pitch was thrown, and everybody was still on their feet applauding, still cheering for Mark McGwire. The next pitch, nobody sits down. Everybody is still standing and cheering and clapping. My hands are getting red and sore. On the *fifth* pitch, Mark McGwire launched the **longest home run** that had ever been hit in Busch Stadium at that time. It was five hundred and twenty-seven feet. It almost dotted the "i" on his name on the scoreboard. It was the most incredible moment, with everybody on their feet standing and cheering. I look around and guys my age had tears coming down their cheeks. Everybody is so happy. We're high-fiving everyone, and everybody is cheering. It was just the most remarkable moment that I have ever had in sports. That's a true story. If you talk to anybody who went to that game, they will tell you they experienced the same thing.

I have been, what we laughingly refer to as, a fine arts photographer for twenty-five years. What that is—it's not journalism. It doesn't record a specific happening. I'm not into memorabilia, which means my photographs were not for any commercial purpose. I didn't do commercial photographs for individuals or ad agencies. The only reason that I took my photographs was to be hung as a piece of art on the wall for someone to look at. I got an idea in 1998. I've been a baseball fan ever since I was eight. My love of the game allows no distractions so I don't take my camera to the games.

In 1998, when Mark McGwire was threatening the home run record of sixty-one, other guys could come close, Sosa, etc. Since I do everything as a piece of art rather than as something for a player, I wanted to show the record of sixty-one home runs being smashed. I got an idea to smash sixty-two baseballs. I called Marty Hendin, in the Cards front office, whom I had known through working with him

Mark McGwire holds the record for longest home run at six major league ballparks...but not Oakland (Pedro Munoz).

on things previously, and said, "Marty, I want sixty-two baseballs." He said, "That's an unusual number, Mr. Marquess, why do you want those?" I told him I wanted to graphically show the sixty-two base-balls smashed, thus showing the breaking of the sixty-one home run record. He said, "Rawlings may be interested in this. Let me talk to Rawlings and see how they feel about it." About two or three days later, I got a call from Scotty Smith, the guy who handles the **baseball** division of Rawlings.

I told him what I wanted to do, and two days later, I got six dozen baseballs sent to me, free of charge. He thought the idea was pretty neat. I started unwrapping all these balls, and I'm like a kid on Christmas morning. I've ruined a four-hundred dollar suit trying to catch one, and all of a sudden I've got seventy two of them in front of me, and they're gorgeous. The first thing I did was I put them in a pile and photographed all those brand-new baseballs because I thought they were really, really gorgeous.

I shoot everything in natural light. I don't do any studio work. Since I've never done commercial work, I really don't understand lighting and I don't really know how to set a shot up. Everybody tries to equate natural light in a studio, and I just simply go outside and use the natu-ral light because I think it has a warmth you can't get in a studio.

I took these balls outside, put them in a pile, the light's really neat. I arrange them a little bit so they're in a pleasant composition, and I shoot it. I took about five photographs with those balls before I smashed them. I still hadn't smashed the balls, but I'm all excited about this. I get the film back the next day, and the colors are just out-rageous. It's gorgeous, and the photographs really look terrific. Forgetting for the moment my idea of smashing sixty-two baseballs, I make some rather large Cibachrome prints. I printed four of these and hung them in my gallery. About a week later, Mark McGwire comes into my gallery, looks at my baseball photographs, says that he's never seen anything like it and is very complimentary. He says,

Each baseball has 108 stitches plus one more in the middle which holds the yarn to the cork.

"I'm going to send you some business." In the next three weeks, half the Cardinal team came out to my gallery and said, "Mark sent us." I sold a ton of these large photographs, and I thought, "I may have something here." My immediate customers were the players themselves who had never seen anything like it. I took a few more photographs and now have nine photographs in the original collection. The next thing I knew, I had an exhibit at the St. Louis Cardinal Hall-of-Fame.

Mark McGwire, on the last day of the season, hit two home runs, to total seventy home runs. The guy that catches it is a guy named Phil Ozersky. While deciding what to do with it, he put it on display at the Cardinals Hall-of-Fame, etc. It just so happened the display was right in front of my exhibit of baseball photographs. I called him and left a message on his voice mail that I wanted to photograph the ball and would only need it for five minutes or so. I wanted to do a fine-art photograph of that baseball. Then he could do whatever he wanted to with it, but we could enter into some sort of agreement for commercial purposes for that baseball. Then he could still sell it if he retained the rights to the photograph. I thought I gave him a really good thumbnail sketch in just a few moments. But I didn't hear anything back from him.

About ten days later, I got a call from an attorney in Florida, Michael Friedland, who was related to Phil Ozersky, and was retained as his attorney to determine what to do with the baseball. I gave him my pitch. Michael Friedland said mine was one of a hundred and twenty-seven they had received that day. He said, "Yours sounds plausible, but we haven't really had a chance to think about everything, but I want you to know that we did get your message, and you are being considered." I started to tell him who I was, but he told me he knew who I was because my exhibit had been right behind the baseball displayed at the Hall-of-Fame.

About ten days later, I got a call from Michael Barnes, with Barnes Sports Group, who was retained by Phil Ozersky and Michael Friedland to generate revenue for this ball. After fourteen pages of documents, through my attorney and their attorney, we reached an agreement where I got exclusive rights to photograph that baseball, and no one else could produce an art photograph of that baseball. I photographed the baseball at the Hall-of-Fame, surrounded by two attorneys, the curator of the Hall-of-Fame, an armed guard and two other people. It took me about fifteen seconds to photograph the ball. I had everything laid out and knew what I wanted to do.

From that point on, my photographic art business, as far as baseball was concerned, was growing at an incredible rate due to all the baseball players' acceptance of it and the viewers at the Hall-of-Fame. Jack Buck saw the photographs and said a few things about them on his broadcast. Apparently people hadn't seen anything like it.

Word got out that I had photographed Mark McGwire's seventieth home run ball. The person that caught Sammy Sosa's sixty-sixth home run ball wanted to know if I would do an art photograph of that ball. They flew his ball in to St. Louis, and I photographed Sammy Sosa's sixty-sixth home run ball. With those two pretty heavy credentials, my business started growing even more, and my name got known more. All my other fine art photography just went out the window. I stopped doing that and for the last five years, I've been concentrating on baseball fine art.

This year, I am in the Major League Baseball Official Guide. I was picked up by USA Today's Gift Guide a couple of years ago. It's been going very well. I've got a calendar coming out for 2004 that is really being accepted gleefully. That's basically what happened.

Ken Griffey, Jr., Curt Schilling, Todd Stottlemyre, his father Mel Stottlemyre, Frank Robinson, Nolan Ryan and a lot of others have been in my store. Every time a team comes in to Busch Stadium, I get a lot of players and managers in the gallery because my gallery is in Union Station which houses the Hyatt where a lot of the teams stay.

I never dreamed that it would pay to be a Cardinal fan.

NEIL UP
NEIL DOWN

Neil Fiala

Neil Fiala, 48, is the Head Baseball Coach at Southwestern Illinois College in suburban St. Louis. The former Frontier League manager grew up a huge Cardinal fan. His dream was to play for the Redbirds...and he did!

In grade school, in the Crestwood area, a suburb of St. Louis, and at Vianney High School, in the sixties, I always dreamed I'd play for the Cardinals. You always sort of dream that because that's what your dream is—to play for the local team. Out of high school, in 1974, I was actually drafted by the Cardinals in the twenty-second round. What's funny about it was **Lon Krueger**, later the Illinois basketball coach, was drafted by the Cardinals that same year as the twenty-first pick. The Cardinals, in the twenty-seventh round that year, drafted Paul Molitor. I talked to Molitor one time, and he said he was only a couple of thousand apart from signing with the Cardinals. It was a small amount—like he wanted ten thousand, and they wanted to give him seven or eight. When you're from Minnesota, like Molitor, nobody knows about those high school guys and if they're any good or not.

I didn't sign out of high school and ended up at SIU-Carbondale. In 1976 I played on a USA All-Star team that went to Korea and

> Former Illinois coach, Lon Krueger, was drafted by the Houston Astros in 1970. In 1974 he signed with the St. Louis Cardinals and pitched one year in their farm system. He was drafted by the Atlanta Hawks. He was invited to the Dallas Cowboys Rookie Training Camp in both 1974 and 1975. He played European Pro Basketball in 1975 and he went to the Detroit Pistons camp the following year.

Taiwan. On that team was Ozzie Smith. You knew he was going to be a good player. In the summer of '76 I played with Molitor in Grand Junction, Colorado for a team called the Grand Junction Eagles. Then in the fall, on the USA team, I played with Ozzie Smith so I was able to play second base with two Hall-of-Fame shortstops, basically in the same year.

Both those guys were really nice guys. They got along with everybody. Molitor was a guy who could run. He was one of the fastest guys there. He had a great arm. He could hit with power and could hit for average. The only thing he did just average maybe was he was just an average fielder. You say, "Well, he may not be a shortstop down the road, but he did everything just outstanding so if he's not a number one pick, I don't know what is." Then of course the next year he was a number one pick. Ozzie was flashy and could handle the glove and back then he swung as good as anybody else—not great, not bad, but he could make the plays. They're both nice guys and got along with everybody and played hard and wanted to win.

In '77 after my junior year in Carbondale, we finished third in the World Series; that year I was drafted by the Cardinals and decided at that time to forego my senior year. I had accumulated enough credits that I was able to graduate college in three and a half years.

At first the Cardinals told me I'd be assigned to Johnson City, Tennessee, but they decided the next day to send me to Gastonia, North Carolina, which was low "A" ball 'cause they needed a second baseman there. I was able to step right in. Hal Lanier, who played in the big leagues with the Giants, was my manager then. It was funny because about every year in minor league baseball I ended up playing for Hal one way or another. His dad, Max Lanier, was a great Cardinal pitcher in the forties.

When I signed with the Cardinals, right ahead of me were Tommy Herr and Ken Oberkfell, and they were all second basemen. We pretty much followed each other up the ladder. Finally, Oberkfell made it, and when he'd move up, Herr would follow him, and I would move up the ladder. When Herr got called to the big leagues, Oberkfell went over to third, Herr went to second and sort of created a log jam for me as it turned out. In '81, I was tenth in AAA in hitting and had a good season, and the next year was hitting .323 and was fifth in the league in hitting in the American Association. I finished in August with a twenty-game hitting streak. They never told anybody till right at the end who was coming up to the Big Leagues or not. Then we got into the playoffs so it sort of extended a few days. You were just hoping and anticipating. Then after the last game when we lost out in the playoffs, Lee Thomas, the Cards Player Director at the time, called and told three or four of us he wanted to see us when we got back to the hotel.

So we thought, "Okay, maybe this is the call." When we got back, he told us, "We're going to call you up. You're supposed to report to the Cardinals out in Los Angeles in three days." As much excitement as it was, it was just as a much a relief. You're hoping since you're a little kid to get a chance to play in the big leagues. I can remember in eighth grade telling somebody I was going to play in the big leagues. That's what my goal was. It was during basketball season that I had said that. So as much as everything else, and as hard as you work, and the years you put in, and everything else, it was as much a relief as it was an excitement to say, "Okay, at least I'm getting the opportunity to get here." Afterwards, of course, I called my wife and called my parents, and they were all excited about it.

Then the next day, we came back to St. Louis. We ended the minor league season on a Tuesday, so we were supposed to meet the Cardinals out in Los Angeles on a Friday. So Wednesday, while we were still there in St. Louis, I had a chance to take my wife out to Musial & Biggies, the restaurant Stan Musial owned at the time, to celebrate. Then I flew out to Los Angeles and met the Cardinals. I was out there for their series and came back home. The first night I was there I got a chance to get in and get a pinch-hit. I was sent in to bunt guys over. I got my first big league at bat on video. Doug Vaughn, one of the news guys on Channel 4, was at that time working for a station in Minnesota. We had played ball together in junior college. He heard my name and he threw on the tape. Back then nobody had VCRs but he got my first at bat on video tape and sent it to me.

The first home game was against the Cubs on a Monday, Labor Day. My family and some friends came out, and we had a chance to get a few pictures in front of the dugout. That was exciting to be taking infield in a big-league uniform at Busch Stadium. I pinch-hit twice during the three-game home stand against the Cubs. Thursday was an off-day, and I got traded to the Cincinnati Reds. I was actually with the Cardinals for about a week in the big leagues.

It was terribly exciting to go in with my home town team and put on that uniform. I lived in St. Louis, and all of a sudden I'm at Busch Stadium. Now, instead of being away in the minor leagues, you get to just drive from home down to the stadium. You don't have to get an apartment or hotel room—you're at home. You get to drive down and go in and dress and be with the big leaguers, to actually be one of them. That was one of the greatest thrills I've had in my life.

Then when I heard I was traded, it was really shocking. I get a call from the general manager. He says, "Hey Neil, are you sitting down or standing up?" I'm thinking, "Uh-oh, they're telling me to stay home and not come back." I said, "No, I'm standing up. Go ahead." He said, "Well, you've just been traded to the Cincinnati Reds. Here's Dick Wagner's, their general manager, phone number. Give them a call. You're supposed to report there. They play tomorrow night at home." It was real succinct. That was about it. I said, "Can I ask you who I've been traded for?" He said, "Well, I can't say because the other people haven't been contacted yet." That was about it—less than a two or three-minute conversation. Doug Bair, a pitcher, came over to the Cardinals and Joe Edelen and I went to the Reds. I always like to say that I helped the Cardinals win the pennant in '82 because they had Bruce Sutter who was a "closer" and they had the "starters" but they didn't have the set-up man. Doug Bair became the Cardinals' set-up man. He'd throw in the eighth inning, and then Sutter would close it down in the ninth.

I told my wife, "Hey, guess what? I've just been traded. I'm supposed to be in Cincinnati tomorrow." Of course, she was upset 'cause here I am getting a chance to be at home. Now all of a sudden, instead of being at home the rest of the year, I'm going to be in Cincinnati and on the road again for the rest of the season so it is definitely shocking.

I never even got to be on a baseball card that said "Cardinals" on it. I was up there so quickly, and left so fast, I never made it. I was on a minor league card. I was on the back of Doug Bair's card because it said Doug Bair was traded to the Cardinals for Neil Fiala and Joe Edelen. I didn't get that opportunity so I've always said Topps should go back through the years and get pictures of players who hadn't made it and call it the "lost rookie cards," and put out a set of those, or "people who just got up there briefly."

I was able to participate in five major league games and I have the box scores for those. One nice thing is when you don't get in that many games, you can put them all on one little plaque and say, "Here's my career." It helps out in recruiting. I can say, "Hey, look, I at least got a chance...." I always tell people I got a chance to get my one hit in the big leagues and retire.

I grew up loving baseball. I grew up loving the Cardinals. I grew up dreaming of playing for the Cardinals...and I did.

Cardinals Fan Mr. "T"

EXPERIENCE IS WHAT YOU GET WHEN YOU DON'T GET WHAT YOU WANT

Lloyd Lowe

Lloyd Lowe, 77, spent his formative years on a farm in Marston, Missouri before moving to St. Louis and graduating Cleveland High School

I started fooling around with baseball—out in the country we would take our old stockings and put rocks in them and make a ball out of them, and we'd use a broomstick for a bat. The town had a team that we used to go watch play on Sundays.

When we moved down to St. Louis, I started learning how to throw a ball and catch a ball. I'd throw it against the house and catch it. I practiced a lot. We kids would get together and play ball in the alleys. Back then, we didn't have television or any other entertainment like the kids do nowadays. Most of the kids just liked to play ball. We'd go up to the high school on Saturdays, although we were still in grade school, and just play games amongst us. Then when baseball season started, we would ride the street car to Sportsman's Park for a nickel and get in there and watch the Cardinals. It was just great fun. You'd pick out a certain player you liked and you tried to imitate what he did, and you'd practice and practice and more practice.

I signed for ninety dollars a month in 1943 with the Cardinals and went with the Jamestown Cardinals in the New York—Penn League. I played Legion ball in 1942. Yogi Berra was on the team, and we had some players turn professional off that team and went to the big leagues. This Jamestown was Class D. In those days, they had Class D, C, B, A, AA, AAA, and then you got to the big leagues. There was a lot of good talent out there.

Even up in Jamestown, New York, we didn't travel in a school bus, we traveled in cars. We'd squeeze fifteen players and all their bags and equipment into four cars. We'd go out to the ballparks and play the ball game, and then you'd go to a hotel, and they'd put four or five of us in a room. When I was playing with the Jamestown Cardinals, I was getting a dollar and a quarter a day for meal money. That's when we were on the road. For breakfast we'd have cornflakes or maybe pancakes, which would be fifteen cents. You'd have a couple of hot dogs for lunch. After the game, you'd go get some scrambled eggs to try to stretch it. Then when you were home, you were on your own and had to pay for your own meals. We had the desire, and you just wanted to be a ballplayer. Almost all of the fellows on the team had a shot at making the big leagues.

In the Texas League, when we would go in to San Antonio, which was the Browns' farm team, the hotels weren't air conditioned. The club houses weren't air conditioned. They might have two faucets for a shower. Things were just different. The heat was really, really bad. But when we would travel on the trains, they were air conditioned. From AA on up, it was usually a train league. As far as flying and all that, it's just unheard of.

It was great to be picked by the Cardinals 'cause they were the hometown team. Little boys have dreams and sometimes the dreams come true and sometimes they don't.

Auto Dealer, Blaine Poland, with Lorrie (Mrs. Jason) Isringhausen.

YA GOT THE LOUVRE
YA GOT THE SMITHSONIAN
YA GOT TRINKET CITY

Marty Hendin

*If you hang around the Cardinals office or Busch Stadium long enough, meet the right people and prove that you're a baseball fanatic, you might get to meet Marty Hendin, the Cardinals' Vice President of Community Relations. And, if Hendin likes you and has time, you might get invited to Trinket City, the long-time nickname for his office. Hidden in the bowels of the Stadium, Trinket City is a Cardinal fan's candy store. The amount and quality and uniqueness of Cardinal **memorabilia** is overwhelming...enough so that most first-time visitors are initially speechless. Few, if any other, Cardinal executives in the history of the club have met more people than Hendin nor served the team so tirelessly...*

When I was in PR, I shared an office with other people, so it might have been '78 when I moved into my own office as Promotion Director. It was an office that had the old-fashioned wood paneling. There was an area around a pillar that kind of stuck out ten or so inches from the rest of the wall. I started putting pictures on it—taping up celebrities who were here. That just started it. When the remodelers came through and wanted to get rid of all the wood in all the offices, I had so much stuff on there, I just said, "No way." It got to the point where they would be coming around, and I would rush out and stand in front of the door and block it with my arms extended.

> In the early 1990s there were over 8,000 sports collectibles stores. Primarily because of eBay, there are now fewer than 2,000.

Then I just started putting stuff everywhere. It's a good conversation starter. I'll say, "Come see my office in Trinket City." "What are you talking about? What's Trinket City?" "Well, you just come see it." The most common phrase when they see it is, "Oh my God."

I have just wall-to-wall covered with different things. The one thing I try to do is get different things that people don't have. There's a shelf that has some of our first-ever beer mugs. There are two shelves that go around about two-thirds of the room. I've got caps piled up on those. Really, the beer mugs I started 'cause I was involved in that. Other than that, I don't have anything that anybody else has in terms of the giveaways we've done here, like the bobbleheads. I have a copy here and at home of every Cardinal Magazine that's ever been published. I'm a big-time Danbury Mint Collector, as are many of our people, so the top of the TV is the more quality stuff. I've got a whole shelf of bobble heads. The main thing is just different things— two pin boards of Cardinal pins and then a lot of loose ones. A lot of autographed things over the years. I got a whole big deal of Ozzie in 2002 from the Hall-of-Fame. I was trying to think what I wanted to do with that. I had the ticket, the credentials and the pins and the autographed stuff, the post cards and stamped envelopes so I put all these in a collage, and it turned out great. I collect autographed books that I keep at home. Something different is autographed CDs of everybody I've ever met here. I want the nicest picture they can sign. I've got tons of those, ranging from a very eclectic mix to Saint Louis Symphony to Nellie to Emmy Lou Harris to Vince Gill to Kathleen Madigan, all types of folks there. The back wall is my little classier wall, where I've got pictures of the three presidents I've met, Reagan, Bush I and Clinton. I have a lot of things from the Hundredth Anniversary Program that I put together. There's a Cool Papa Bell autographed picture.

I always say that I would never have believed, as a kid growing up, that I would be meeting the people I meet, celebrities, politicians and business leaders and doing the things I get to do and going to the places I get to go.

I guess I'm most proud of having the World Series things and the three presidents' pictures and the one most memorable to me is a statue of Gussie Busch. I was involved in getting the statue we have of Gussie here at the ballpark. I have the artist's drawing of the statue autographed by Gussie.

I don't even want to know what the most valuable piece I have. I don't want to know what I've spent buying stuff. My problem is that for a long time I had to buy three of everything, one for here, one for Trinket City West at home, and one to send to my son. Now that he's moved to an apartment, he told me not to send him stuff anymore—so I'm saving some money there.

A lot of celebrities are Cardinal fans. A lot of country-western guys and gals and others—John Goodman, Vince Gill, Bobby Knight, Billy Bob Thornton, Itzhak Perlman, George McGovern, George Michael, **Mike Ditka**.

My favorites players over the years are Ozzie and Steve Kline. Steve is probably the best guy I've ever worked with. He's never turned us down for something in the community. Everybody loves him. He goes out of his way to talk to people here in the ballpark. He knows more people in this ballpark than I do. He goes and sits in the ushers meetings. He sits in the Sports Service meetings. Sometimes, it's tough to get guys to come out for pre-game ceremonies. But Steve Kline comes out, 'cause he knows he's not warming up until sixth inning, and he volunteers to come out and talk to people. He's just that kind of guy.

Cardinals Care has given 5.7 million dollars over seven years to area children's agencies. We've built baseball fields. Right now, we're doing one of our more successful things. We take a bunch of players and wives and buy teddy bears and divide into groups and go to the hospitals and go room-to-room with the hospital people and give the kids the teddy bears and signed tee-shirts. Soon, we will have our eighth "field dedication" where basically Cardinals Care has gone into the neighborhoods and put a lot of money into taking a field and making it a much more spectacular baseball field. This one is right

When Cardinals catcher Joe Girardi played for the Cubs, he caught a ceremonial first pitch from Mike Ditka. Girardi had a football curled behind his back. After catching Ditka's pitch, Girardi fired the football at Ditka which Iron Mike caught easily.

down the street from where I used to live, and we're going to name it after Jack Buck. That's going to be a big one. We're working in the communities, through the fields, to the kids, to do some great things that we're all so very proud of.

Winter Warm-Up will have its eighth year. Last year we made six hundred thousand dollars over the three-day weekend for Cardinals Care.

The fans make me the happiest with their loyalty and their knowledge and the pride we all have here that we're the best. I remember when we got McGwire. Everybody said, "What do we need to do to keep him?" Jocketty said, "The fans need to make him welcome." One of the TV stations put me on camera that night and said, "What would you want the fans to do to make Mark McGwire feel welcome?" I said, "Do what they always do." You don't see fans in other ballparks applaud a good catch by an opposing player.

When the Dodgers wives came in here for the '85 playoff, they went back to everybody in LA and said, "You gotta wear blue." When the Royals came in this year, they went back and said, "Hey, we've got to wear blue." People say it's like a college football atmosphere here. The opening day is a religious holiday here! We do pep rallies for the playoffs. Every radio station is on every corner doing a different pep rally.

The fans here are great. They don't mind giving of themselves, giving a lot of time, taking off work to volunteer for Cardinals Care charity.

I hope to be here as long as they'll have me.

A view of Marty Hendin's "Trinket City"

Chapter Three

I Saw It On the Radio

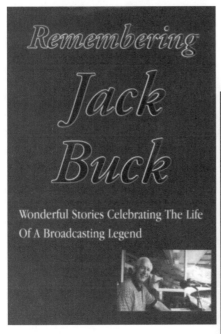

I Never Met Mike Shannon But I've Known Him All My Life

N o professional sports team has ever had a bigger radio network than the St. Louis Cardinals. No sports team has been blessed with better announcers than the St. Louis Cardinals. No sports team has ever had more fan-friendly broadcasters than the St. Louis Cardinals.

Arguably, the two greatest play-by-play men in baseball history, Jack Buck and Harry Caray, graced the Cardinal airwaves from 1945-2001, including fifteen seasons together.

When Harry Caray's outstanding Chicago eatery opened in late 1987, the menu stated: "Pork Chops—go to Ditka's" referring to Iron Mike's house specialty a mile away. They realized Ditka's had a superior product. This chapter is predominately about Harry Caray...for Jack Buck, go to: *Jack Buck, Forever a Winner* by Carole, Julie and Joe Buck, a wonderful book with the real inside view of the Cardinal legend.

As for Harry, older Cardinal fans know that Eddie Einhorn drove him to the cheatin' side of Chicago, where apparently he had to repay a debt to Satan. It is irritating to these Cardinal fans that many younger baseball fans are unaware that Harry served the Cardinals far longer than he announced for America's Loveable Losers.

HELLO AGAIN, EVERYBODY

BEA HIGGINS

It was a wild ride for Bea Higgins during the 26 years she served as Harry Caray's personal secretary...initially at an ad agency, later full-time in St. Louis.

When we got the Griesedieck account, the boss I worked for, Oscar Zahner, believed that beer and baseball went together. And he was instrumental in getting Harry here. He came in 1944, doing hockey and a few things. Then the baseball broadcasts started in 1945. He had been working in Kalamazoo, Michigan. Paul Harvey, who would later become famous, was the news director there and had hired Harry to do sports.

When Harry started, Gabby Street was with him and none of the articles I've read mention Gabby Street. He really was a father image to Harry, a wonderful man. Gabby was in his eighties when he was broadcasting with him. They just enjoyed each other's company so much. Gabby died in 1951. Then Gus Mancuso came on. He used to be a catcher with the Cardinals. Then, later, Stretch Miller was on. And then Jack Buck. Oooh, Jack was so wonderful, too!

When Harry first started, he kind of talked a little fast. And I remember the people at the brewery calling my boss and saying, "I don't think he's going to work. He talks a little bit fast." My boss said, "No. He's good. He's got something. Just hang in there." And, of course, my boss turned out to be right.

Harry also broadcast Cardinals and St. Louis Browns road games via Western Union ticker. That was set up in the Paul Brown Building. I'd go over with the engineer and get everything set up, watch him broadcast. The ticker tape is just saying, "ball one. ball two," and he's leaning back, saying, "It might be. It could be. It is." You know, practically falling on the floor.

One interesting thing: after he broadcast the games for a while, he had never had these kinds of paychecks before. He said there were two things he always wanted to get if he ever had any money: One was a new suit at this exclusive men's shop in St. Louis, the other was a convertible. And he got both of them.

I can't remember what the suit looked like, but I remember he called and I met him downstairs on Eighth and Olive, where our building was, and rode around the block with him in the convertible. He was so thrilled with these two things that he always wanted and now he was able to buy.

After I got married and started raising my children, I quit the advertising agency. I kept handling all of Harry's mail out of my home until he left St. Louis. He was a fan's person. I know with the mail, he read every letter and signed every letter. And he'd get upset if a fan didn't like him, because he wanted to be liked.

To me, the mail went either way. They loved him or they hated him. There wasn't any in-between. They loved him, adored him. Or, they didn't like him at all. When I was answering his mail or doing something for him out of my home, I would always have the broadcast on. But I wasn't really listening to who got a strike or a ball. I was listening to what he was saying. And, by the end of the evening, I'd say, "Uh-oh, I'd better write that down. I'm going to get a letter. Or he's going to get a call from the brewery. Or from a player."

Somebody would make him mad and he'd want to answer them. And I'd say, "You can't say that." He'd say, "Well, what do you mean?" I'd say, "Because you just don't say those things." And he'd say, "Well, that's what I want to say." I remember one day, I said, "I'm not going to answer that. Answer it yourself." And the next day he called and said, "Are you off your muscle?" And then he'd say, "Well, answer the damn letter the way you think we should answer it."

One other thing I want to mention about his mail. We got letters—obviously, people wrote for them—from blind people very often saying, "We can almost see what you are saying." And, you know, that's quite a feat. His mail was absolutely amazing. I know when he had his accident in 1968, I went to the hospital and I'd say there were fifty big brown bags full of mail—easy. I've got a picture of me standing there with all this mail in the room. I never thought he'd walk again—or at least for years. And he said, "I'm going to walk before spring training." And he did. It was sheer determination. But he had that determination."

After Harry's departure from St. Louis in 1969, I didn't talk to him all that often.

The last time I saw him, I had been in communication. He wrote me a nice letter when my husband died, and he sent his book when that came out. We really hadn't kept in touch like I wanted to. It just gets away from you. But I did see him in 1993 while I was working at another job in Clayton (Missouri) and he was staying at the Ritz, which was only two blocks away.

We were talking on the phone, and he said, "I'm going to walk up and see you." He came up, and we had a nice visit for a couple of hours and that's the first time I'd seen him since he left St. Louis twenty-four years before. He seemed to be very, very happy when I saw him the last time and I was so happy about that.

They loved him here in St. Louis. People came in droves whether the Cardinals were winning or losing. That's the kind of pull that he had. The main comment about his broadcasting was, "He makes you feel like you are sitting right in the ballpark."

When the Cubs won their last World Series in 1908—any team can have a bad century—there was no radio coverage…because radio had not yet been invented.

HEAR ME NOW, LISTEN TO ME LATER

I knew Harry because he lived just a couple of blocks from where our restaurant is. I started working here in '68 and, of course, he was coming in here then. When the Cardinals were in town, he'd come in sometimes twice a day. He'd come in before the game and have lunch and whatever. And then end up here at some point at night after the game, if not immediately after. He used to make the rounds pretty good.

I happened to be at work the day Harry was fired by the Cardinals in 1969. Harry walked in and nobody at that point had heard he got fired. He asked if he could use our private dining room to have a press conference, and I said sure.

There wasn't a large entourage at that point. He said, "Have somebody get me a Schlitz." And I said, "Harry, you know we don't have any Schlitz." At that point, all we carried was Anheuser-Busch products. He goes, "Well, I want a Schlitz. Send somebody over to the store to get me a Schlitz." And I said, "Harry, you don't want to do that." He said, "No, damn it, send somebody to get me a Schlitz." Again, I repeated, "Harry, you don't want to do that." He said, "Damn it, Carl." And I said, "Okay, you got it. Who am I to argue?" So I sent a guy across the street and he came back with a Schlitz, and Harry, during his interview, made sure it was visible.

Harry regretted that move all the rest of his days, because he was an Anheuser-Busch guy and truly loved Gussie."

——*CARL COWLES*, Owner, Busch's Grove Restaurant, St. Louis

I knew Harry Caray when he was in high school. He went to Webster Groves High School here in St. Louis. I had a cousin who went to Webster Groves. Harry and my cousin were a couple of years older than I was and, through my cousin, I met him. As a matter of fact, at one time he was kind of a wannabe basketball player. This was before the days of the **NBA**. It was AAU ball, good basketball. He was on a club with my cousin and several other athletes from Webster Groves High School. Through my cousin, I ended up on the team, too. Harry and I kind of sat on the bench together.

——**BING DEVINE**, Former Cardinal General Manager

What impressed me the most about Harry Caray was the fan reaction to his work. I first met Harry in the pressroom in St. Louis my first year, where I was in awe of everybody. The impact Harry made on the community was remarkable. The people in St. Louis just loved him.

The other great thing was he would be a fan on the air. He rooted openly. That kind of shocked me, because I was brought up by Red Barber in New York. Our whole idea was you don't root at all, because there were three teams in the city. There are people coming from all over, and we don't want to be selling product only to Dodgers fans. We want to sell them to everyone. To see someone like Harry go completely the other way was remarkable.

And if he was annoyed with the team, he would say it. I remember one time in St. Louis, the Cardinals were just furious at him because he said, "Once you get past (Ken) Boyer and (Stan) Musial, it's like having the weekend off." The other seven players were livid. But that's Harry.

Without putting a label of provincial on the Midwest—and I don't mean that—I think over the years if the announcer is in any community long enough, something happens. There is some chemistry. The people get the announcer they want, and he knows what they

In March 1954, the Lakers and the Hawks played a regulation, regular season NBA game using baskets that were 12' high rather than the usual 10'...the next night they played each other in a doubleheader. True facts, believe it or not!

want. He follows their direction. For Harry and Chicago and St. Louis, it was absolutely perfect.

But knowing him, had he gone to New York, he might have had the love and affection there, too, for all I know.

———**VIN SCULLY**, Dodger Announcer for over fifty years.

On Sunday mornings after church my mother would fix a big breakfast and then Dad would stick us six kids in the car and take us for a ride. This was the only day mom was away from all the kids. We would drive through the countryside in Illinois listening to the ball game with Jack Buck and Harry Caray. We always were on a mission to steal corn. We would steal the corn and take it home, then mom would fix a big dinner of corn.

———**CATHY LEONARD**, Bleacher Season Ticket Holder

My dad bought me an old Volkswagen Bug. I drove up and down the hills of Black Earth trying to get a station from Peoria, Illinois to hear the last game on Sunday of the '64 season. You couldn't get KMOX during the day.

On an old reel-to-reel tape from 1969, I have this tape of what was rumored to maybe be Harry Caray's last game, the game against the Mets when he, at the end, was kind of somber about everything. He said he didn't know what his future would hold, and if he'd be back with the Cardinals or not, but he thanked all the Cardinals fans and management for all the years in St. Louis. Then **Charlie Finley** hired him in Oakland. A year later, he went to the White Sox, and the rest is history.

———**STEVE SCHMITT**, 56, Black Earth, Wisconsin

When Harry Caray first started announcing the Cardinal games on the radio in 1945, he'd describe every fly ball to right as "all the way out to the Griesedieck beer sign on the right field wall." Once TV came in, everybody could see how far out the fly balls really went. Then we knew that Harry sometimes exaggerated just for the sake of getting the sponsor's name on the air.

> Late Oakland A's owner, Charles O. Finley, grew up in Northern Indiana and loved Notre Dame. When he bought the A's, he changed their colors to Notre Dame's green and gold.

The huge scoreboard in left-center field was scaled down when Sportsman's Park was sold. It was a manually operated scoreboard. Watching the scoreboard was exciting. Nobody had a transistor radio back then to get immediate news at the park. People would gasp as the numeral plank was drawn up telling how many other teams scored during their most-recent inning. It was a dramatic way to keep track of the pennant race.

The Cardinal games in those days were on several different low-power radio stations. In 1943, Dizzy Dean and John L. O'Hara and J. Taylor Grant were on KWK, which was a part of the Falstaff Beer Radio Network. Then O'Hara and France Laux did both the Cardinals and Browns games in 1945 for WTMV and WEW. These were low-powered, five-thousand watt stations with limited coverage compared with the fifty-thousand watt broadcast later of KMOX. I remember the Cardinals' owner, Fred Saigh, wanted to play a Sunday night game in the nineteen forties because of the humid summer days, but the protestors came out of the woodwork, and he was never able to do it.

————NATE WILLIAMS, Middleton, Wisconsin

When I was sixteen, seventeen years old I went to a lot of games. After the games, I would get autographs. I'm in the Marriott one day and I see Harry Caray and a couple of other people coming down the hallway laughing and talking. People are asking him for autographs. I used to carry this book around and anytime I'd go to a game, I'd have players autograph this book for me. It had a lot of different pictures in it, and I'd get the autographs on the pictures or on the inside cover. I opened the book to one of the inside pages and said, "Mr. Caray, I'd like to shake your hand and say hello. My grandpa used to bring notes to you at the stadium." As a youngster I was very aware of the scent of Budweiser. It was almost like Harry had cologne on and it was Budweiser, kind of overwhelming. So I shake his hand, and he takes my book, and he says, "What's your name?" I say, "My name's Craig." He signed my book and hands it back to me, and he says, "Nice talking to you," and he pats me on the back, and they walk on and go out the door and head over toward the stadium. I grab my book and just waited for it to dry. I'm looking at it and it said, "Harry Cow, Holy Craig," right there in the center of my book.

————CRAIG BALL, 34, Maryland Heights, Missouri

Harry Caray was a pretty good gin rummy player. One of the things he always said after a few hours' playing was, "The Big Possum walks late." I hated when he said that, but he ended up using that on his broadcasts quite a lot. He'd also say, "What are martinis mixed with?" He'd lay his cards out on the table and say, "Gin."

——JEROME HOLTZMAN, Retired Sportswriter

Harry Caray was my guy. I used to listen to Harry every night from 1960 until I got interested in girls in high school. Harry made things exciting. You wished you were there. He had that distinct voice and he made you want to be at the ball game. I remember in 1978, I'm in West Lafayette, Indiana at a Howard Johnson's on a recruiting trip and I flipped on the TV. I hadn't heard Harry's voice since 1969—we didn't pick up any Oakland games when he was announcing there and we didn't pick up any White Sox games on this side of the river. I'm in the bathroom, and I'm hearing Harry's voice. It was a White Sox game. He had the effect on me of thinking I was twelve years old again, listening to him. When Harry died, my cousin and I drove to Wrigley Field. The shrine they had outside of Wrigley Field was basically Budweiser bottles. We went down and contributed to the shrine.

——NORM RICHARDS, St. Charles, MO, Former Houston Astros Scout

I think what impressed me most about Harry Caray—above and beyond the fact that he was Peter Pan, above and beyond the fact he was in many respects a guy who because of his orphan upbringing in St. Louis always thought the other shoe was going to fall and thus he figured "I better cram twenty-eight hours into every day" was the fact that when you had the opportunity to visit with him in a casual but private atmosphere, you found another man. His voice would change. His octave level would change. He was always remarkably honest.

That was the essence of Harry. Harry loved tweaking us. Harry loved being a "Peck's Bad Boy," and I think this goes back to an element of his St. Louis childhood, which wasn't very comfortable. I've read innumerable stories about Harry crying during the holidays over very acute feelings of loneliness.

Harry had one quality very few of us ever achieve. Harry developed the ability to tell management and the people he worked for to go straight to hell and get away with it, because he was so damned talented. And sponsors were so in love with this guy. His relationship with

Budweiser. He literally kept Falstaff Beer on the map with the White Sox back in the early 1970s. True Value was in love with him.

I remember one time being in spring training down in Florida decades ago. The late Jack Drees, who himself was a legendary broadcaster, and I were having dinner. Then we began going down Highway 41, stopping at a couple of joints. Finally, it's about one-thirty or two in the morning, and Jack said, "Do you want to have one more belt?" I said, "Sure."

We stopped off at this little honky-tonk, walk in and there are about ten hard-bodies dancing on the dance floor. I look over and there's Harry standing in this pack of girls dancing. He yells out, "Come on in, kid. There's plenty for everybody."

———CHET COPPOCK, The Sporting News Radio Network

Well, Harry and I were together twenty-five years. He saw my entire career and saw my good years. We had a lot of great years together. I guess it was probably after my career was over when Harry thought I was a great player and talked about it. He sang my praises very highly through the years.

Harry made a lot of great Cardinal fans back in those days, because after the war there weren't many cars around and people didn't travel. Harry made all these fans in Arkansas, down in Tennessee, all the southern states, Kansas and other places. We were the team for the West. We had all those fans. But Harry made them great fans through listening to him and Cardinal baseball.

After his stroke, Harry made a remarkable recovery. When I saw him his mouth was turned, his arm was down and he couldn't do much. I figured this thing is serious. Six or eight weeks later, he was back doing the games again. He was tough.

I would be with Harry and Gussie Busch and Jack Buck. We played cards quite a bit after my career was over. He was a pretty good card player. We'd play Honors, a game that Busch kind of invented. Face cards count so many, you could go high or you could go low. You could go around King-Ace-Deuce, play that series or you could go down the other way. It was an interesting game because you didn't know if a guy could go high or low. Harry loved playing cards.

———STAN MUSIAL, Harmonica Player

For a while I really had Harry Caray down pretty good, imitation-wise. I did him every day. We got a kick out of it. I did it in front of Harry. I did it on the Cardinal team bus. When people imitate you, you've got to be somebody. They don't imitate people who aren't anybody."

He loved baseball to the point where he thought fans sometimes might be cheated by lackadaisical play. He was not ashamed to talk about it. I remember things he said about Kenny Boyer. He loved Kenny Boyer. Harry never said anything because he disliked somebody. He said it because he thought they could do a better job. It wasn't malicious.

If he ever said anything about you, and he heard you were looking for him, he was right there for you. He'd come walking into the clubhouse. He'd stick his face right in your face. He was not embarrassed to put his face in your face and say, "You got a problem with something I said?" He did that with Tracy Stallard in 1965. It was Stallard's first season with the Cardinals. Tracy was supposed to do Harry's pre-game show. He didn't show up. Harry marched right in the clubhouse. I was there. I saw it. Harry walked up to Stallard and got right in his face. He said, "If you ever do that to me again, I'll bury you. If you don't want to be on my show, tell me. But don't ever try that again."

I don't think I saw him in anything that matched. That's why I enjoyed him so much, to see him in a pair of shorts out there. I always looked forward to seeing him in the spring. I called him "Coach." I called him that for a long, long time. I think Harry made a lot of people better people, by either coming out to the ballpark or listening to a broadcast. I was glad to be a friend of his. I learned a lot from him. He'll be remembered for a long, long time. Baseball has lost a lot of great people, front-office people, broadcasters. It will go on forever. But baseball will always have a place for people like Harry Caray.

———BOB UECKER, Ticket Master

The rock group, ZZ Top, was visiting Wrigley Field one day to sing the National Anthem. They were sitting on the bench. Harry came by to do his pre-game show with the manager at that time, Jim Lefebvre. Here's two guys with Blues Brothers hats, blue jeans and long beards and mustaches and sunglasses. Harry sees them and says, "Hey, who are you guys? I'm Harry Caray. Are you guys rabbis?" They said, "No. We're ZZ Top." Harry asks, "What kind of a religion is that?"

———BRUCE LEVINE, Chicago Sports Writer

This was around 1984. The Cards were in Chicago. We're on Rush Street. It's late, really late. I said, "Name me eleven guys who hit fifty or more home runs in a season." There were about fifteen guys in there drinking. So Harry started. He named them and named them and named them. All of a sudden, he got up to ten and couldn't remember the eleventh guy.

I knew who it was, and Harry said, "All right, damn it, I can't think of it." So I said, "Oh, I don't know. I knew there were eleven." Everybody stood around and said, "I don't know, uh...."

So Harry finally said, "That's it. This is bulls——. I've got a book back in my room." He left the bar at around four in the morning. He got in a cab and went back to the Ambassador East. He rummaged through the room, woke up Dutchie and then came back to the bar about a half-hour later. But in the meantime, I had told everybody in the bar, "Ralph Kiner."

When Harry walked back into the bar and had the book up over his head, we all shouted at the same time, "Ralph Kiner."

Well, he walked over to me and said, "Dreesen, I can forgive you for a lot of things, but I will never forgive you for cheating me out of half an hour of quality drinking time."

Years later, I saw Harry down on the field before a game. I said, "Harry, how are you doing?" He said, "Tom, I haven't had a drink in two years." I said, "Really!" He said, "Yeah."

He said, "You know all that stuff how people tell you that you can have just as much fun not drinking as you can drinking?" I said, "Yeah." He said, "They're full of s——. I've never been so bored in my entire life."

——**TOM DREESEN**, Comedian, Los Angeles

I remember my granddad at the old farmhouse in Jefferson City, Missouri, would sit in the bedroom and would have the radio blaring out the Cardinal games because he was so hard of hearing. The kids would be outside running around the yard and yelling and doing the things kids do playing. He would holler out the window, "You kids be quiet out there. I can't hear the ball game."

Then we'd go in the house, and when we'd be in the house, the only time he came out of that bedroom during a Cardinal ball game, he'd be wearing these bib overalls. He'd come out between innings, open the refrigerator and grab a couple of cans or bottles of Bud. He'd put one in each pocket, go back into the bedroom and resume listening to the ball game.

My dad would do the same thing. He'd sit down right next to that radio, and he'd have the Cardinal game on. If us kids were making too much noise, he let us know about it. He never missed a game, never! We'd be in a restaurant eating dinner, and he'd have to go out to the car, "Just going to get a score in the game." He'd be out there and just couldn't tear himself away. He'd be sitting in the car listening to the ball game. He'd get mad, and the Cards could be getting killed by ten runs, and he'd never turn that game off. Whereas mom, if she sees them get too many runs behind, will turn it off and walk away. She will not watch it if they're losing by more than two or three runs. When dad died in 1993, we buried him with his red Cardinal cap on. Then we had a Cardinal pennant on the casket, inside the cover.

I remember, when I was younger, going to a lot of games. I've seen Stan Musial and Bob Gibson play and all those guys. It seemed so hot and I hated going to the games when I was younger. There were a lot of doubleheaders, and I would be like, "You mean there are two of them." I was so bored, and it seemed like it was a hundred and fifty degrees. We would be all dressed up to go to the games. Now I go to as many games as I can. I can't get enough.

—————KATE SCHEPKER, 48, Davenport, Iowa
(her mom is pictured above with a young Al Hrabosky)

There are still times when I am almost glad a game is not on TV just so I can kind of sit and listen to it. You can picture it in different ways. You don't have to worry about instant replays, you don't have to worry about what angle they are going to show you, you can just play it in your mind and sometimes that's the best way. I had a transistor radio under my pillow at night. My dad would have supported me with the radio under the pillow and my mom probably would have said go to bed.

—————ED "DAL" WRIGHT, Season Ticket Holder

In '54, Jack Buck was second banana and was for fifteen years. He was almost third banana for a while because Joe Garagiola was in the booth for two years. It was Caray, Garagiola and Buck. The St. Louis fans did not really totally warm to Jack at first when he was the solo announcer because they were so used to the drama of Harry Caray. Jack's sophisticated delivery and his wit wasn't fully grasped at first, and it took a while. I was telling Wayne Hagin this. "You're not trying to fill Jack's shoes, but Jack was loved here." I pointed out to him that Jack Buck's announcing of the game was accurate. You knew immediately where the ball was hit. You knew what inning you were in. You knew how many were out and how many were on and who was batting. He let you know this every two or three minutes, and you didn't realize he was telling it. Jack was really skillful at that. Wayne does the same thing. He just works it into his broadcast. "People like you now, Wayne. It'll take a few years for them to love you, but they like you and appreciate your style of broadcasting because you are as accurate as Jack was."

———**DON MARQUESS**, co-owner, Fox Productions

I became a Cardinals fan when I was nine years old. I would listen to France Laux, an announcer out of St. Louis. He was awfully good. He was as good as the ones that followed in my memory. It seems to me he was the voice of the Cardinals for at least ten years or maybe more.

I grew up in the Champaign-Urbana area. My mother took in roomers from the university and that summer there was a fellow staying at our house called Carl Berlinger. He would come home after work and pitch and catch with me, and he would talk about St. Louis. He bought me a Spalding Base Ball Guide. I pored through that. I loved the statistics. The Cardinals had this great year, won the pennant and that was with Rogers Hornsby and Grover Alexander and Jesse Haines. We had a crystal radio set, and we heard the games. My dad took me down to the fire department where they had set up a loud speaker and a couple hundred stood there and listened to the World Series and heard those dramatic moments. It was wonderful in those days with the radio drama—you could see the whole outfield in your mind's eye. The next year Hornsby was traded for Frankie Frisch of the New York Giants. It hit me hard because I loved Hornsby.

My radio wasn't that good and I could hardly hear and sometimes I couldn't get the Cards at all. I would go out in the backyard. The house right behind us had a radio with a very loud speaker and the games would come in on it real well. I would crawl down under the bushes behind that house and I'd lay there on a hot summer day and enjoy the ball game. That happened again, again and again and I don't think the people who had the radio ever saw me back there listening.

——BUD SPERLING, 87, Chevy Chase, Maryland

The St. Louis Cardinals are also responsible for introducing me to one of the best friends I've ever had, Mike Shannon. I've never met him, but, oh the many pleasurable, tense, exciting and frustrating hours we've shared. Whether he's extolling the merits of a "cold, frosty Busch" or pronouncing that "Ol' Abner's done it again," Mike's voice has never failed to offer reassurance, induce a smile and make me feel like I'm right there with him in the next seat. Much like Harry Caray was, Mike is one part broadcaster, two parts fan. I like knowing he is as excited about the Cardinals as I am.

——TINA WRIGHT, Nashville, Tennessee

When I was a kid, my dad worked three jobs but he always made sure he was off on Sundays, and we made sure we would listen to the games. I remember long drives to Grandma's, and lying in the back seat with the sun shining in, listening to Jack Buck. Things like that are such a good childhood memory that makes such a warm feeling. When they were on TV, we would all watch. That was the thing we all had in common. My mom died of cancer a few years ago, and when she was sick, that was what she looked forward to was watching the games. We made sure we were there to watch the games with her.

——DIANA CAMREN, 30, Cardinal Fan

I was asking an usher, Bob, Section 263, "Bob, I'm just curious. You're here every night. The other night someone got hurt and I couldn't see who it was so I looked around to ask someone with a radio what was going on, but I couldn't see anyone listening on the radio. So, do you think, since Jack Buck died, that fewer of the fans are listening to the radio during the game?" He said, "You know. I never really thought about it that way, but looking around, I don't see that many either." I'm just wondering if everything changing—a lot of people who are die-hard baseball fans, will they not be as close because Jack Buck was so much a part of their memories and so much a part of what was going on?

——CRAIG BALL, Cahokia, Illinois native

I'd rather listen to the games on the radio than to watch on television. My problem is that Memphis doesn't have a very good station. They do NASCAR and that kind of garbage. For a long time on sports talk radio, they would rather talk about a game than have the actual game on the air, which used to just drive me nuts. Yesterday's game was not on the radio here—they had NASCAR! That's horrible. I know a lot of people like NASCAR, but I'm not one of them.

———GEORGE McINGVALE, Hernando, Mississippi

We were riding up in the elevator one day, and Jack Buck was on the elevator with us going up in the stadium. He was talking to William, my little guy about four years old. Jack was talking back and forth, just general conversation with everybody on there. William did not realize who the man was at all. We get up to our seats, and we have our radio on. He's looking all around. He says, "Mommy, where's that man who was on the elevator with us. I don't see him around me." I said, "Sweetie, he's on the radio." He said, "No, he was on the elevator with us." He just didn't understand how Jack Buck could be on the elevator and on the radio at the same time. When he got older he figured out that was the man on the elevator with us.

———JULIE REESE, Warrenton, Missouri

From where I'm from, it's nothing but cotton fields, sand and mosquitoes. Back in the 1970s the Cardinals were broadcast by KMOX all through the South. It was rare to run into anyone other than Cardinal fans in the 1970s here in this area. That all changed in the 1980s with cable television. I bleed Cardinal red because my family is a generation of Cardinal fans. That started back in the 1970s, listening to the Cardinal games. Listening to Lou Brock, he was my childhood hero. During the summertime during my generation, we didn't have summer recreational things. We didn't have a summer swimming pool, we had fishing holes and baseball. I grew up in a community that loves baseball. Baseball was very much a part of the lifestyle back then. It's not as much now because of softball replacing it pretty much in this area.

———JOHN CARMICHAEL, Black Oak, Arkansas

Cardinals President Mark Lamping presents Marion Ingber a plaque commemorating over twenty years of never missing a Cardinals home game. Amazingly, for the last eight years of that streak, the Ingbers have lived in Pebble Beach, California.

Chapter Four

Fandemonium

BOB COSTAS WAS NEVER AS YOUNG AS HE LOOKS TODAY

Bob Costas

Move over, Dick Clark, and meet your heir apparent, Bob Costas. Costas, 50, grew up on Commack, Long Island, listening to KMOX on his father's car radio. The Syracuse alumnus arrived in St. Louis in October of 1974 to do play-by-play for the ABA's Spirits of St. Louis and never moved away. Arguably, the busiest and hardest working of the "big-time announcers," he is nevertheless unceasingly cooperative with almost everyone.

D uring the McGwire-Sosa home run chase in 1998, the national press descended upon St. Louis for that momentous weekend in September when the Cubs were here. One writer, from *Newsday* in New York, said that the combination of passion and civility among St. Louis baseball fans is what makes it the best baseball town in America, and I agree with that. Cardinal fans have tremendous passion for the game, they are extremely knowledgeable. The Cardinals have a rich history which the fans very much appreciate, but they will also show appreciation for opposing players. You see very little of the kind of ugliness and mean spiritedness that you can see in other stadiums and arenas. It's that combination of passion and civility that distinguishes St. Louis fans.

I think it's also important in recent years that the new ownership went out of their way to make the ballpark reflect Cardinal history and to disguise the fact as much as possible that it was one of the "cookie cutter" stadiums from the late '60s and early '70s. All of the other ones, Three Rivers, Riverfront, Veteran's Stadium, they all were just soulless bowls. They managed to make Busch Stadium into a place that felt like a ballpark and had little touches that were not only pleasing to the eye, but acknowledged Cardinal history. That is a big part of it too. Even though the game has changed a lot, and it's more reliant now on power, Cardinal fans have grown up with teams that won in subtle ways. The real old timers remember the Gas House Gang, or the teams of the '40s. Middle-aged fans remember the teams of the '60s. People in their '30s remember the teams of the '80s, where taking the extra base, laying down a bunt, playing hit and run, the smart subtle plays that make a difference in close, well-pitched ball games. Cardinal fans have a tremendous appreciation of that. That, in general, is what sets them apart.

I'm going to give you one memory now, because the other people are going to give you Musial, Brock, Gibson, Flood and Boyer, Mark McGwire, and Ozzie Smith. So I am going to go down a different path. I am going to talk about one specific night in 1979. The Cardinals played an extra inning game against the Astros at Busch Stadium, and the Cardinals then had a part-time outfielder and pinch hitter named Roger Freed. Roger Freed was the quintessential baseball "every man." He looked like a guy from a weekend softball league, and he was a very clumsy outfielder, but he had some power. Vern Rapp had been his manager in the minor leagues and he helped pave the way for Freed to come to the Cardinals. He didn't cut a dashing figure, he didn't have much finesse in the outfield, but he was a fan favorite and one year he hit close to .400 as a pinch hitter.

The Cardinals are losing 6-3 going to the bottom of the 11th. The Cardinals load the bases with two outs in the bottom of the inning against Joe Sambito, who was then the best left-handed reliever in the National League. Freed comes off the bench to pinch hit. Not many fans were even in the ballpark at that point. The paid attendance was only 6,349. It was during kind of a lull in the Cardinals fortunes; they weren't really a contender, it was before Herzog got there. There might have been 900 people in the park, or even less, that were still around by the time Freed comes up to bat. In this sort of impossible every man's "Casey at the Bat" situation, he lines a home run over the left center field fence…a two-out, pinch-hit grand slam home run that turns a three-run deficit into a 7-6 win and is clearly the single greatest moment of Roger Freed's life, or at least his baseball life. Stuff like that may happen to Barry Bonds with regularity, but it didn't happen to Roger Freed all that often. Roger Freed actually passed away a few years ago. I'm sure that he replayed that night in his head every day of his life thereafter. It was just so classic and so unexpected. The fans just loved this guy so much because he was so unassuming and just happy to be in the big leagues. Freed cut such an unlikely figure on the field and Sambito was pretty close to untouchable at that point. I can still see him rounding the bases and the combination of excitement and surprise on the faces of the fans. Even some people in the press box were kind of high-fiving over the kind of joy of it all. That's a Cardinal memory that sticks out for me, that I think a lot of other people are not likely to mention.

Growing up on Commack, Long Island, I knew of the Cardinals and their history. I often listened to KMOX on my father's car radio through the crackle and static. KMOX would come in sometimes pretty clearly. I heard Harry and Jack Buck and I knew there was a certain romance about the team. I got here in October of 1974. The Cardinals had just concluded a regular season in which Brock stole 118 bases. It was a particularly exciting baseball summer in St. Louis. People were still buzzing about it in the off-season. I noticed how KMOX's programming became very baseball heavy starting around early February. Even in December and January, if you were doing a sports talk show, at least half the questions would be about baseball. The football Cardinals had a good team then under Don Coryell, but still half the questions would be about baseball. On January 10, you would still get more questions about baseball than about basketball or hockey, so you could tell it was a baseball town.

HE DROVE BY THE CUBS MUSEUM OF PROGRESS. IT HADN'T OPENED YET!

Gene Siglock

Gene Siglock grew up in Alton, Illinois, dreaming of playing for the Cardinals. Instead, he was a Prudential Agent for 25 years and now is in the courier business.

It was about 1959 and the Cardinals had gotten Gino Cimoli from the Dodgers. Gino was a handsome Italian guy, dark blue-black hair and the dark complexion. Joe Cunningham had been traded so he and Stan were my two favorite players. My first name being Gene, I was playing high school ball then, so I picked up the nickname Gino.

My dad worked at Carter Carburetor as a machinist right across the street from the ballpark. So a lot of times we'd go to the games and my mom and dad would go over and eat at Johnny Molina's restaurant, and they'd let my buddy Joe and I go over and try to get autographs in the clubhouse. We're standing over there outside the clubhouse trying to get autographs and my mom and dad are walking towards us down Dodier. I can see them about a hundred feet away. Here comes Gino Cimoli out of the clubhouse. I'm all excited. I go up, and I was always real polite, "Mr. Cimoli, Mr. Cimoli, will you autograph this baseball for me?" He says, "Get out of the way, kid." He shoves me out of the way and walks down the street toward my parents. Just as he got to them, my mom, all of a sudden, reached over and grabbed his left forearm with both of her hands, just got him in a grip. He just stopped dead in his tracks. Now I'm about fifty feet away, but I can hear what they're saying. He just looks down at his arm and looks up at her and he says, "Lady, you better let go of my arm or somebody's gonna get hurt." She looks up at him with her

97

right index finger in his face and says, "Yeah, and it's going to be you, Buddy, if you don't give my son an autograph. You're his favorite player, and his nickname is Gino." He just stood there for a second and didn't do anything. Then he turned around and looked at me for a minute and waved me over. I ran over real quick, gave him the ball, and had him autograph it. She let go of his arm then, and he wanted to go down that block, but he crossed the street right in the middle of the block, went to the other side and went down about a hundred feet and came back across the street. The funniest thing was she would never own up to doing that. Every time I tell somebody about this, she says, "Oh, I wouldn't do that. I wouldn't do that." She just turned eighty-eight in July, but it was about six months ago that she finally owned up to it. It came up some way in conversation. "Yeah, I did it." It made her mad the way he just brushed me aside. I saw him several times after that, and he would stop and talk to me—not surprisingly.

It was Ron Swoboda's rookie year—about 1966—and he was about eighteen years old when he came up with the **Mets**. We'd always go down early for batting practice to try to catch some foul balls because the baseballs back then were three dollars apiece, and the major league baseballs would last forever playing Indian Ball or playing sandlot. My buddy and I are down in the right field corner, and it was only three hundred and ten feet down the line. There was an old wooden bench sitting down there at the visitors' bullpen. The Cardinal's dugout was on the third-base side at the old ballpark. Now they don't let them play pepper games, but then Swoboda was in a pepper game. He was batting with Gil Hodges and Richie Ashburn and a big coach by the name of Rube Walker. His forearms were as big as my thighs, a really big powerful guy. Swoboda was getting a little bored with this pepper game and every once in a while he'd just kind of slap at the ball a little bit harder. He just popped one up and hit the facing of the upper deck. I turned around, and it came right to me, and I made a basket catch.

> After the Mets had played their first nine games in their inaugural 1962 season, they were 9½ games out of first place.

He had two more baseballs laying there so he picked up the second one and they played again for a few minutes. He swung down on one and it bounced and Hodges reached for it, and it tipped off his glove and came right to me. So I had the second baseball.

So then they went along, and a little bit later he hit a high line drive. Walker jumped for it and missed it. I caught it. So, Swoboda was out of baseballs.

He comes walking over to the stands and says, "Hey, Buddy, give me one of those baseballs back." I thought he was just kidding. Back then I was about 5'10" and about a hundred and thirty-five pounds. Swoboda wasn't much older than I was, but he was about 6'2" and I guess two-hundred-ten or -fifteen anyway. I said, "Oh, yeah, sure, buddy, I'm gonna give you a baseball back." He said, "Listen, you wise guy. Give me one of those baseballs or I'm going to kick your butt." He steps up on this wooden bench, grabs my right arm and tries to twist it behind my back. He's gonna climb up in the stands and take one of these balls away from me. I was trying to push away from him, but he had a good grip on me. All of a sudden this great big arm came around his neck and grabbed him. Rube Walker had grabbed him in a choke hold. He's saying, "Let go of him. Let go of him." Swoboda wouldn't do it. His eyes are starting to bug out of his head, and his face is turning purple. I'm almost starting to laugh 'cause it's funny, but he's still got a good grip on my arm and twisting it. Finally, Gil Hodges comes over and tells him to get the heck off of that bench and get down in the club-house. Finally, he walks off the field. As he's going to the dugout, someone had taken one of those big pins and stuck it right next to the support for the railing. He saw it there, and he picked it up and threw it at me. Luckily I had my glove 'cause I batted it away so it didn't hit me. There were about four or five hundred people in the stands who saw it happen and everybody's booing him as he's going off the field.

So the game starts, and unbelievably the Mets are kicking the Cardinals' fannies, going into the bottom of the ninth, it was 9-2 in favor of the Mets. Swoboda hadn't been hit one fly ball in the air, but every time a ball was hit out there on the ground, we were all screaming and hollering at him and trying to get him upset. The Cardinals got the bases loaded with nobody out and Bill White hits a fly ball right down the right-field line, and the ball's just barely fair. Swoboda camps under it, and he's right even with me, maybe fifteen—twenty feet away from me. I'm screaming at the top of my lungs, "Metal glove. We'll listen for the clank. Don't let it hit you in the head." I'm almost hoarse now because I've been screaming at him the whole game. The ball hits his glove, and it drops right between his feet and just stopped. Instead of picking the ball up, he looked right over at me. I swear I thought he was just gonna let the ball lay there and come over and dive into the stands and put a whippin' on me. After about a two or three-second delay, he bends over and picks the ball up, throws it home, and he threw it all the way over the catcher on the fly. Three runs scored, and White ended up on third base. The Cardinals ended up scoring seven runs and tying the game, and we beat them with a run in the bottom of the tenth, 10-9. My buddy, the minute the game was over, said, "Let's get out of here." And we did.

I think **Gil Hodges** had chewed him out for something earlier. But, when I wouldn't give him one of those baseballs back, boy, he just lit up like a Christmas tree. What was so hilarious was that everybody down that sideline now has heard what he did before the game started and how he grabbed my arm and tried to get the baseball away from me. Everybody down that right field line was screaming at him when he dropped that ball, but of course I was the loudest and I was the closest.

I played high school baseball. I had a forty inch vertical leap. I only weighed a hundred and thirty-five pounds, had a twenty-eight inch waist, and I finally got just about six feet. When I was a freshman in high school, Ron Holtman was the coach at Marquette High School in Alton. He let me try out for **varsity** because I could catch the ball so good. We used to play our games down on the riverfront in Alton, just about where the gambling boat, the Alton Belle, is now. He had me stand in shallow center field, and he tried to hit high drives over

> The title character in the current sports comic strip *Gil Thorp* (no "e") is named for Gil Hodges and Jim Thorpe.

> The word "varsity" is the British short form of the word "university."

my head. I made one of those diving, over-the-shoulder catches just like Jim Edmonds made a couple of years ago. He called me in, and he said, "Okay, you're starting center field. I don't care if you hit zero." He stuck me out there between two football players and told them, "You let him get anything he calls for."

We were going to about twenty or twenty-five baseball games a year, and I would always take my glove. I had just bought a new Rawlings ball glove, and it had the stitching where when you caught the ball in the webbing, the glove would close automatically, and it would just stick in there. It was really a nice glove. All my buddies kidded me and called it "The Basket." So we go over to Sportsman's Park, the last game of the year in 1961. The Cardinals were playing the Cubs. Of course now, that would be a sellout. Back then the Cardinals were sixth that year and the Cubs were dead last, and there were about a thousand people in the stands. It was Team Day. We got a front-row seat in right field for a dollar. At the old ballpark, the box seats only went between the first and third bases, they didn't go into the outfield.

The game starts. There's a left-handed batter up for the Cubs. You know how they call all the rookies up at the end of the year, so he had been called up from the minor leagues. On the first pitch, he hits a line drive out towards the screen of the pavilion but the ball starts curving. It started out about fifteen feet fair. There is nobody sitting between me and the outfield wall in the old ballpark. Now in the old ballpark, the outfield wall came over into the stands, and it separated general admission from the main grandstand. Then there was a yellow line painted on the wall, 310'. The ball starts curving, and I know it's going to be foul. I had my glove on my hand. I jumped up, and I'm running full tilt down that front row, which is pretty wide. The old seats didn't automatically pop up, the ushers would have to put them up after the game so nobody was sitting down there. All the seats were up except one. I looked out of the corner of my eye, and I saw that seat was down, and I stepped up on it and jumped up and out as far as I could go. I was stretched out as far as I could go, and the ball came straight over my head right into the webbing. Absolutely perfect. It had to be a one-in-a-million thing. 'Course, when it hit that webbing, the glove closed. That was the trick of that glove. You just kind of left your hand limp and tried to get the ball into the webbing. I followed the ball into the glove, and all of a sudden, I felt something hit my forearms and something brush my hair, and POW, everything went black.

I hit that wall head on. What saved me from really bad injury is I was looking up. My chin and my forearms and my breastbone hit the wall. If I would have just had another second, and looked down, I would have busted my nose and broken all my teeth off. I hit that wall a ton. Some people were reaching down from general admission, and one guy's fingers brushed my hair. That's what I had felt from up above. My buddy said that if I would have bounced off that wall, I probably would have broken my back because I was so high up there. He said it just looked like a bug hitting a windshield. He said I just hit that wall and just slid down and flopped over on my back between the rows of seats. That's the first time I had ever been knocked cold. When you're unconscious, your hearing comes back before your sight does. I remember hearing Harry Caray's voice saying, "Holy cow, folks. It's a great catch by a fan down in the right field corner, but I think he's hurt. It looks like he's hurt." I remember thinking, "Wow, is he talking about me?" All of a sudden, I felt something hit me in the face. I looked up and saw one of the ushers had grabbed a white towel and stuck it in ice water and came down and was hitting me in the face with it. That brought me around. I had split my chin open and had bled all down the front of my shirt and my forearms were all bloody. But luckily, the forearms took the brunt of hitting the wall, and then the point of my chin. I guess that's why it knocked me out, I hit right on the point of the chin and it split my chin down to my Adam's apple. They brought a stretcher down, and I said, "Oh guys, I don't want to go on a stretcher." So, two of the ushers got on each side of my arms and carried me down to the first-aid room, but I still had the ball. When I did come back from the first-aid room to my seats, I heard a smattering of applause for catching the ball. I walked out and held it up as I walked down the aisle, but I was hurting pretty bad. The funny thing was that nobody knew this particular player. When I went to school the next day to show the ball off, they said, "Who hit it?" When I mentioned his name, nobody knew who he was. Three years later the Cardinals traded a pitcher by the name of Ernie Broglio for this player. He was a left-handed hitting outfielder, Lou Brock.

Several years after I caught the ball, for my birthday, my wife got us tickets to the Baseball Writers' Dinner. We went to the Gold Room at the Sheraton Jefferson over on Tucker Blvd. Lou got an award there, so when he went up the stage, I went up front to the edge. I had the ball and wanted him to autograph it. As he came down the steps, I said, "Lou, Lou, autograph this ball for me." He said, "Oh, buddy, I can't. I've got to go to the john so bad." I said, "Lou, with your speed, you'll make it." So he stopped and signed it real quick and went running through the door. I talked to him afterward. Lou said, "I know it would make your day if I said I remembered it, but that was my first at-bat in the major leagues and I just remember as the ball went foul, I turned around and didn't see the catch. I remember some commotion down there."

My oldest son and I went up to a Cardinal-Cub game in 1984. In **Wrigley Field**, they had opened a little sandwich restaurant down the right field line. Up above it was a private club that cost thousands of dollars to join. All you had to have was a ticket stub for that day's game, and you could go in and get these deli sandwiches, shaved turkey and ham, an ice cream sundae. Prices were pretty reasonable compared to the rest of the park. Your deli sandwich and some ice cream weren't much more than getting a hot dog and a soda out in the park proper. It was decorated real nice. They had these big wooden tables that had memorabilia sealed in clear plastic on the top of the table. They had taken old seats out of the ballpark, three on each side, so each table held six people. Then they had a big counter and the cushions for the bar stools at the counter were made out of old bases. The waitresses all had these outfits on that looked like the ladies' outfits from "A League of Their Own." They had TV monitors on up there and if the Sox were playing, they'd show their game. If the Sox weren't playing, they'd show a tape of "This Week in Baseball" or

More NFL games have been played at Wrigley Field than at any other stadium in the country. Mile High Stadium in Denver was in second place until demolished in 2001.

something related to baseball. We got in there and got the second to last table, and there were only the two of us sitting at this big table. I can look out the door and there are about three hundred people out there waiting to get in. I stopped the waitress and said "Tell those people we're glad to share the table with some of them as long as they don't mind sitting with a couple of Cardinal fans.

So this guy sat down, by the name of Bob Browning. I always remembered his name because the Reds had a pitcher by the name of Tom Browning at that time. He and his wife came in and sat down with us and we started talking. We found out that he was best friends with Jim Frey who had just become the Cub manager that year. They had gone all through grade school, high school and college together. Through Jim Frey, he got three seats right behind the Cub dugout in the front row, right where they go down the steps. Meanwhile, I had real good seats in St. Louis, in Section 140. Mister Busch's private box used to be right in the front row of our section. I got to meet a lot of people then because of the World Series and the playoffs, Skitch Henderson, Chub Feeney, etc. Celebrities would be walking up and down the aisle, and my seats are right on the aisle. I'd jump up and shake hands with them and sometimes get autographs from them. Browning and I talked, and we decided that we would swap some game tickets with each other. Later on Frey became the general manager, and, of course, I about cried when he got let go in the early nineties, 'cause that was the end of that. These seats were so great it would be like sitting right in front of the coaches' box in St. Louis. In Wrigley, there's no foul territory. The only bad thing about it is you really had to be alert because if a ball came up there, you didn't have much reaction time.

One of the first times we went up there, the kids were in school, and my wife and I went. I had an extra ticket, and my boss at work wanted to go so bad that he took a vacation day to go up there with us. We go in and sit down and the ushers will just drive you crazy. I finally just took my ticket stub and stuck it in the bill of my cap. About every five and ten minutes before the games start, they're coming around checking to make sure you belong down there. They don't want anybody sitting in those seats unless you have the ticket. I'm sitting in the middle, my boss is sitting toward home plate, and my wife's sitting toward the outfield. We're right behind where the players go down the steps so we're about a third of the way down the third-base line and maybe no more than fifteen feet off the foul line. You're so close, you could hear the players talking.

So I'm sitting there. The Cardinals had batted around once. It was about the top of the fourth inning, and Vince Coleman was leading off. Thank God for the gray road **uniforms**. I've got my ball glove there—I'm left-handed. My wife had gone up and gotten some pizza. She brought me a slice, and it was real hot so I took my ball glove off and laid it on my right knee. I bent over and was blowing on the pizza to cool it off. I had just sat back in my seat and Coleman got an inside fast ball. Even though he wasn't a big guy, when you get an inside fast ball, and really turn on it, you can really smoke it. I saw the ball was gonna just miss my boss's nose and was gonna hit me right over my right eyebrow. I'm thinking "neck muscles do your thing!" All I could do was just slam my face forward right into that slice of pizza. The ball was so close that it actually grazed my ear. That's how close it was. If that would have hit me, it could have killed me. I played ball until I was forty-five years old so my reaction was pretty fast, but it was hit so hard I just didn't have time to even think about the glove. I heard this loud whack and thought, "Oh, golly, somebody right behind me got hit and hurt bad." I looked around and luckily nobody was in the seats right behind me but two rows back and about four seats down, the guy just got his bare hand up in time and the ball was hit so hard that it busted that bone on the outside of his hand. It came right through the skin and just showered everybody with blood. The ball went off his hand and all the way down in the left field corner and the guy with the glove down there caught it. That's how hard it was hit.

Maybe three or four weeks after this happened, a little boy was sitting about three rows back and about two rows closer to home plate, and

The Yankees were the first to put numbers on the back of uniforms...circa 1930...Lou Gehrig was the first athlete to have his number retired.

he got hit above the ear, and it fractured his skull. The Cubs ended up paying his family fifty or sixty thousand dollars in medical bills. I think they did it voluntarily because there's no liability for a batted ball. If a player throws a bat, that is a liability issue. You don't expect a bat to come flying in the stands, but a ball, you just kind of assume the risk.

The fans in Wrigley are nice. They'll give you the business, but you never feel like you're in fear like you would at Shea. You would never go to Shea and wear any Cardinal apparel or you wouldn't get out alive. Wrigley is just good natured banter. I really enjoy going up there. We try to go up there at least one Cub-Cardinal game every summer. When we had those seats, we'd definitely go.

For years I took a megaphone to the games. I never used any profanity. In 1987, we were at Wrigley Field sitting in those good seats and the Cubs were playing Montreal. Hubie Brooks was playing shortstop for Montreal and Tim Wallach was their third baseman. It's so close there you can hear the players talking when they're having infield practice between innings. Hubie walks over to Wallach, probably about the bottom of the third inning, and he says, "The Cardinals are going against Dwight Gooden in New York today." Wallach says, "Yeah. Gooden's pretty tough on them. He'll probably shut them out." It kind of ticked me off, but I didn't say anything. The game goes on for an inning or two. I looked up at the manual scoreboard, and the guy drops a "10" for the Cardinals in the top of the first inning. I couldn't resist that—I had the megaphone there. I had it turned all the way down to a "one." Pasqual Perez was pitching that day. He had the Cubs shut out. He's just going into his windup, I flipped the megaphone on and I just said, "Hey Wallach, Brooks, look what the Cardinals just did to Dwight Gooden in the top of the first inning," thinking they were professional enough they'd wait until after the pitch was made. The minute I said that, they swiveled around to look at the scoreboard, and the Cub batter hit a hard one-hopper right between Wallach's legs. If it would have been about three inches higher, his voice would have been about ten octaves higher. So, the ushers come down and take my megaphone away, like it was my fault.

People don't remember this now because you can go anywhere and buy a real major-league uniform exactly like the players wear. But that wasn't available until the early nineties. The teams really guarded those uniforms. They had some type of a fear that people were going to sneak out onto the field in a real major league uniform. You could always tell the uniform—it was such a bright white. The Cardinals are one of the most expensive uniforms because there's a company by the name of Levy where the ladies hand embroider the bird on the backs of the uniforms. I was in Joe Cunningham's office in 1987 and I'd been bugging Joe for several years to get me a real Cardinal jersey. He would never tell me no, but would just say, "Well, I've got to get you together with Bill Smith from Rawlings." One day I took Joe a check for about thirty thousand dollars for our group night. He got a phone call. While he was on the phone, a guy knocks at the door, and says, "Hi Joe." Joe cups his hand over the phone and says, "Hey, Gene, there's the guy you want to meet." I said, "Who's this?" He said, "That's Bill Smith, from Rawlings Sporting Goods." I stood up and shook his hand, and he said, "What's going on here? What do you want?" I told him I wanted a real Cardinal jersey with my lucky number 33 and my name on it. So Bill looks at Joe and says, "Joe I'm not supposed to do this. You're going to get me in trouble." Joe says, "Hey, look, the guy's been a group manager for me. He's been a season ticket holder for years. Just do it for me. Make him up a uniform." So the guy says, "Okay, you want your last name, SIGLOCK, lucky number 33." I said, "Yeah." He told me they were running off a Cardinal order right now, and this was on a Friday. He told me, "Call me a week from today after lunchtime, and I will have the uniform for you. With all the lettering and everything, it would cost about three hundred and thirty bucks." I asked him what he wanted for it, and he said, "Well, we'll just do it for you, but your group night is when they have the fireworks display, so how about a few tickets." I said, "Well, that depends on how many tickets—if you want fifty or so—no." He said, "No, seven or eight tickets." I said, "You got it." So I got him the tickets.

The next Friday I call out there like he had told me. He told me to hold while he went to check on the uniform and was gone a long time. When he came back, he said, "I don't know what to tell you. It's been made up, and it's crossed off the list, but it's not here so apparently they've boxed it up and shipped it down to the ballpark with the Cardinals' order. Let me track it down." I said, "No, don't worry. I'll just call Joe and he'll track it down for me." I call Joe and tell him what happened, and he gave me the name of Buddy Bates, who was the clubhouse guy. Joe was a notorious practical joker—nothing mean or anything like that, but he loves to pull peoples' chains. Buddy gets on the phone and says, "Gene, where are you?" I said, "I'm over in Illinois." He said, "Well, get your fanny over here so we can get you outfitted and get you out there for batting practice. Your locker is going to be between Jose Oquendo and Tommy Herr."

Years ago, they didn't have the name plaque like they do now—they would individually sew the letters onto the uniform. The team would give the Levy Company the next uniform number to go out, and it just happened to be—guess what number—33. Now I'm saying, "Hey Buddy, let's quit kidding around. I need to come over to get the uniform 'cause I want to wear it for my group night." He thinks I'm some rookie just pulling his chain. Everything I say, he's changing around. I said, "Come on, who do you know that the Cardinals had in the minor leagues whose last name is Siglock? That was when they had all those injuries in the middle of the year, and he said, "Look buddy, I got Rod Booker starting at second base tonight, and I never heard of him until ten o'clock this morning." Everything I say, he kept saying, patronizingly, "Well, I'm sure that Rawlings Sporting Goods sent me a jersey with your name and number 33 on it by mistake." I had no way of knowing then, but that was the next uniform number coming up. Finally I had to get Joe back on the line to convince him I wasn't some rookie.

Now he's real embarrassed. He asked if I was coming to the game that night and told me to come into the Cardinal office and ask for him. My wife, kids and I get to the game, and I didn't know what he was going to do so I sent them on down to our seats and I went in and asked for him. He comes and gets me and takes me down to the clubhouse and I got to meet Jim Lindeman, then the Cardinal first baseman, and several of the Cardinals. They signed some autographs for me and bought me a soda. He gives me the whole rest of the uniform, the real Cardinal stirrup socks, the pants, the cap—like another two hundred dollars worth of stuff, and he won't take any money for it. I'm having a blast down there talking with them.

I'd always wear the uniform to the All-Star game. A lot of times people really thought I was a player. When we were in Minnesota, the players were actually dressing in the hotel, and my son and I were walking over to the ballpark, and I just had the uniform shirt on, and all of a sudden, I hear tires squealing. This cab comes through a red light, pulls to a stop right in front of us, and the guy slides over to the passenger side and shoves a baseball and an ink pen in my face and asks for my autograph.

Now you can go out and buy any uniform, but back then you couldn't possibly buy one.

Cardinal Fan Jim Clauser

WISCONSIN: COME SMELL OUR DAIRY AIR

Steve Schmitt

If you're looking for arguably the best Cardinal fan in the country, you would be well-advised to start in the middle of nowhere. That, of course, would be Black Earth, Wisconsin. Go to the largest shoe store in the Midwest, The Shoe Box, and ask for Steve Schmitt, 56, the owner. If he's not there, head two miles west to a sports bar called Rookies, which has a real Whiffle Ball field behind it and a Cardinal Museum inside. Steve Schmitt is living testament for what enthusiasm, passion in your pursuits and a great attitude will do to transform anyone's life. He'll be smiling, chattering a mile-a-minute, darting here and there, lovin' it all...but ask him about the Cardinals and he "steps it up" another notch.

His team, the Madison Mallards, in the Northwoods College League outdraws every team in the Cape Cod Summer College League as well as many minor league teams. Hang around Steve Schmitt for awhile, and a lot of things are gonna happen and most of 'em are gonna be real good! He'll meander all over the place with his conversation, disappear for a time, return and resume in mid-sentence. When you leave, there will be a smile on your face and a great feeling in your heart.

In 1956 I was walking around in my home town of Black Earth, Wisconsin and I'm trying to get KAAY out of Little Rock, Arkansas, a rock and roll station, or KOMA, the Coma in Oklahoma, but somehow I got KMOX. All of a sudden, Musial's up in the bottom of the eighth, and he hits a shot off the pavilion roof. It cleared the bases and a guy I'd heard of but never heard "live" was almost jumping out of the booth—Harry Caray. I'm amazed. I thought, "This is the greatest." I didn't know too much about the Cardinals. I had listened a little to Blaine Walsh and Earl Gillespe back in the fifties in the Milwaukee Braves heyday. I loved baseball but the craze just never really hitched with me or anything, All of a sudden, the next night I'm trying to find KMOX—where is this radio station? I caught it again. I don't remember the details, but it was another exciting game.

The next day I write to: St. Louis Cardinals, Busch Stadium, St. Louis, Missouri—no zip code. "I am Steve Schmitt. I'm nine years old, and I'm a Cardinals' fan." They sent me back 4" x 6" black and whites of Wilmer "Vinegar Bend" Mizell and Don Blasingame and Musial and all those guys—I was hooked! It was just amazing. I'll never forget it. That was a great year for me.

Like everybody else, I started a scrapbook. I collected cards. I did the Whiffle Ball thing. I kept the stats. I did all the stances of the Bill Whites and the **George Crowes** and Gino Cimoli and Javier and everybody. How they hit, I tried to hit. Of course, when Cunningham hit left-handed, I hit left-handed. I did the announcing in the Harry Caray style.

I played full nine inning Whiffle Ball games with my friend. We kept track, and I had a big lead, and he came back and beat me thirty-two games to thirty. We would go nine innings, like Whiffle Ball, we'd use the plastic bats and a little golf-size Whiffle Ball and play in our back yards in Black Earth. You hit a shot off the porch, it was a double; off the roof, if you caught it, it was live if it rolled down; if it went over the roof, it was a home run. We had our ground rules. We thought it was great. If we had enough guys, of course, we'd go play a pickup game somewhere. We lived for that. I'll never forget that summer. We had such a great time.

I collected a lot of Cardinal cards which I still have. I had a neighbor, who was a little older than I, who went in the Navy and his mother gave me all his cards, and I still have those. I owe this guy a lot 'cause in those cards was a '53 Mantle, Jackie Robinson. They mean a lot to

George Crowe's brother, Ray, was Oscar Robertson's high school basketball coach...Red Auerbach was Bowie Kuhn's high school basketball coach.

me, but they aren't worth anything to me, because they'll all end up with my grandkids.

I begged my folks to take me to County Stadium in Milwaukee to watch the Cardinals play the Braves. There was no freeway in those days, all two-lane roads. They took me in 1957. There were only two years that the Cardinals took birds on the bat off their uniforms, and that was the first year. I remember seeing Ken Boyer with just the "Cardinals" across the front.

My favorite would have to be Stan Musial. I loved them all. I liked George Crowe when he came off the bench to pinch-hit. I liked Gino Cimoli and Carl Warwick and, of course, Joe Cunningham and Schoendienst and all those guys. I guess they were all my favorites—they're all definitely my favorites.

I never went to old Sportsman's Park. I went to Grand and Dodier last year during the playoffs and sat there with a buddy of mine just for the memories. They had a big sign up down there. I listened to all those games, but never had a chance to go to that park.

Where I grew up in Wisconsin, there weren't any other Cardinal fans. None of my buddies were ever Cardinal fans. There were a lot of Braves fans and Yankee fans and Cubs fans, a few White Sox fans, still a few Red Sox fans. But I had nobody that I hung around with that was a St. Louis Cardinal fan. Now, today, there are all kinds of Cardinal fans. These guys come in the store every day. I love it. They tell me their favorite stories. I had a family come in yesterday, and they saw my signs. I have a big Cardinal with a bat on the outside of the Shoe Box and St. Louis logos all over the outside of the store. Cub fans stop in. They'll argue with you that they're the number one Cub fan. I say, "That's wonderful." Because Cardinal fans don't argue who's the number one Cardinal fan—we just have so much in common. That's one thing about Cardinal fans. I don't know about other fans, too, but there's no competition. It's amazing to me. Nobody's trying to outdo the other guy with a story. Cardinal fans are different.

The hardest time trying to get a ticket was for Mark McGwire's September 8, 1998, game when he hit the sixty-second home run. I had been there for home run number sixty-one the day before. I called my daughter, Emily, and told her she had to get down there. I made reservations for her through TWA Express, and she went to the airport that night, but there was some kind of mix-up. She went back home crying because it didn't work out. I said, "Emily, we'll try tomorrow morning." I got her in from Madison to Chicago, and she came down for that Tuesday game. There was a guy in the street, and I bought a couple of tickets from him for about thirty rows up behind the dugout. I paid four hundred bucks each.

Before, a lot of times, I would go and just get a single ticket, which wasn't too bad to get. I got to see home runs numbers 61, 62 and then 64, 65, and then went back for 69 and 70.

My big thrill is to go to spring training, go to Jupiter. I've been doing that for several years and I go down and see the first four games. I get to talk to my buddies, Dave Duncan and Marty Mason, Jose Oquendo, Joe Pettini and Boots Day. They are all good friends. They always order shoes and western boots. They're characters. I leave them alone. I don't hound them. That's a big deal for me. And, I always go to Opening Day in St. Louis. I wouldn't miss that. That's a big deal. A lot of times after the last sale on Saturday night here at The Shoe Box, about six o'clock, I'll drive to St. Louis– it takes about six and a half hours. From The Shoe Box in Black Earth, Wisconsin to Rockford to Bloomington to Springfield and into St. Louis, about three hundred and seventy miles. I sometimes get to Mike Shannon's for the last call for one bottle of Budweiser and back to the room. I can get down to St. Louis by about twelve-thirty, one o'clock. The next day I'll go to the game, leave after the game about four-thirty or five, and get back about eleven-thirty.

I love the National League. I love the Pirates, the Cubs, the Reds, the Giants, the Dodgers, even the Mets and the Astros and the Expos even though they came a little late. I love all the National League teams. The Senior Circuit is my favorite, by far. I love Wrigleyville, that whole area. If you took all the cars out of there, and came off that El train, it would be just like 1940 or 1930. Not a whole lot has changed. Cub fans are Cub fans, and I respect them to no end. It's just that we're Cardinal fans, and we're a little different. And a little better. As Jack Buck said, "Maybe the best thing Chicago could do with the Cubs and White Sox is to merge them, and then they'd only have one losing team." There's "C-U-B-S—Completely Useless By September!" The National League gives the Cubs a lot of credit over the years—they've held the rest of the National League up from the bottom for a long time. But, no, I love Cub fans. There are a lot of wonderful Cub fans that come in the store. Some are elderly and some are young, but we always have a good time. We have this certain bond, as long as we're guys in the Senior Circuit.

My grandson and my daughter have gotten foul balls. I guess if I've gotten a foul ball, I've given it away. I'm looking at balls here from a lot of good players over the years. These are all gifts. I've never bought a signed baseball. I have so much Cardinal memorabilia that I had to buy a restaurant and decorate it. I bought a place and called it "Rookies" and it has a full-size Whiffle-Ball field and there's Cardinal memorabilia on the walls and on the ceiling. There are six thousand baseball cards in the men's bathroom behind glass. Ninety per cent of the memorabilia is all St. Louis Cardinals. It's located right outside of Black Earth. It's quite a place. I've had people say that outside of Cooperstown, it's pretty amazing.

My dad owned The Shoe Box in 1951, and then I bought him out in the early seventies. I deal with a hundred and ninety major shoe companies. I just had a call from Tom Tresh and Bob Turley. Bob Turley and I talked baseball for a while, and Tom Tresh ordered a pair of shoes. We have dress shoes and western boots and golf shoes—you name it we've got it.

Lots of major league ballplayers have been here in the store—Fergie Jenkins, Maury Wills, Ron Kittle, Hal Lanier, Tom Lawless, Joe Cunningham, Gaylord Perry, Johnny Blanchard, Jimmy Wynn, Tommy Davis, Ryne Duren, Joe Charbonneau—that's probably just the tip of the iceberg.

When I go to spring training, I'm pretty low-key about being in the shoe business. Some of them order shoes from me. I don't bother or hound them while I'm there. If they want shoes, they get hold of me. They can talk to me. I never invade their privacy. They'll see me up in the stands and they'll come over and talk to me. Red Schoendienst called two weeks ago and told me he needed three pair of shoes. He wanted a light-colored slip-on, a dark-colored slip-on, and a lace shoe with a soft sole. He has no idea of stock numbers or anything so I just sent him three pairs and I get a check a week later, with one of his 6" x 8" signed cards that I don't have. Those are definitely my kind of guys.

I get caught up here. I'm at the store ninety hours a week. I don't have a lot of time to think about things, but it's a big deal. Ryne Duren's a big buddy of mine, and everybody loves him. He's on the bus somewhere or out eating and he gets his cell phone out and he'll have me talk to someone. It's a big deal for me. A couple of months ago he said he had four guys who wanted to talk to me. The first guy was **Bill Mazeroski**, and then Harmon Killebrew and then Fergie Jenkins who I know through another party, and then Nelson Briles, who I had never talked to before. After Gibson went down with his broken leg, Nelson Briles came back and won like eleven games for us. That was a big treat to talk to him. I went down to the St. Louis Browns reunion last year. For two days we sat around and talked to those St. Louis Browns guys, Roy Sievers, Don Gutteridge, Ned Garver, and all those guys. It was amazing. That was a great treat for me. I finally could get away from The Shoe Box for a couple of days and just talk baseball with those old guys.

After 9/11, I flew to Pittsburgh, spur of the moment, for a game, and flew back the same night. I remember a couple of years ago, the Cardinals were in Denver and were snowed out on a Saturday. There was only that one trip to Denver scheduled that year so they rescheduled the Saturday game to Sunday and made it a doubleheader. This was my chance to go somewhere and see eighteen innings of baseball. What a fantasy that would be. I get United Airlines and get to Denver, and they did it as a split doubleheader, but I still got to see one game. I just flew back that Sunday night. I love doing things like

Phil Niekro lost one game in high school. When he was a freshman, he lost to a rival team from East Liverpool, Ohio. The winning pitcher was Bill Mazeroski, a senior.

that. It's hard for me to plan anything ahead of time. It depends on how busy we are here.

Tony La Russa has been my favorite Cardinal manager. I would never say anything negative from Fred Hutchinson to Solly Hemus to Joe Torre to Whitey Herzog or Tony La Russa. I don't really know if I have a favorite—I love them all. I had an old buddy who just passed away at eighty-two years of age. He's been a customer of mine and a friend of mine probably for twenty-five years. He's never called me by my name—every time he saw me, he always called me Solly Hemus. He was one of my favorites. As a matter of fact, he was buried in a Shoe Box sweatshirt. What a character he was.

I don't know if I would say we're successful, but we're always busy. I love what I'm doing. I spend most of my time here. I own a restaurant, but I don't go out there for lunch or for a beer at night. I run my butt off here and love it, and I take care of the Madison Mallards. During the game, I'm doing everything from cooking hot dogs to changing the paper towel rolls in the men's room. We draw good crowds.

The Madison Mallards are college kids and the league is like the Cape Cod League. We have a good time. I took an old ballpark and put a bunch of Cardinal memorabilia around and hung a bunch of flags and put a bunch of banners up and put truckloads of paint on the walls and the bleachers. We put a party deck out there. We're having a wonderful time. The players are all freshmen and sophomores in college. They are all good kids. We host an All-Star game every year. We have a combine and a home run hitting contest. We have three kids from Baylor, Minnesota, University of Illinois, three guys from Notre Dame. The first year we did nine hundred seventy three fans a game. Last year we did nineteen hundred seventy two fans a game, and this year we're up to forty-two hundred and fifty-six fans a game. I have a good manager, and he's picked out some great kids. I painted the whole courtyard and the walkway green, and with duck-prints and hung a bunch of flags and banners up. I've got an open-air suite that I call "Baseball Heaven." I have a big "Welcome to Baseball Heaven" with a halo over Maynard, our mascot." I do "Baseball Like It Oughta Be," all over the park. We try to be customer friendly. I have about seventy people working out there, and they're all great, and I love them to death, but when the gates open at five forty-five, at five thirty-five, we'd better be going. It's a never-ending battle. The minute that door opens, and the first fan walks in, everything should be finished. We should all be at our stations with smiles on our faces and ready to go.

I've never thought about whether or not I'm the biggest Cardinal fan in the country. I've got a gentleman who comes in and he went to school with Stan Musial. I had the Cardinal batboy in yesterday, Nate Pfitzer. He's twenty-two years old and is still the Cardinals' bat boy. His grandma lives in Madison, only twenty miles from here. I've met so many big Cardinal fans. I think Cardinal fans are very different from other fans. I can see Cubs' fans arguing "I'm a bigger Cub fan than you 'cause I saw **Andy Pafko** play in 1945. I saw Charlie Grimm playing." But I don't think Cardinal fans are that way. All I know is every day at The Shoe Box, I play the St. Louis Cardinals' movie, and I have for fifteen years. It's a highlight of the history of the St. Louis Cardinals. It goes on at seven in the morning and goes off at nine every night, seven days a week, little shorter hours on Sunday. Cardinal fans come in and want to know where I got it, and so I've begun to keep extra copies here if they want to buy one. While I'm at the store, I always wear something with a Cardinals' logo on it.

I can't ever imagine going to a ballpark and having negative feelings. The Cardinals can lose, but just hours later, they can come back and get five runs in the first inning.

If, when I was a little boy, I hadn't picked up that KMOX Harry Caray broadcast, I don't know where I'd be now. I don't think I would have been a Braves' fan, and something about Earl Gillespe's voice and Blaine Walsh's voice, and those guys were great, but now that I think back, they were absolutely wonderful, but they didn't do anything for me—not a thing. I just don't think things would have been as good. I rarely have a chance to come up here to my office, but right there is a 1968 World Series pennant up there with all the pictures on

In the very first set of Topps baseball cards, the first card (#1) was Andy Pafko.

it. I've got Cardinal jackets here. It's unbelievable. My life wouldn't have been half as good. I've got a great life. I've got a wonderful life. I think of the Stan Musials and the Red Schoendiensts and Ken Boyers—there's no end to it. Mike Shannon's call when Ozzie did the home run off of Niedenfuer, I'll never forget it. Mike tells Jack, "Jack, he's trying to pull the ball." You never hear that on replays because they don't go to that part of the highlight. But, there's Mike Shannon, and two pitches later, Ozzie pulled a home run.

Who can forget Bob Gibson. Wasn't he something? In 1968, he started thirty-four games, completed twenty-eight, thirteen shutouts, ERA 1.12. The question is: How did he have nine losses that year? With any luck, he would have won 30! Gotta go now.

Rookies Sports Bar, Black Earth, Wisconsin including authentic Whiffle Ball stadium..

BITS AND BITES—
BEGGED, BORROWED AND STOLEN

The most money I've ever made in one day would be when Mark McGwire hit the sixty-second home run—I sold about twenty-two cases. That's over three hundred dollars in commission, and I made about three hundred in tips. A big night! I remember the moment that he hit the sixty-second home run. I was pouring a guy two cans of beer. He had given me a twenty. Mark hit the home run. Everybody went crazy and celebrated for five or ten minutes. Then I went back over there to give him his change for the two beers. He told me to keep the twenty, and he handed me a fifty. That was seventy dollars for nine dollars worth of beer. So at that historic moment, that's when I got that tip money. My other fans, beyond that, were pretty much five, ten extra—that's how I made so much money that night. He made money for us. During that time, the place was filled. Most of the people had left after his last at-bat. I loved Mark McGwire.

——RUSSELL, THE BEERMAN, 54, Spanish Lake, Missouri

We heard about the Celebrity Bartenders promotion at the Westin Hotel after a Cardinal game. It was Jason Isringhausen and Jim Edmonds who were going to bartend. One of my girlfriends went over there early before the game to check out the bar seating, get in good with the bartender, just to check out the lay of the land. After the game, we walked into the bar at the Westin and it was packed. We couldn't get a seat anywhere close to the bar. However, one of the hotel employees had remembered my friend being there earlier, and actually made room for us at the bar. Well, Edmonds and Isringhausen came in to bartend. It was something else!!! They had no clue—the only thing they knew how to do was hand somebody a cold bottle of Bud—there was no way they even had an inkling about how to make a mixed drink!!!!! Not only that, they didn't even attempt to run the register, so they ended up handing out beer to everybody and not charging. It got really, really, crowded. So we ask Jimmy Edmonds for a shot of Goldschlaeger. He was able to muster up a shot glass and pour the shots. We asked him for another one and he was so flustered he couldn't find any more shot glasses because no one was behind the bar to clean the barware. I yelled to Jimmy, "Jimmy, just give us the bottle!" He took a look at us, looked at the bottle, and was more than glad to hand it over to us, just so he didn't have to round up shot glasses. We passed the bottle around a couple of times between seven of us. We then we handed it back to him and he put it on the back bar!!! That night was just so great!!!!! Vina was there, Tony La Russa showed up and everybody had a great time!!! They were signing autographs and all. One time I turned around and there was La Russa just inches away. I was so flabbergasted, I reached out and twisted his nipples. He was stunned. You can't get that kind of clarity sober. The best part was they were just handing out drinks right and left, and they never even attempted to figure out the cash register system. It was just a hoot to see them behind that bar running back and forth. They really worked their rear ends off!!!!!

——MAUREEN KELLY HOENER, 46, St. Charles, MO

I take my glove to the game, but I haven't gotten a foul ball. I carry it in my van almost everywhere I go. If the kids are playing ball, and I'm not in a hurry, I stop. I'm part of it. I love baseball. I really do.

I don't go to many games. To tell the truth, I'd rather watch it on television. The beer's cheaper, the restrooms aren't crowded. I like going to the games, I go down on the MetroLink when I do go 'cause it runs just a short distance from the house and takes you right to the ballpark. You don't have bent fenders and the big expense to park.

When I go down the steps to my basement, I have a life-size cutout of Ozzie Smith there. He has a bat in one hand and a glove in the other hand like he's being interviewed. People are kind of surprised because they think he's standing there. I made it. It was a six foot, five foot roll, and I glued it on the cardboard and cut it out with a razorblade. That gets a lot of comment. I've got my scorecard up there when I played at Fantasy Camp. I was named the most valuable player on our team. Each team had one. We had eleven men on a team, and I played short center. I always played outfield when I was a kid, and I don't remember ever dropping a fly ball. I used two hands.

——CLARENCE VOLLMAR, 77, Florissant, Mo…
Cardinal memorabilia collector and Cardinal Fantasy camper…

I didn't know Frank Mankiewicz—a big Washington power-broker—but after a little while he found out I was a Cardinal fan, and we sat together a good deal. He was very helpful on giving me inside information on what was going on. He was press secretary for Bobby Kennedy. We loved to stump each other. During the latter stages of the McGovern campaign, I was right on deadline, and my editor, John Hughes, called me in Washington. He wanted some information to make it really zing. I called up Mankiewicz's office and got his secretary. I told her how urgent it was, and she said he was working on something vital. She says his door is locked and no one can go in. I told her to write this down and slip it under his door—"Who was the outfielder for the St. Louis Cardinals, whose uncle was Buster Keaton?" All of a sudden I heard this phone pick up, and there was Mankiewicz. He says, "Who was it?" I said, "Ernie Orsatti" Then he gave me the information I wanted for my story.

——BUD SPERLING, 87, columnist for the *Christian Science Monitor*

The managers and coaches talked about Tony Pena and how he was going to do all these wonderful things, but he was the clumsiest guy on two feet. All he did was fall down and break something every spring. That, to me, was the most frustrating thing. A close second behind him is J. D. Drew. With all that he could do, he's such a panty-waist that every time he gets a hangnail, he's off for three days.

——KAY HOENIG, Cardinal Fan

On the Cardinal Cruise a few years ago, there was this guy who was just an indescribable jerk. He was not part of the Cardinal group but kept leeching onto us. He was standing there talking to Ray Lankford. Ray kept trying to push him off onto me. I had been carrying my camera around and as an embarrassment to Ray, I said to the jerk, "Hey, would you like to have your picture taken with Ray Lankford?" He said, "Yeah!!!" I said "Okay, Ray, smile!" and he mouthed a foul word to me. All of the sudden Ray looks at the guy and looks at me and says, "Hey, wouldn't you rather have your picture taken with her than with me?" The guy says, "Yeah!!!!" Ray reaches for my camera and I told him to back off, stand there and smile. The guy puts his arm around Ray a little bit, and I take the picture. Being so close, when I took the picture, it was overexposed quite a bit, and Ray's eyes bugged out because he didn't want to be in the picture at all, and this guy had this really cheesy grin. At the Winter Warm-Up, I had made multiple copies of the picture and had given them to different people in our group. Ray was one of the people signing autographs at the Winter Warm-Up that year. We all decided we were going to take these pictures up to him and have him sign them. We're sitting at a table right outside the main signing area, and we were talking about it. There was a lady sitting at the table and none of us had any idea who she was. She started laughing as we were talking about it. I looked at her and said, "Would you like to help us out?" She says, "This sounds great, yes." I told her if she did this I would pay for her to get an autograph of his on whatever she wanted. She said, "No, I just want to be a part of it." I give her an 8x10 copy of this picture. Ray has no idea who she is. She stands in the line and she plays this thing so good. She gets up there and lays it down on the table in front of him. Ray looks around and says, "You weren't on the cruise, right?" She says, "No." He says, "Where did you get this picture?" "Some lady is out there in the lobby selling them." "Ray stands up and screams out my name" We were obviously rolling at this point.

——MICHELLE DITTON, St. Louis

A guy named Joe Vonder Haar went nuts on this fantasy camp concept. He brought his brother who is a short, squat guy, heavy-set, but not a bad athlete. His brother Virgil has now become the batting practice pitcher for the Cardinals. He had never pitched before in his life. He showed up there. He's a left-handed pitcher, and obviously they like him. He wears number sixty-six; most of them wear a number like ninety-nine. He just wears his uniform from the camp. He was telling me the other day that there were people yelling at him from the outfield, "Boy, that Ankiel's really let himself go, hasn't he?"

——MARTY HENDIN, Cardinal Vice President of Community Relations

After Ozzie hit his home run in '85, I thought, "This is the end of an exciting day, and I'm going to take tomorrow off so I'll stay up late tonight and go hang around down where the celebration is. On my

way down to the Landing, I was searching where all the noise was coming from, and I happened to run into a guy on the street. He was a pretty scraggly-type character. He had a gym bag with him, and I found out he was selling some hats and novelty stuff. He said, "I might have something you want. He showed me a couple of hats, but I already had them. He said, "I have something you don't have. I'll guarantee you don't have it." He pulled out a hat—blue with orange trim, the Mets colors, and it said, "Hernandez sucks." He told me it was five dollars, so I bought it, for the laugh. I put it on underneath my Cardinal cap, and went down to the landing. We were all drinking, and everybody kept pulling off my Cardinal cap 'cause they could see this blue cap underneath it, and they thought it was a Dodger cap. As soon as they looked at it, they started laughing. They wanted me to go up to the band and show it to them and told me they would get a laugh over it and would give me a free drink. I was game. I go up there, and the guy tells the whole bar about the cap. I get my free drink and I'm happy. I was up there talking to the owner, and all of a sudden, this girl tugs on my shirt sleeve. I thought, "Boy, this is going to be a great night." See a great game, get a free drink, and…. Then this girls says, "Do you know who that is over there?" I said, "No." She said, "Well, that's Keith Hernandez." She said, "He showed me his license." I just rolled my eyes back in my head. I thought of that line in Casablanca, "Of all the gin joints in all the world," when I decide to have some fun, there's a guy right here that I've been making fun about. It was like, "I'm gonna wake up tomorrow and people back in my hometown are gonna read the paper and see that this guy got upset and started a ruckus at the bar." She pulled me over there where he was. It was actually Hernandez, but he was pretty cool about it.

I told him, "No one is going to believe this really happened. Could you autograph my ticket to the game?" And he did! It was pretty incredible.

——**KEN THOMPSON**, Ballston Spa, New York native

All the ex-Cards who go to Fantasy Camp are regular guys. You can sit down and talk with them and they tell great stories. Bob Forsch, Lou Brock, Danny Cox, George Hendrick, Tudor, Tewksbury. A lot of the guys I have the home phone numbers of most of them. It's just amazing the instruction you get down there. Jack Clark and George Hendrick were my coaches. I couldn't hit a baseball to save my butt when I went in there but then I was hitting .400 when I left.

Danny Cox and George Hendrick have to be two of the funniest people I ever met. Danny and George were our coaches together. Each team has their own name. Our team was called The Silent Cox. There was one team called Ten Gardeners and a Hoe, because they had ten guys and a girl. The gal was Ann Carroll, who was there doing a story for Fox Sports Midwest. On our team, one guy had a prosthesis with his leg cut off from the knee down. We called him "CHA." We had a guy seventy-six years old on our team—who could play. George was always giving this guy a hard time. The old guy gets a hit. He's running down to first, makes the turn, and George goes, "That's the way to hit it." The old guy looked at George and says, "Take that, you p——."

Each day, if they catch you doing something, they fine you. One day, the catcher, instead taking his mask off and throwing it, took his glove off and threw it when he tried to catch a foul ball. They fined him for it. There were numerous times when guys would walk up to bat without their helmet on and they would fine them for that. One guy tried to slide home but he was like fifteen feet short, and he got fined big time. Usually the fines were a buck. The money goes right to the foundation.

——**JOHN EPPARD**, Carson City, Indiana, Cardinal Fantasy Camper

The hardest ticket to get for me was the one for the night McGwire hit number five hundred. I looked for about two hours, and nobody was selling that night. Not at any price, there were none to be sold. Then a foreign guy walks up to me, and says, "Are you needing a ticket?" I said, "Yes, how much?" He said, "Here, just take it." I said, "No, I don't know how much they are, but I'll pay you." He said, "No." We go into the stadium, and I offer to buy him beer or soda or peanuts, and he said, "No, don't worry about it." Then just right before the game, the Cardinals come out. We're sitting on the first-base side about halfway up over the dugout, and he goes, "Which one is Mark McGwire?" This was the night he hit five hundred. I could not believe it, and I said, "What?" He said, "Where is Mark McGwire?" I said, "He's on first base." He said, "Where is first base?" He was about twenty-five and was working here short term as an intern or something. He said his company gave him the tickets about three months previous so he could go to the ball game. It ended up being game five hundred. Here I had been ready to pay two hundred bucks for a ticket to go to this game and to see this milestone event.

——JEFF DINAN, Friends Tire Company

Russell the Beer Man. He is so important to us that we paid his way on the 2003 Boston and New York trip. Russell has let me run tabs. I've said, "Sorry I don't have any money tonight," and he said, "That's okay, Cathy, you can just pay me tomorrow." Every year Russell buys something new with his tip money. One year it was a Cardinal red Mustang convertible which he still has, like an '87, '88. We had a party that we started 20 years ago called Bleacher Fest. It used to be just the people who sat in the bleachers and worked the bleachers, back when we were caged in but now it's open. They were after the last game of the season, bring out some bar-b-que grills. One year we were running out of beer and I said I'll go on a beer run. Russell walks over and gives me the keys to his brand new Mustang and says here take my car. I said, "Russell you must be nuts." He said, "Cathy, I trust you with my car." Dumbest thing Russell ever did.

——CATHY LEONARD, Bleacher Season Ticket Holder

We tease Delores, next to us, who is the sixty-nine-year-old. Delores keeps score in every game. She's got the Bob Carpenter book. She goes to every game, too. She's got her own unique way of scoring.

We tease her about being old because she's watching the game, she's listening to it on the radio, and she'll still miss plays. She marks it WW for "wasn't watching." So we tease her and tell her she should put WL for "wasn't listening" either. There are enough people around there who are scoring that she can always catch a misplay from someone. It's just a whole big family down there. It seems like whenever somebody gives us box seats, we might sit there for the first half of the game, but we're anxious to get back to our family in the bleachers. So, we can be two rows behind home plate, and you know for sure by the seventh….You just miss your friends. People aren't fun in the box seats. They're usually on the cell phone.

Lucy came up with tee-shirts with the bleacher rules on it. The number one rule is no cell phones in the bleachers. You're supposed to be watching the game. Get off the phone.

We've got a chant for cell phones. They'll stand up and surround the people, "No Cell Phones! No Cell Phones!" And it's so loud, you can't hear the conversation. It forces them to hang up. That's the number one rule.

——JEFF KROEMER, Cedar Rapids, IA

Cardinals Fan John Denver

THE NAKED AND THE DEAD (ALMOST)

Garrett Koch

Garrett Koch, 50, of Hazelwood, Missouri, is a computer trainer for EDS. When Mark McGwire hit his 70th home run in 1998, Koch captured it on film and had the great shot made into a poster. He took the poster to spring training in '99, determined to get McGwire to sign it.

As we got to Roger Dean Stadium in Jupiter, Florida that day, my whole focus is on "Where is he?" and "How can I get to him?" I am just driven. We enter into the stadium. The first thing my wife wants to do is buy souvenirs, and I'm not even thinking of that. I've got my cardboard tube mailing container for this poster and my marker and I'm ready to just go for it. After having seen a bunch of players come out that we did get signatures from even Red Schoendienst and some of the all-time greats, I'm still pumped and looking forward to this one opportunity I might get. We sit on the right field line, in the grass area, close to where the relief pitchers sit. That's where McGwire would go when he got pulled out of the game. He comes and sits down with them. He stood up between innings and signed stuff.

My brother, his wife and two sons are over on the left field stands. My wife and I sit there on our blanket along the right field line. McGwire is playing a rather terrible baseball game—made two errors by the seventh inning. In the bottom of the seventh, he gets up to bat. The crowd has been getting bigger and bigger and closer and closer and more intimidating to try and get close to the foul line. At every between-innings segment, there's a rush over to the right foul line so I decide just to stand there and wait for him through the game. The bottom of the seventh comes, and he hits a wimpy little nubber right back to the pitcher. He comes walking down the foul line. The electricity is going through all the fans standing there. I am ready with marker. As he comes walking down the line, we call and cheer and clap and watch him walk right out of the stadium, right off the field. I am just dumbfounded. I can't believe he's walked out and not signed anything.

Well, I'm not beaten. I've decided I'm going to get out there and find him somewhere back there. I say a quick word to my wife, and I head outside the stadium toward the direction he went. I find a gal standing there with a large-lens camera, looking as though she's done this before. Through this gate that she's looking, and I get to that point, and sure enough McGwire comes through that area, and I get a quick picture of him there. He continues to walk to my right down the sidewalk to the street. I start walking down that way thinking I'm going to beat him down to wherever he's going. I continue until I get to the clubhouse. Little did I know, at this point, that while I was walking down to this clubhouse, that he had dropped off his stuff, went back inside over to that right field line and had signed things for the fans that had been standing there.

I get down to the clubhouse and it says "Minor League Entrance." I consider myself minor league in various areas of my life, so I pop on in there—it didn't say "Minor League Only." I walk in and there's a reception desk. A young lady was behind the desk, kind of preoccupied with a few individuals. I notice on the right side, there were a couple of vending machines and a closed door that I'm thinking is the way back into the clubhouse locker rooms. I quickly decide I need a soda, and pull out a dollar and nonchalantly walk over to the vending machines and stick the dollar in and take a quick look over to the receptionist again. She was not paying any attention. I hit a button to get a soda. Nothing comes out. I hit another button. Nothing. I hit a third button. Nothing. Finally when I hit a button, a diet drink comes out. I don't like Diet Pepsi, but it didn't matter at that point. I got my soda. Another quick check at the receptionist—she's not looking. I grab the handle of that door, it opens, and I duck in, not knowing what's on the other side. Fortunately there's nothing there but a fairly blank hallway. There's nobody standing there, nobody noticed me come in, I realize what I've just done. I've got family

You Can't Be **Famous**
Unless You're a **Cardinals Fan**

John Daly

Rob Reiner

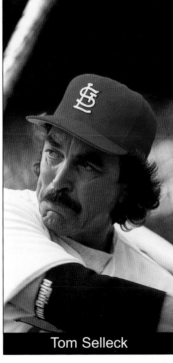

Tom Selleck

Yasmine Bleeth

Michael J. Fox

Stephen Tyler

Robert Wuhl

Kenny Rogers

Lea Thompson

Scott Bakula

George McGovern

Tony Orlando

Tommy Hilfiger

Ann Jillian

Isaac Bruce

John Schneider

Thomas Gibson
"Dharma's Greg"

Billy Bob Thornton

Jack Klugman

Donny & Marie

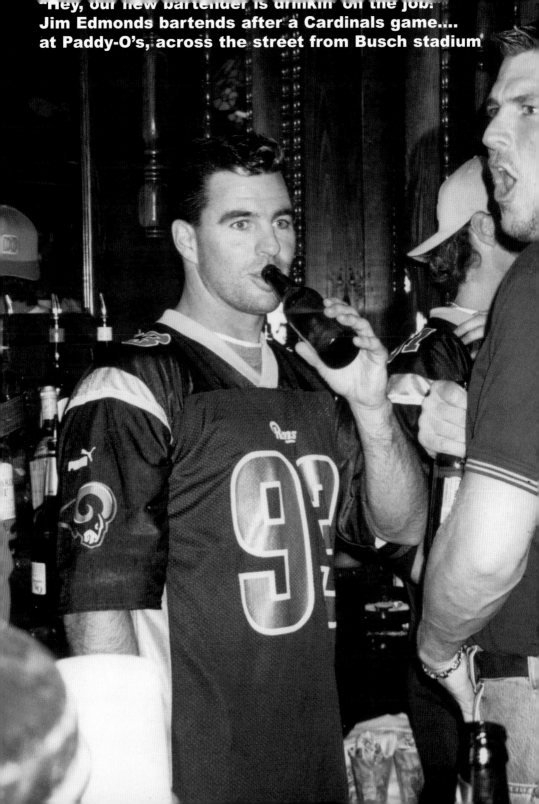

"Hey, our new bartender is drinkin' on the job!"
Jim Edmonds bartends after a Cardinals game....
at Paddy-O's, across the street from Busch stadium

Cruisin' with the Redbirds. Clockwise from upper left: Joe Buck, Fredbird, Walt Jocketty, Lou Brock, Cardinal fans Pat Blassie and Pat Eilermann and Bob Forsch

On the high seas. Clockwise from upper left: Al Hrabosky, Dal Maxvill, John Tudor, Tom Pagnozzi, Redbird fan Mike Hoenig and Joe Cunningham.

Scott Rolen, Mike Shannon, and Johnny Pesky at Fenway Park

NASCAR driver Kenny Wallace's racecar. The die-cast version is one of the top-selling models ever.

Former Cardinal pitcher Danny Cox (left) with Kenny Wallace

Atop the Marriott–1998...Cardinals fans desperate to see a McGwire home run

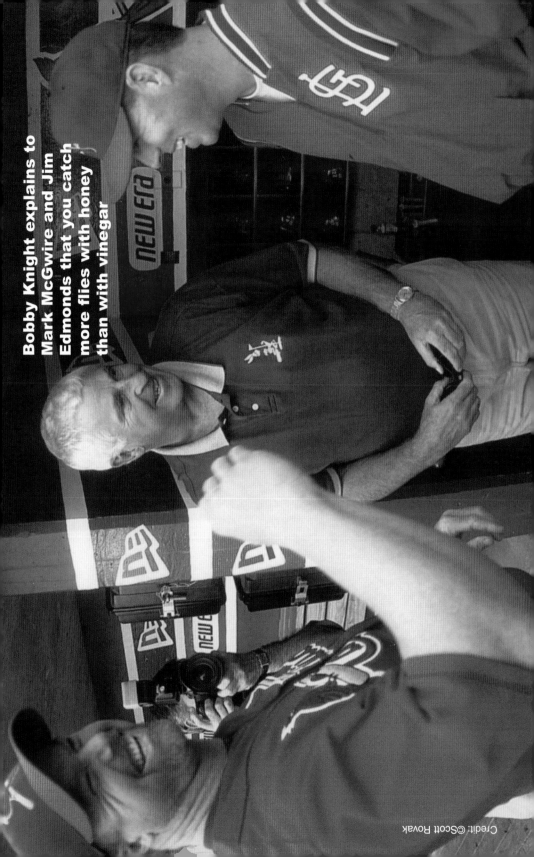

Bobby Knight explains to Mark McGwire and Jim Edmonds that you catch more flies with honey than with vinegar

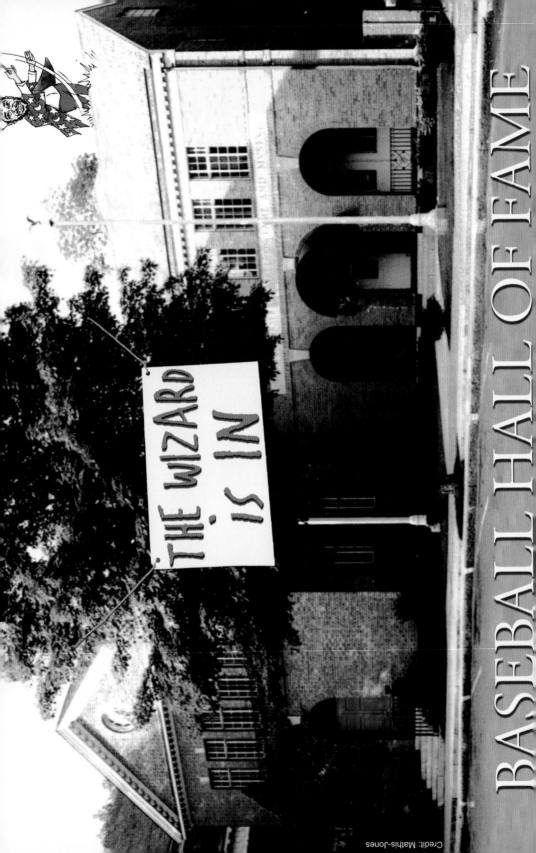

THE WIZARD IS IN

BASEBALL HALL OF FAME

Jason Isringhausen admires the unique airbrushed shirt of Debbie Gruber... butt we know what you're thinking!

TIME

THE WEEKLY NEWSMAGAZINE

CARDINALS' STAN MUSIAL
Thirty days hath September.

Stan Musial HOF 69

Happy Holidays!

outside that I may never see again because I may get arrested at this point. I headed down the hallway and realized that someone has entered from the other end of the hallway—looks like probably a trainer or a coach. I figured he was going to stop me and throw me out or have me arrested. As he approaches, I'm looking at a hallway that forks off from the hallway that we are both approaching each other on. I'm hoping I can get to that hallway before I get to him, but it didn't work out. He crossed the hallways, comes to me, says, "How you doing?" And, he walks past. I was dumbfounded that I hadn't been arrested, and here I am inside of the clubhouse where all I wanted to do was get my poster signed.

As I head down this other hallway, a main hallway down the center of the facility that must be a half a mile long, I start down it more or less investigating what's there. I'm passing these minor league coaches' offices and realizing more and more that this is kind of ridiculous. I don't know what I'm going to find here. As I get to what I thought was the center of it, there's another cross hallway, so I look in both directions and see no one, I just see other offices. I continue on down the main hallway, still with this Diet Pepsi in my hand. I thought my family must be wondering where I was, and I didn't know if the game was still going on. I get to another hallway, a third hallway, that has signs on both sides of the hallway indicating it was for "Major League Areas." So I thought I must be getting close. As I start to approach the far side and get into this major league area, it suddenly occurs to me, "What am I actually going to do here? Am I going to walk into a locker room and find Mark McGwire standing at his locker, possibly nude, after showering, and ask him to sign my poster? And what am I going to do with this Diet Pepsi?" So I decided to just get out of there.

The next step I take is toward a hallway to the left and I realize there's an entrance there to the home-team major league workout room. I thought it would be cool to see what kind of machines are in there. No sooner do I take a step inside, then there's Mark McGwire about ten feet away, standing in front of a mirror wearing nothing but a towel. Here's the hero that I've been looking up to, that I could get my poster of his most heroic moment in Cardinal history signed. That dumbfounded me so much that I was totally speechless. He's looking in this mirror and his eyes immediately start over to me as I enter his peripheral vision.

Here I am, this dumb-looking guy with a Cardinal baseball hat, wearing shorts and a camera around his neck, holding this cardboard tube. Obviously, we both intimidated each other. He looks at me and, for what seemed like two hours, I was trying to think of something to say. I can't stand it. I have to say something first. The only thing that comes to mind is, "Do you want a soda?" I beat myself up for—probably to this day—as to what else I could say—anything! "Do you know where I can find J. D. Drew?" Anything but "Did you want a soda?" He says, "No. Who are you? How did you get in here? Who let you in?" Suddenly, I realized that he'd had a bad day. He's getting closer as he's asking these questions. I realize I've blown it. Not only have I accosted my hero, but now I've intimidated him and basically got him mad. As he starts walking toward me, I see nothing, but this huge white chest getting bigger and broader and taller. Even my peripheral vision is getting filled up with his arms. As he's asking me these questions, I'm speechless. About the time he's two feet away from me, a hand comes onto my shoulder. I turn to look and it's one of the trainers. I look back at McGwire who is starting to walk away and I realize "I'm not going to get my poster signed. I've ruined a possible chance to actually meet Mark McGwire and possibly make a friend." We didn't even exchange names, shake hands, say "Hi." I turned and start walking toward the trainer, and he said, "Sir, you need to leave." I felt like I couldn't even move. I did not want to leave the area, but it was over. I'd met my hero in the worst possible way you could imagine.

THE DOs AND DON'Ts OF WORKING WITH MARK McGWIRE! DO!

Don Todd

Don Todd, 55, grew up in Pinck-neyville, Illinois, but has lived for many years in Lincoln, Illinois. He is retired from a handicapped development workshop.

I won an auction on a Mark McGwire bat at the '98 Winter Warm-Up. This meant that I would get to sit with Mark McGwire while he signed autographs. Also, I would get a Big Stick Mark McGwire bat, and he would sign that for me before he signed the other autographs.

I worked at Lincoln Developmental Center at the time, which is a place for developmentally disabled individuals. Michael, one of the individuals in my case load was a big St. Louis Cardinal fan and a big Mark McGwire fan. I decided that I would buy a picture of Mark and take that with me and ask him to sign it at the same time.

The auction ended on Sunday, and I had to be at the Regal Hotel on Monday at eleven thirty. McGwire was going to be there at noon to sign autographs. I went into one of the rooms—kind of like a press room—and waited. I had my picture. One of the Cardinal people came in and gave me the bat. I asked, "Do you think Mr. McGwire would mind signing this picture?" They automatically told me I couldn't take the picture and ask him to sign it, but I never gave up on the picture. Another person came and walked me to the stage about noon, and I asked him. He said the same thing—that I had paid for the bat, but I couldn't get the picture. They took me on to the stage, and I sat down at the table where Mark was going to come in. In a few minutes, his body guard walked in and introduced himself. The crowd was just humongous, a very big crowd.

In a few minutes, Mark came in. He was a very cordial person, shook my hand, asked me how I was, where I was from, and we talked a little bit. We sat down, and he asked me how I wanted the bat signed. He wrote "To Don. Mark McGwire. Number 25." Then he started signing autographs for other people. He signed and signed and signed. He hardly ever stopped, but one time when he did, I said, "Mark, can you do me a favor?" He said, "Sure." I told him about Michael, the individual that lived at Lincoln Developmental Center. He said, "Oh, I'd love to sign that." He signed the picture, "To Michael, from Mark McGwire." and I gave it to Michael, and he just loved it. I thought this was a real neat thing for him to do.

I went back to the Winter Warm-Up the next year. I bid on another opportunity to get an autograph, but this time they didn't have anyone sitting with Mark. I was part of the crowd, which is what I usually am, but as I got up to the table where Mark was, he said, "Hey Don, you ought to be up here with me." I couldn't believe that after a year, especially the year he had gone through, being thrown with so many fans, he still remembered me—remembered my name, and it was just like we were friends. It was such a fantastic feeling. Here was this man who had just broken Roger Maris' record; I think he had just met the Pope, yet, here he was, and he remembered me. That tells you the kind of guy Mark McGwire is.

ENOS WASN'T GOING BALD
HE WAS GETTING MORE HEAD

Don Saforek

Don "The Barber" Saforek is a legendary Cardinal fan in the Hawkeye state. Raised in Kalona, Iowa, he was an outstanding soldier in the Pacific Theater during World War II and was delighted when his uncle asked him to go to the 1946 World Series.

He and I headed for St. Louis and got to the stadium about an hour before the game. I was anxious to go in and said, "Let's go in and see them." He said, "No, we've got to get some tickets." I said, "What? You don't have any tickets?" He said, "No. Don't worry about it. Come on. Let's take a little walk."

We went across the street to the parking lot. The first thing you know, he's showing me Al Brazle's Cadillac, Murray Dickson's Cadillac, Max Lanier's—the pitchers had them all lined up in a row in the parking lot. I said, "Yeah, these are fine, but what about tickets?" He said, "Just relax." Pretty soon a little black kid came into the lot and said, "Tickets, tickets." I said, "Get 'em." My uncle looked at them and said, "What have you got?" He told the kid, "Oh, no. You're way out of line. Get out of here. I don't want to talk to you." Now, this was only about twenty minutes before the game. I was saying, "You're crazy. Take those tickets." He told me to just wait a minute. Pretty soon, another one came by. Now, it's about ten minutes before the game. He looked at his tickets and told him, "No, no, you're way out of line." I said, "Aw, come on." Now, it's about five minutes before game time, and we ended up buying tickets for the same price it would cost you to go in the gate. That was the first day.

We stayed all night. The next day he said, "Well, we have to go stand in line for tickets." At ten-thirty in the morning at old Sportsman's Park, they were lined up practically around the stadium. We stood there and made a little headway, slowly. There are three guys ahead of us. All at once, the three of them, practically in unison, yelled, "Hey, Enos." Pretty soon, a guy waved at them as he was heading in to get dressed to play ball—it was Enos Slaughter. They were from his home town. As soon as he saw them, he came right over to talk to them for about five minutes. I'm on cloud nine—Musial and Slaughter, together, were my heroes. The big surprise I got, as they're talking, Slaughter took off his hat to scratch his head, and I saw he was bald. I did not know that—that was the biggest surprise of my life, he was only about thirty years old. As a barber, I never did like bald heads.

Two Americans were caught in Mexico attempting to smuggle drugs, one was a Cub fan and the other a Cardinal fan. They were brought before the captain of the firing squad who informed them that he would grant each one a last wish providing that it was reasonable. The ugly Cub fan said he could die in peace if he could hear Harry Caray sing "Take Me Out to the Ball Game" one more time. The captain said, "This is your lucky day. We have cable in the palace, our head of security is a moron and a Cubs fan, and he tapes every game." The captain turns to the Cardinal fan and asks if he has a reasonable last wish. The big, good-lookin' Cardinal fan replies, "I sure do, *senor*!" The captain says, "Well, what is it?" And the Cardinal fan says, "Shoot me first."

HE PRAYED THAT HE WOULD PLAY FOR THE CARDINALS. GOD ANSWERED HIS PRAYERS. GOD SAID, "NO."

Terry Rush

Minister Terry Rush of Tulsa is a Fantasy Camp junkie. He is the author of Silver Voice, Golden Heart— *a nifty book on Jack Buck.*

I didn't like going to church at all—it was so boring. I was a baseball player. I was born to play baseball. It was in my blood. When I was a little kid, I vowed that "whenever I get big, to never go to church." I was going to play ball with the St. Louis Cardinals anyway. Now, I have missed both goals, and I have been preaching for over thirty years, and never did get to play as a real St. Louis Cardinal player, but I do get to play through the Fantasy Camps.

After my wife and I married, we began to study the Bible with another couple. My wife was a very devout Catholic, and I was just a nice guy. Neither one of us knew anything about the Bible when we began to study. I didn't know that the Bible had a message for people. I honestly thought that it was a gift that you got at graduation when you were in eighth grade. I didn't know it had any life in it, and that's what I was picking up in churches. It wasn't that the churches were dead, it's that I was. I wasn't getting it at all.

I wanted to be a big league ballplayer so badly. I would get a package of big marshmallows and slit the package and let those things dry out. Then when it came Little League game time, I would stuff one of those hard marshmallows in my jaw. It had that image that I was chewing tobacco. The problem was that when you spit "white" it just didn't seem right. But, you want to have that image of being a pro ballplayer. I couldn't wait for the spring to start. Back in those days, we got three TV channels, one of them was CBS, and you look for the Game of the Week, and you find that the Cardinals are going to be on two times in the summer, or maybe three—that's all you got to see them. I just could not wait for the Saturday or those two or three weekends—to get to see the "real big guys" play ball.

When I got to go to my first game, we drove about five hours to old Busch Stadium to see the Braves play the Cardinals. I wrote Stan Musial a letter and said, "Mr. Musial, I'm Terry Rush. I'm eleven years old. I'm coming down there, and I'm going to be seated in this section in this row. Can you come out and meet me?" He never came out to meet me, and I just was crushed. I thought that when he wasn't batting or in the field, he could run up there and say "Hi," 'cause I would've if I'd been playing ball. That was a disappointment. We went to a doubleheader. I felt sorry for people who only got to go to a single game.

Then I grew up and became a minister. In early 1984, I read there was going to be the first Cardinal Fantasy Camp in St. Petersburg, Florida, and it had Shannon and Flood and Cunningham and Gibson and McCarver and Maxvill—I cried. As a grown man, I cried thinking about having forgotten how much those men meant to me, and they never knew it. Maybe if I could go one time to that camp, that God would open doors for anybody who was interested. I understood that they would not be thrilled to find out that there was minister at camp. I expected it and understood it. I mentioned around church in Tulsa about the idea of going to the camp. A family heard about it and they said, "Let's do this. You have a way of encouraging people, and we don't. We have money, and you don't. So, let's be partners." So they sent me.

I'm excited and stupid and scared—all of that—when I go down there. It was a week-long camp, and I almost couldn't enjoy any of it because I didn't know how it was going to go, and I didn't know what was next. Whatever was happening at the moment, I could hardly enjoy it because I was so excited about what would happen next.

And, I was a good enough ballplayer to be mediocre! I loved the game and accidentally made a few catches here and there. The pros always made fun of it. They taught me to catch. I wasn't a catcher and they taught me to be one, but I could never catch a pop-up.

All of the non-pros are called rookies. One of the rookies in camp was, at the time, the quarterback for the Chicago Bears, named Bob Avellini. All week long, in front of everyone, he bragged to Gibson, "I'm gonna show you what a real hitter's like." That was a mistake. Gibson was about forty-four years old at the time and was in mint condition. Gibson never said a word. When it came Saturday, everybody is anxious to see Bob Avellini bat against Gibson. McCarver's catching and Gibson's throwing. Avellini steps to the plate and Gibson winds up. You hear this crack, like a rifle shot, hitting McCarver's mitt. Avellini just kind of tremored. He had no time to move. Everyone just awed over the next pitch—same way, just cracked like a rifle. Avellini just sort of jittered his elbows. He never moved the bat. Third pitch—same way, struck him out on three strikes. Avellini never saw the ball. McCarver said, at the banquet that night, he had forgotten how afraid he used to be to catch Gibson.

I've been to about thirty-five camps since that first one. When I came back, that first time, I was just thrilled to death. Then we soon got a letter from Randy Hundley saying that for fifteen hundred dollars you can do a mini-camp at Busch Stadium. I couldn't go back and ask that family for money. So I sold things of my own, saved up the money and sent myself. That was a real stretch for me to do that, but I really believed that this thing would work.

It broke open so big that the church picked it up and said, "We'll send you." In the first camp, the media ignored me, and players weren't thrilled over me being a minister. In the second camp, it was reversed. The media wouldn't leave me alone. Instead of avoiding me because I was a minister, they were intrigued because I was a minister. Nothing had changed, except that God had just broken open the doors. The media, television, radio, newspapers—I was in all of it. The second morning we were there, I opened up the *St. Louis Post-Dispatch*, and there's a color picture of me in the Sports Section. You can't imagine what a thrill that was. It was just weird.

Curt Flood, who was my childhood hero, had been polite to me the first camp, but he was awkward about me being a minister, but the second camp, he was hugging me. He nicknamed me "The Preach," introducing me to the other big leaguers reminding them, "Hey, Red Schoendienst, remember the preacher?" "Oh, yeah." This was because I wrote Curt's mom. At camp, I had given him a book of mine, and he had kinda laughed it off. I didn't realize it might embarrass him that a preacher gave him a book. He later wrote me and said, "Hey, Preach, I liked the book and my mom liked it." I thought, "Well, I'll write his mom a letter and just sort of water the seed here a little." I didn't know her name so I just said, "Dear Curt Flood's mom." Well, she was in her eighties, and it meant so much to her that someone would remember her that it just won him over. He adopted me and never let go. He told me one time at camp, a year later, "You know, Terry, you're an amazing guy, because mom's got six of us kids, and she'd die for everyone of us. She has our pictures on her little nightstand beside her bed, and you come along. All of us kids are moved across the room to the bureau, and your picture's on the night stand." I went to see her one time in Oakland. Then the family asked me to speak at her funeral. It was an amazing thing for me to get to be a part of their family. I still stay in touch with my Flood brothers and sisters. When Curt died, I spoke at his funeral.

It took a long time for the baseball people to come to me to talk about God. If they want to know about God, I never bring it up. I wait till they come to me and say, "Hey, can I talk to you?" And, inevitably that happens. I'm just available. So it has let me mingle with these guys in a non-threatening sort of way.

I met Orlando Cepeda in one of the earlier camps, and Curt and I were in Curt's room. Cepeda called his room, and Curt said, "Come on down here. I want you to meet a friend of mine." Orlando, this huge man, walked in and Curt said, "I want you to meet Terry. He's a minister for the Memorial Drive Church of Christ in Tulsa. This is Orlando Cepeda, Catholic." Cepeda said, "Buddhist." And Flood said, "Ahh, he's Catholic." And, again, Cepeda said, "Buddhist." I knew what had happened, and Curt didn't. God said, "If you want to help a Buddhist, you become a Buddhist. If you want to help a person under the law, even though you're not under the law yourself, you become under the law, that you might win someone over." The next day we were at batting practice, and Orlando was our hitting coach. Whenever you hit, you went to the next station, so I made sure I hit last. When I finished, I took my helmet off and laid my bat down and said, "Orlando, when you go to the Buddhist Temple this week, could I go with you?" The man started shedding tears—because nobody had shown any interest in his religion. I went with him to the Temple, and to this day, whenever **Orlando Cepeda** and I are in the same building, when he walks through the doors and sees me, he gives me this huge bear hug—just because I showed interest in him.

On occasion, in Busch Stadium, back in those days Hrabosky would take some glue and put on the Fu Manchu beard and mustache and wig. The crowd just loved it when he would come out all grizzly. I go out to the mound and Hrabosky can't breathe. He's got this mean look on—but the man can't breathe. He's going, "Terry, Terry." Everybody in the crowd thinks he's this big bear, and he's standing there telling me, "I used too much glue, and I think I'm gonna pass out. I can't breathe." I want you to watch out for me."

I was catching, later that day, Gibson was batting. The ball came in and he swung. I thought he hit the ball, and I thought his bat exploded. It was the loudest noise I'd ever heard. He was just standing there. He wasn't running, and I couldn't understand, with that ball in the outfield, why he was just standing there. I said, "Bob, that is the loudest noise I ever heard in my life. Did your bat blow up? He said, "No, Preach, I hit you in the head. Are you okay?" I knew to say that I was okay, but I didn't know why he was asking it. We just kept standing there, and I said, "Where is the ball?" He said, "It's in your glove." I looked and there it was. I could not figure that out. The umpire said, "Do you want to throw a few?" I knew then something was wrong, but I didn't know what, and I didn't want to say yes,

> Orlando Cepeda used more bats than any player in history. He felt each bat had exactly one hit in it. When Cepeda got a hit, he would discard the bat. He got 2,364 hits in his career.

because I wanted to play. He had swung at the ball and missed it, and, on his backswing, he had hit me in the head and knocked me unconscious. I never did understand what they were talking about, and we went ahead and finished the inning.

I went over to the dugout, just sort of shaking my head, going, "What was wrong with those guys and that conversation? I don't get what they're talking about." I took my mask off and it was dented in on my left eye. It makes me very proud in life to say that Bob Gibson knocked me unconscious at Busch Stadium. Not many guys can say that.

I made the mistake, and so I learned from my failures, I learned that you can talk to just about any of these guys as long as there's no one else around. My mistake with Curt in the very beginning was I gave him my book in front of a group of guys. I didn't even think about that making him feel awkward. He was not so much against the book because he read it later and liked it. He was uneasy, being a jock, about what the guys looking on thought.

I was in a Fantasy Camp in Jupiter, Florida and we played ball a few days. Right before our big game on Sunday, Darrell Porter, Lou Brock and I are speaking in chapel down along the first-base line. The fans are in the stands, and we're standing there speaking with them. I was sharing with them. I said, "If McGwire was an active ballplayer and the Cardinals were to announce they had traded Mark McGwire straight up for me, the fans wouldn't be able to believe it. It just could not be possible. But there was a greater trade made, and that was when God traded Jesus, his son, straight up, for us. It was just impossible that could happen, but we don't think of it as to how impossible it was until we think of McGwire being traded for me—and that the trade actually has been completed. All he wants is for you to realize that you're on his team—that you've been traded for. When it was over, Porter and Brock were speechless. Brock told me repeatedly throughout the rest of the day, "Terry, wow, I never thought of that. That was really, really good."

Immediately after we concluded the chapel, this lady came down on the field there and said, "I'd like to meet you. I knew Lou and Darrell, and that's who I came to hear today. I've never heard of you, but I've never heard anything like that. I'm Carole Buck, and I have a radio program in St. Louis. I want to know if I could interview you next week." So, we struck up a great friendship.

In the span of time, I sent her a couple of my books, and she really liked them. We just became instant friends. Then, as Jack was very ill, I would stay in touch with her, because I knew she was hurting and the family was hurting. A couple of months after Jack passed away, Carol called me here in Tulsa and said, "Terry, I want to know if you would consider writing a book about my husband. I don't want it to be about baseball, per se. I want it to be about his generous heart because he was so good to help people in the community and the fans. I agreed, of course. I have been writing it, and it's completed now, *Voice of Silver, Heart of Gold, the Mutual Admiration of Jack Buck and his Fans*. It's a heartwarming book.

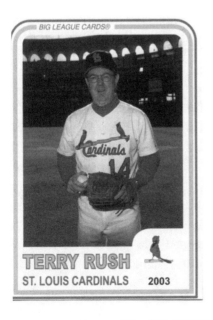

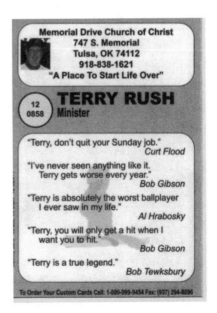

BLIND LOYALTY

Mike Hoenig

Mike Hoenig was raised on a farm just outside Fort Madison, Iowa. He was born blind due to an optic nerve disorder. A regular on the Cardinal Winter Cruise, Mike is a popular figure on his Busch Stadium visits.

In the Quad Cities, there's a Cardinal fan club. I just happened to stumble onto it one day. I was there for another meeting, and I heard them talking about Red Schoendienst and I thought to myself, "Gee, they know a lot about the Cardinals." Well, it was a Cardinal fan club. They sponsored trips every year down to St. Louis, and I went on one. Another friend there and I kind of hooked up, and they invited me to go on the Cardinal cruise in '90. I just started meeting Card fans that way and through spring training. I've really met a lot of people through these.

Listening to the games on the radio gives me a much better description. The best example I can give you is Joe Buck. He's a great announcer, but when he's on TV, he assumes that everybody is seeing what's going on so his description changes dramatically. The Cardinals were in the playoffs in '96, playing the Braves. I was out in D.C. and couldn't pick up the radio broadcast. Joe Buck was doing the TV. At a critical part of the game, Cardinals had runners on, and he said, "You don't need me so…." Well, I actually wrote him a letter after that and said you need to understand that there are people who are blind or for whatever reason can't see what's going on, and you still need to use your excellent descriptive skills to tell us what's happening." I guess the down side of radio is that you do sometimes get announcers who don't seem to put a lot of enthusiasm into what they're doing, and that really changes the complexion of the game a lot.

Dan Shulman, who does the Sunday Night Game of the Week a lot, is very good. Jon Miller's pretty good. When I first started hearing him, I thought he was kind of dry, but over time, I really came to like him. He did the World Series the last couple of years on radio, he is enthusiastic, and he knows the game very well. I really like listening to him.

Jack Buck was my favorite announcer, as he was everybody's, and I'm still adjusting to losing him. Of course, I like Mike Shannon, but there are times when he kind of loses focus a little bit. He's gotten into this thing where he'll say, "Swinging—home run," and I just can't get into that. I like Wayne Hagin. He's a very descriptive person. Of course, I know I'm biased because I met him on the cruise and think he's a great person.

Jack Buck understood who his audience was. During his Hall-of-Fame speech, he talked about the fact that he was broadcasting to blind people and to shut-ins and to people in prison. He took it so seriously and, especially in his heyday, he just put so much enthusiasm into every call. You just felt like you were in the game from start to finish.

Actually, there are a lot of sports fans who are blind. I went to the School for the Blind in Vinton, Iowa. Baseball is a sport you can understand easily. It translates well on the radio so there were a lot of us who were Cardinal fans when I was in school there.

Harry Caray was very entertaining. Sometimes in his later years it was a little hard for him to always be right on track with names, but, gosh, you couldn't dislike him. He was funny and a lot of times I'd listen to the Cubs games just because Harry was on.

When I go to St. Louis to the games, I sometimes fly down using air miles. I have a friend who has driven me down. Fortunately, when I get down there, I usually have places to stay. I get real spoiled. Last time I stayed with friends in Brentwood. We went to the zoo, went to dinner, and went to lunch every day. I took some time off during the week and just enjoyed being decadent for four or five days.

Baseball is a great entertainment during the summer, and actually all year, because there is always something going on. It has introduced me to a whole group of people I wouldn't have known—also, something to be loyal to. It would be a big void if it were gone. Cardinal fans are probably more knowledgeable. You will go somewhere and the fans will be talking about the night before and the game and who did this and who did that. Other people look at you like—how do you remember all that stuff? That's part of being a good fan.

Being blind, a blind person is just like anybody else except that, you do things a little differently. The other night there was a new acquaintance in our group. I have a sister, and the new person made some comment about, "Well, I hope you take care of little brother." I don't think I need to be taken care of any more than anybody else does. With the Cardinal organization, the fact that being from out of town and the fact that I'm blind probably has made it a little easier. With Fred Hanser and Dan Farrell, it's becoming more than, "Oh, aren't we being nice." I think they are honestly sincere in their treatment of me.

"Proud Papa" from the Marquess Gallery in St. Louis.

Chapter Five

On the Road Again

Bird Watchin'

AT BANK ONE BALLPARK, THE P IN SWIMMING POOL IS SILENT

Pat Bieniecki

Pat Bieniecki runs Cardinal Travel with her brother, Dal Maxvill, former Cardinal star player and General Manager.

C ardinal fans are like nothing else in the world. They're fun to be around. Cardinal Travel started in '69. On the tours I do, the people are like family. I've paired people up. I've got a couple now who are engaged. Both lost their spouses about four years ago. Last year we flew out to San Francisco and then motorcoached up the coast sightseeing and then saw the games in **Seattle**. On the way out to San Francisco, I assigned these two fans next to each other. They're the kind of fans who can talk about a game that happened years ago and tell you how the pitcher performed, and who made the last out—both he and she are serious fans. All the way out to the coast, I sat behind them, and they never stopped talking—talking baseball. They just became friends and then first thing you know they showed up at the airport for one of our trips, and she's got on an engagement ring. He's probably seventy-five and she's about sixty-five. It's great, and I love it.

One day in '79 my brother Dal Maxvill and I were talking business, and he said, "I sure wish you would come to work for me and be my bookkeeper." He and Joe Hoerner had formed Cardinal Travel. I told him my kids were still little and I didn't want to work until they were older. He said, "Well, could you come in after they go to school and

> During the Seattle Mariners first year in 1977, they measured their distance to the fences in fathoms. A fathom is 6 feet. For instance, where a park may have a sign that denotes 360 feet, the Kingdome would have the number 60.

maybe work four hours a day?" I ended up working full-time very, very shortly thereafter. Now I can't get out of here.

I grew up in Granite City, Illinois. My earliest memories are sitting on the living room floor playing a game with Dal, and Cardinal baseball would be on the radio. We would go to a park and watch softball teams 'cause my mom and dad were great fans of ball, period. I can remember going to old Sportsman's Park when I was about eight and Dal was about twelve. We took the public conveyance over to Sportsman's Park. I remember during the seventh inning stretch we were standing. I was standing as close to Dal as I could get 'cause he was my big brother. He had his little ball glove with him and he was sure he was going to catch a foul ball. He stood there, and he looked down at me, and he said, "I'm going to play on that field one of these days." I remember looking at him and thinking, "He sure will 'cause he's my big brother."

When he signed with the Cardinals and went to the minors, we were all excited. I can remember one day I came home from work. My mom and dad were sitting on the front porch waiting for me. They said, "Honey, go in and change clothes. We're going to the ball game. Dallan got called up today." That's his real name, Dallan. He was going to be in uniform that night at the ballpark. I was very excited.

Dal was the first major league player to hit a home run outside of the United States. They were playing in Montreal. He never hit home runs. At that time my husband had been drafted into the service and we were in Albuquerque. I was working for a construction company. Whenever the newspaper was brought in, I would always ask for the sports page to read during my lunch hour. My boss said, "You're the only woman I know that reads the sporting page." I said, "Well, my brother is a major league baseball player for the St. Louis Cardinals." He didn't believe me. I was reading the box scores this one day, and there that home run was. I highlighted it, and just picked that paper up and went into his office and stuck it in front of him and said, "That's my brother."

Because I was raised with the Cardinals, seeing my brother play there for them was a dream come true. I wish our parents had lived long enough to see him become the general manager.

Last year, my agency had eighty-eight people going to Boston and New York; then I had another fifty-one come in for New York only. The one thing Cardinal people do is they make no bones about who they are. They've got their Cardinal shirts. They've got their regalia. They've got their hats with their pins on it. When we go to the airport, it's hysterical. I get there early because they start looking for me, and I don't want anybody to panic. I like to watch the gate agents and other people in the area as all these people come in wearing these red shirts.

I think the Phoenix ballpark, Bank One, is the best. The refreshment stands, the restrooms—spotless when we were there. The very first year they played, I took ninety-eight people out there. We could only get seats way down the right field line, almost to the swimming pool, but my people don't care—as long as we're in the ballpark. I try to get much better seats than that, but for a large group, I can't always get it.

I have a lot of women who travel together, and women are baseball fans. I always have more women on tours than men. As a woman would get up to go to the restroom in Phoenix, she'd come back and say, "Oh my God. You have to see the restrooms." They were huge, and there were no lines. You go to Busch Stadium, and you miss two innings.

The first or second year that Dal was GM, I wrote him a letter. I said, "Dear Mr. Maxvill, I just want to let you know what a good job I think you are doing with the team. Congratulations. I do have one complaint. As a woman, and I'm sure you realize a lot of women go to the games, they have to stand in line and miss whole innings to go to the restroom. I guess we will have to cut down on the amount of liquid we drink to avoid that situation." In parentheses I said, "I'm sure Anheuser-Busch doesn't want us to do that." I made sure that the letter went on long enough that I had to go to a second page. My next paragraph said, "Congratulations Mr. Maxvill on the wonderful job you are doing. I know that your parents are very proud of you. Cordially," then I signed my name.

He took the letter in to Fred Kuhlman, who didn't know me, and he said, "Dal, maybe this is something we need to look into." Dal said, "Yes, we probably should, but I want to let you know one thing—that's my sister."

FURTHERMORE, TODAY MARKS THE NINTH ANNIVERSARY OF THE LAST TIME SAMMY SOSA HIT THE CUTOFF MAN

Dick Fox

Dick Fox, 61, grew up on a farm near Lost Nation, Iowa, listening to Harry Caray and Jack Buck. He is now retired and lives in Celebration, Florida and Cape Cod.

(Left: Dick Fox with Christie Vilsack)

I almost gave up on the Cardinals early on because of players named Tom Poholsky and Tommy Glaviano. I collected baseball cards—when I was looking for Stan Musial and Ted Williams, all I ever got were Tommy Glaviano and Tom Poholsky. I can picture those cards perfectly in my mind to this day. They drove me nuts. Even though they were Cardinals, I had a bazillion of each of them and got tired of seeing their uniforms. The only more ubiquitous was Wayne Terwilliger of the Washington Senators.

After college, we lived in New York City. My college roommate was playing minor league baseball in Williamsport, Pennsylvania for the Met system, where Whitey Herzog was director of player personnel. One day at a swimming pool at a Holiday Inn in Williamsport, Whitey Herzog asked me to go on a scouting trip to Philadelphia with him that afternoon. The Mets had the first pick in the baseball draft and were torn between this pitcher he was going to scout that day named Jon Matlack and a catcher from Hamtramck, Michigan, named Ted Simmons. Thank God, he took Matlack... because Ted Simmons ended up being my favorite Cardinal ever. It seemed like every time the Cardinals really needed a run, and Simmons came to the plate, one way or the other he got 'em home. He was a very underrated player compared to other catchers of that era.

Over that period of time, for various reasons, I got to know some of the Cardinals, particularly Tim McCarver and Joe Hoerner. I remember having lunch one day with Steve Carlton at the Tin Lizzy in New York. He was pitching against the Mets that night. Carlton said, "The Mets might win the pennant this year, but they're not gonna beat me tonight." Ed Charles hit two home runs for the Mets, and they ended up beating the Cardinals, 6-0, to clinch the pennant. Carlton was a wonderful guy. He was smarter than most ballplayers. He was more introspective than most ballplayers. As a result, I feel he's the victim of an undeserved reputation. He was a great guy, as were most of the Cardinals then. After the Mets beat the Cardinals that night, I ran into a lot of the players at a place in New York called Mr. Laffs. As we're sitting there, they're all very, very despondent. I asked them, "What's wrong?" They looked as if they'd just lost their best friend. One of the Cardinals said, "This is it." I said, "What do you mean—this is it?" He said, "Bing Devine is going to hit the panic button. He's going to break the team apart. He's going to trade Curt Flood, and Curt Flood won't report, and it's going to create a problem. McCarver, Carlton, they're all going to be gone." Sure enough, they knew what was going to happen—Bing Devine broke the team up. The Cardinals of the late sixties had very, very unusual chemistry, even for that time. They had been to the two previous World Series. They very well could have gone to at least three more in the '70s if no moves were made. It was just a wonderful time, and it was really sad that had to happen.

Whitey Herzog was just such a great manager. When he was with the Mets, all the players really respected and liked him. You know you're a good coach, or a good manager, when the scrubeenies—the guys who aren't playing—really like you a lot. That's the way it was with Whitey with the Mets. That's why it was so exciting when he became the Cardinal manager. The problem with Whitey managing the Cardinals is that after him, every other manager we're ever going to have is gonna be downhill…at least for me.

You can have La Russa. The biggest reason goes back to 1998, when Mark McGwire saved baseball. McGwire should have won the "Most Valuable Player" award, the Cy Young award, the Rookie-of-the-Year award, the the Manager-of-the-Year award. He should have won every award baseball gave that year. Instead La Russa said, "Sammy Sosa deserved to be the Most Valuable Player because the Cubs went to post-season play." The Cubs went to post-season play! They made the wild-card by winning a playoff game to get into the wild-card game…and La Russa felt Sosa was the MVP that season? The on-base percentage for McGwire was so much higher. McGwire drove that season. Sammy Sosa was aided by far more official at-bats, the short porches at Wrigley Field, the prevailing winds coming off Lake Michigan and better hitters surrounding him. If Sammy Sosa played at Busch Stadium, he wouldn't hit forty home runs if he batted from second base using a corked fungo bat.

On the other hand, in my book, all baseball statistics became meaningless the day Brady Anderson hit his fiftieth home run. If Brady Anderson walked in here right now and sat down, even with the sideburns, we wouldn't recognize him. That was the end of baseball as we know it.

In late August, 1998, the scene is a great sports bar in Naperville, Illinois called George's Place. After dinner, we were sitting with the owner, George, a big wonderful Greek guy. At that time, Sosa and McGwire were tied with fifty-five home runs each. I said, "George, for McGwire or Sosa to break Maris' record, they gotta hit seven home runs in twenty-five games. That's a lot of home runs. There's going to be incredible pressure on them. They're not going to see very many good pitches. Why don't you call your bookie in the morning and find out what the odds are that they won't break the record?" George said, "That's a great idea. You're absolute right. It is going to be exceedingly difficult to hit seven home runs in twenty-five games. I'll call him in the morning, and if the odds are good, let's get some money down on that one, yessiree!" About twenty minutes later, his son, who was bartending, walked by and said, "McGwire hit two more tonight." George facetiously said, "Hell, maybe he'll hit 70"… and he did.

About thirty years ago, I worked late one night, got up early the next morning and worked hard and fast because we had to leave at noon for the three-hundred mile drive to St. Louis—"we" being my wife and her parents. We were staying at her brother and sister-in-law's house and going to catch a Cards-Mets series.

We go to the Cardinal game. We had a great time. We had a little liquid fortification against the unknown, and we go back to her brother's house where we're all staying, and we talk. We have more liquid fortification against the unknown. We stay up late. Back home, I knew I could get up in the middle of the night and go to the bathroom without seemingly waking up. That night I got up and took my usual step pattern, but ended up in my in-laws' bedroom. Their suitcase was spread wide open at the foot of their bed. I relieved my social pressures into their suitcase. My mother-in-law, I found out later, was shaking my father-in-law, "Les, Les, wake up. Dick is peeing into the suitcase." He's saying, "Marge, Marge, go back to sleep. You're dreaming." Well, you probably won't be surprised that they're no longer my in-laws. That's okay, they smelled funny some-times...but they were great Cardinal fans.

We had good friends who lived in Belleville, Illinois, Barb and Ed Brennan. Ed Brennan was a dead ringer for Tom Seaver. I kept telling him that, and he never believed me until we went to a Mets-Cardinals game one night. After the game, we were in the inner sanctum wait-ing for Tug McGraw. The elevator door opened and there was Tom Seaver by himself. Seaver looked straight at Brennan, Brennan looked straight at Seaver, and it was like they were looking in a mirror. To complicate matters, Barb Brennan was almost a dead ringer, or looked very similar, to Nancy Seaver. Anyway, we're going through the parking lot on our way to our car and somebody starts yelling from a door of a big motor home. "Tom, Tom, come here." We look over, and it was Stan Musial. Ed Brennan said, "What should I do? He thinks I'm Tom Seaver." I said, "You're bluffing it tonight, pal, I want to meet Stan Musial." We did. We went in the motor home and all the time, Stan was very gracious, thinking that Ed and Barb Brennan were Tom and Nancy Seaver.

In the summer of 2003, a friend of mine participated in RAGBRAI, which stands for the Register's Annual Great Bike Ride Across Iowa. It is a seven-day journey involving about 20,000 people. There is a group out of Chicago called the Chicago Urban Bicycle Society;

mainly a diverse club of people, including a couple of sports writers from the Tribune. There are 85 people, and they bike RAGBRAI annually. Every year, on a Thursday night, they have a huge banquet in some neat place. For some reason, they are always able to get the Governor of Iowa and the Governor's wife to this banquet. Even though we were outsiders, we were invited to this banquet because my friend knew the main guy from the *Chicago Tribune* that put it together. He said, "Yeah, why don't ya wear like your Cardinal cap and your Cardinal shirt—that would kind of give them a little bit of a hard time," which I did. We were at the Bloomfield, Iowa Country Club. Even though there are only 85 guys in this group, they rented the Bloomfield Country Club—a very nice club for a town that size. It took me about 30 seconds to realize that I had been framed. The huge sign said, "Welcome Chicago Urban Bycycle Society," but the acronym was "C.U.B.S." The good news was the Governor's wife, Christie Vilsack, was a fun lady, a closet Cardinal fan, even though she was surrounded by these Cub people. It was a great time—even if they were C.U.B. fans…but the word bicycle was misspelled on their sign!

The reason many people are Cub fans is, basically, they are people that can't afford World Series tickets.

Here are your 1996 World Series tickets.

PICTURE THIS

Tim Samway

Tim Samway has lived a dream life. The big Irishman is a successful paper executive who has turned his hobby of photography into being the unofficial photographer of the Boston Red Sox. All of his considerable photo fees are donated to the Boys and Girls Clubs of Boston.

He recently relaxed in his gorgeous New Hampshire home and discussed the amazing invasion of Cardinal fans to New England.

All the people around said, "Have you ever seen so many hats and jerseys from an opposing team?" I don't know where they came from because Fenway is always sold out. But just to see them, and I'm not being patronizing, but they were just some of the nicest, most knowledgeable fans. It really was a treat to be in the ballpark with them. And I saw them in restaurants and out on Yawkey Way. I don't ever remember seeing so many hats and jackets from another team, not even the Yankees, yeah. That was the nice part about it.

The one thing I remember going into the series was Johnny Pesky talking about Mike Shannon. Johnny was his manager in the minors in AAA in Seattle, and it was '61 or '62. Apparently, the Cardinals lent Shannon to the Red Sox 'cause the Red Sox had somebody hurt and they needed an outfielder. Pesky had Shannon for that year and Pesky said he was just such a great kid, and then the next year or the year after that, Shannon, was the big star of the World Series. Pesky always says, "Whenever I see Shannon, I remind him that I gave him his start." Pesky was very anxious for his friends to meet the great Mike Shannon. He introduced me to Mike Shannon and the two of them just started with the needle, typical old-time baseball jabbing at each other and pulling each other's chain.

Shannon really trumped Pesky because Shannon looked at me and said, "Would you take a picture of Pesky for me so I can put it up on the wall of my restaurant?" Pesky said, "What the hell do you want a picture of me for?" He said, "Johnny, in St. Louis, you're a hero." Johnny, for all the years I have known him, has taken that. He takes it in stride. I just remember one time somebody was giving him a hard time, and he said, "Were you at that game?" The guy said, "No." Johnny said, "Well I was." When Shannon said, "You know, John, in St. Louis, you're a hero," the place broke up. Of course, he was referring to the famous play in the '46 World Series when Enos Slaughter scored from first while Pesky hesitated throwing home on the relay from the outfield.

Let me tell the Johnny Pesky story. Right after the 1946 World Series, Pesky goes back home to Oregon completely bereft. And he has to come back to the Boston College-Holy Cross football game. Now back then, B.C. and Holy Cross were actually big time in football, and they were playing a nationally ranked game at Fenway Park. He decides to wear sort of an old cap and dark glasses, and come to the game incognito, because, again, he didn't want to be recognized. Late in the game, a guy for B.C. punts the ball, and a guy from Holy Cross who is catching the ball, fumbled it. B.C. recovers. And everyone is swearing!

All of a sudden, some leather-lung ten or fifteen rows behind him stands up and shouts out, "You should have kicked it to Pesky. He would have held on to it!"

Shannon introduced Scott Rolen to Pesky. Pesky wanted to meet Rolen. They came out on the field and the three of them were talking, and Pesky's telling Rolen about how he knew Shannon. I was just standing five feet away. I have a photo that I love—Pesky talking with Rolen. I don't care if Rolen ever plays another game the rest of his life, he showed me so much as a man who must have been raised very well-mannered. He treated Pesky like Pesky should be treated, as a veteran. He was leaning in to John to listen to him. He was looking him direct in the face, and John was gesturing with his wrist and his body and his feet and everything. Scott Rolen just was looking at him and just really paying attention and asking questions. It's one of those baseball things I'll always remember. I have seen the reverse many times.

It was fun to read the Boston papers as the Cardinals were coming to Boston. A lot of us had forgotten a lot of the details of the '46 and '67 World Series. Just rereading all those stories and what great series they were 'cause there isn't much film around from '46. The other part about it was all of my friends who said, "Will they please get rid of this inter-league play?" changed their minds with the three games we played the Cardinals. That is what inter-league play must have meant. And, to be honest with you, I can't tell you to this day who won any one of those three games? And it didn't really make any difference. I just remember them as being an event at Fenway Park that I truly, truly enjoyed. I never did really like the inter-league play, but I sure as hell liked those three games with the Cardinals. It was just terrific to be there.

Scott Rolen and Johnny Pesky.

IT WAS A QUGPATCH IS WHAT IT WAS

Joe Rangel

Joe Rangel is a longtime Cardinal fan from the Quad-Cities... an area he feels is twice as good as the Twin Cities.

Carlos Alfonso, Lisa Crowell, and Kate Rangel

Lisa, my step-daughter works for Iowa-Illinois Gas and Electric in the shareholders department. She gets a call from this guy out in San Francisco who has to get some information so he can get his taxes done.

A couple of days later, he calls her back and says, "I really appreciate what you did. I'm Carlos Alfonso, the pitching coach for the San Francisco Giants. I'd like to do something for you and your family. We're going to be in Chicago playing the Cubs this weekend. If you'd like, I can get you and your family some tickets." Lisa says, "No thanks, we're Cardinal fans." He said, "Well, I'll tell you what. I'll give you the hotel number where I'm staying in Chicago, and if you change your mind, give me a call, and I'll have some tickets for you."

Lisa tells her mother—my wife—Kate, the story. Kate tells some fellow workers—Cardinal fans—the next day. This co-worker says, "Well, if he can get tickets to the Cubs game, he can get tickets to the Cardinal game in St. Louis."

Lisa calls him. He called back the next morning. Kate answered the phone. They get to talking baseball and how much she likes Willie McGee. At that time, Willie McGee was playing for the Giants. He told her he could get ten tickets for the game in St. Louis, six for Lisa and her friends and four for Kate and me and our friends. He told us they were staying at the Adam's Mark Hotel and said there was a little nightclub down there called AJ's. "Maybe after the game, we'll meet you down there."

So the day comes to drive three hundred miles to St. Louis, and we don't know if this Carlos was legitimate or not, but we made our plans. We were teasing the girls that this guy wasn't going to leave any tickets. We get down to St. Louis and went to the Will Call window. It's not open yet so we go into our rooms at the Adam's Mark.

I got to thinking, "I wonder if Carlos is even here." I call up the front desk and said, "Could I have Carlos Alfonso's room?" They said, "We don't have anybody here registered by that name." So we were really teasing the girls then. I decided to try to call Willie, so I called the desk and said, "Can you put me through to Willie McGee?" Sure enough, they rang it through. A little boy answered the phone. I asked for Willie McGee, and this boy said, "Dad, telephone." I'd never met him before, but I tell him my name and asked if Carlos was here, and he told us that he was here. So then we wait around and when Will Call opens, we go up to see if they have any tickets for Joe Rangel. The man said, "Yeah, we've got tickets here for you." We picked up the tickets, and we really got excited then.

We go to the games, and they were real nice seats, right behind home plate. After the game, we go down to AJ's trying to find Carlos. At this time, Kate's carrying a sweatshirt with her that has Willie's picture on it and says, "What about Willie?" which she was hoping to get autographed. The shirt came about as a sort of joke because she was always saying that to us when we were picking out ballplayers in a computer game. Because she said it so much, we had a sweatshirt made up with his picture on it that said, "What about Willie?" There's a little hallway you have to walk through to get to AJ's, and the elevators are right there. We're standing in that little hallway, and we don't know what the ballplayers look like, but all the kids do. They were there getting autographs as the players were getting off the elevators. We're don't know what Carlos looks like, but every time someone walked by that we thought might be him, we'd whisper, "Carlos, Carlos," to see if the person would turn around. Willie came through this hallway and wasn't stopping to sign autographs, but Kate yelled at him and held up the shirt. He saw the sweatshirt that Kate had with his name and picture on it. When he saw it, he just stopped in his tracks. He came back and said, "Hey, that's a nice sweatshirt." He autographed it for Kate, and we had our pictures taken with him. I said, "Hey, Willie, that was me that called you up this morning." Then he remembered the call, and the funny thing was, he said, "Hey man, I thought that was you." Willie said that! I had never met nor talked to him before. Then we stopped some ballplayers and asked if Carlos was there. They told us he was here but they didn't know where he was. Finally, Matt Williams came and got us and took us in to the bar and introduced us to Carlos. We finally get to meet him. We talked to him for a while. A great guy! We talked to Willie again. We had our pictures taken with all of them. It was great!

Cardinals Fan John Goodman

WHEN ST. LOUIS CALLS,
YA GOTTA ACCEPT THE CHARGES

Jan Pasuit

Jan Pasuit, 56, is a retired teacher living in Freedom, Pennsylvania, near Pittsburgh. Her father, a U. S. Steel executive was originally from Missouri.

Starting when I was about ten years old, I would go to Missouri and spend the whole summer with my cousins. My dad always showed me things about baseball like how to pitch and other things. I had this love of baseball and spending the summers, all three months, out in Festus and DeSoto, Missouri, I became a Cardinal fan in about '56.

I was a big baseball fan. I bought the Sporting News. I have a male cousin who is a year younger, and he and his mom lived with my father's parents so I had a ready-made boy to play baseball with. I guess you'd say I was a tomboy. I frankly was quite good at throwing a ball, batting and doing all sorts of things like that.

But now it's '98. We figured that McGwire wouldn't hit 61 or 62 until the end of the season. I already had tickets for the last three games, which I had bought early in the '98 season. I worked part-time as a computer instructor for a large company. They knew I was a big Cardinal fan, and it was fairly easy, if my boss had some warning, to get me covered. It was obvious when the week started that the way things were going that I'd better get myself down to St. Louis so I talked to my boss. On Wednesday—it was like a miracle—U. S. Airways had e-fares, and it was a reasonable rate to fly down. I talked to my husband, and he said, "I know there's no way I'm going to stop you." I said, "I've got to go *now*." He said, "Well, I know you'd absolutely corrode if you didn't go down. I know you'll get tickets—I don't know how, but you will." So I flew down. The Cardinals weren't hiring anybody to work as extra ushers, but I managed to get a ticket for "home run 60" from a scalper for not too much.

Now the tickets for '61,' and that's the one that we're talking about, were going for a *lot* of money—like two hundred—and I was getting desperate. It was about twenty minutes to game time. The temperature was way in the nineties. Frankly, I was melting. I was standing in front of the Marriott Hotel right across the street from Busch Stadium where everybody walked by. There was a person who would sell me a ticket, but I think it was for three-hundred dollars. I was considering it, but there was a part of me that said, "You can't do this. We don't have that kind of money."

Then a fellow walked past me, and then he walked back to me, then he sort of stood next to me. He said, "Are you a baseball fan?" I pretty much talk to anybody, and he didn't look dangerous, and there were thousands of people around so I said, "Oh, yeah, I'd give anything for a ticket to a game. Do you have a ticket?" He said, "Yeah, I've got a ticket." I said, "You don't have an extra, do you?" He said, "Yeah." I said, "How much?" He said, "Well, I don't really want to sell it. I'd give it away if you were really a fan of the game." I thought, "Oh God, here I am roasting to death and this guy sounds like he's a psycho." Then he said, "No, I'm really serious. It's an extra ticket. I had come up with a friend, and we had sort of a fight last night. I just wanted somebody to go into the game with me, but the person has to be a real fan of the game."

Then he gave me a test. He said, "Who are your favorite Cardinals?" I said, "Well, right now, it's Mark McGwire, but given my age, and I can see I'm a little bit older than you, my favorite Cardinals were Bob Gibson, and when I was a kid in the fifties, I really liked Kenny Boyer and Bob Smith." He sort of lit up, and I think he knew I was really a fan because I could name guys from the fifties. We chatted a bit, and then he reiterated, "If you want to go to the game, I'm serious." Then I thought, "Oh, this is a pick up." I said, "You need to understand that I'm married," and I showed him my wedding ring. He said, "Oh, no, no, no. It isn't that." He said he was from Charlotte and had flown up with his friend for the game. I said, "Okay, let's go for it." We go up and went through the gate. I thought, "Lord, I don't believe I am doing this." Then I thought, "Wait till my sister, my dad, and my husband hear this story."

We go in, and he had wonderful tickets. I think they were in Section 240, which, heaven knows, probably would have cost five-hundred, six-hundred dollars. I said, "Well, surely let me pay you something." He said, "No, you can buy me hot dogs and soda." We sat down and chatted until the game started. We just immediately started talking tons and tons of baseball. That was the game where Mark hit 61. It just seemed so natural that when he hit 61, we high-fived and hugged and yelled.

Then at the end of the game, I took him down to meet my cousin. I had to wait until she finished working—till all the people had gone. Then he said, "Do you want to walk outside and get the special newspaper. I said, "Sure," and we walked out and got the newspaper. He turned and said, "Well, I guess I'll see you." We looked at each other, hugged again, and I have never seen him or heard of him since. It's just been one of those incredible experiences.

Somehow, I just knew, when I walked through the gates with this man, that McGwire would hit sixty-one that night. I felt the situation was so odd that he was going to do it. It was almost like a religious or a cosmic thing. If a miracle would happen, that this man would be so kind as to take me in to the stadium, for free, and not be a weirdo, and we actually had a very nice time chatting baseball, that home run 61 would be it. He was just a fan of good baseball, more than a Cardinal fan. He liked the Cardinals, but he particularly liked McGwire and what he was doing.

Cardinal Fan Marc Springman

Coach: Lawless, Tudor
Height: 6 Ft. 3 In.   Weight: 220 lbs.
Birthday: 6/ 19 / 55
Position or Title: 2nd/3rd Base
Hometown: Godfrey   State: IL
Heroes: My Mother and Father
Nickname: Catdaddy
Sport/Activities: Golf, Travel, Baseball

St. Louis Cardinals Legends Camp - Roger Dean Stadium - Jupiter, Florida - February 7-11, 2001
Sports Twins Photography © 2001

THE CARDINALS ARE AN ITCH THAT DOESN'T GO AWAY WITH ONE SCRATCH

Debbie Gruber

Debbie Gruber, 48, is supervisor of house-keeping for K's Merchandise in Decatur, Illinois. She lives in Clinton, Illinois and attends about ten games a year at Busch.

I've been a Cardinal fan all my life, ever since I could pay attention to my dad talking about the Cardinals and listening to them on the radio. My mom's been a Cardinal fan for a long time—we're both in there together—we love the Cardinals, just love them.

Marlon Dixon works at a hardware store in Decatur and he makes airbrush shirts on the side. My friend is married to him, and she had him do a shirt with pictures of some rock singers and also had her daughter's face put on it. Then I got to thinking that if he can do that, then why can't he do me ballplayers. The first one I had done was Willie McGee because he was my all-time favorite player. I took him a picture of Willie McGee and said, "This is what I want done. Can you do it for me?" He said he could. He just enlarges the picture upon the wall, and he puts the shirt up on the wall and enlarges it on the shirt. He airbrushes from that and he gets the details so fine that it looks just like the guy. He just airbrushes them on there and then he heat-sets them so you can wash them and they don't fade. If you have one face done, he'll charge twenty dollars for the shirt. The Gold Glove shirt I had done—Fernando Vina asked me to get one made exactly like it for him. So now Fernando's going to have the same kind of shirt I've got. That shirt's going to cost me forty dollars. I'm not going to ask for anything from Fernando for it, I'm just going to give it to him. I also did that last year with a picture of Eduardo Perez.

He asked me if I could have one of the shirts made with his face on it for his dad. That was pretty cool. I had another shirt of Eduardo made for myself and then I had one made of Andy Benes for my mom 'cause she wanted one autographed by him. Fernando happened to be signing a baseball for me that day, and he asked me if I could get a shirt made with his face on it for his mother. So a couple of the ballplayers have shirts that I've had made for them for their relatives.

I've never seen any of these shirts anywhere else so I don't think anyone else does them. I've had people stop me and ask me about them. It's kind of neat because when I'm wearing one, the players will stop and talk to me about them. They're kind of a conversational piece, and I've never had one of the ballplayers not sign it. Marlon just does them in his spare time as a favor for me. I've tried to convince him to go in business doing them, but he doesn't really think that much about doing it.

I went to Montreal last year with my mom to go to a Cardinal game. I had taken my mom to Cooperstown, and then we went to a Cardinal-Mets game. I looked at the map and saw it was only about a six-hour drive up to Montreal so we just drove on up there to see them play. We'd never been there, and we've tried to go to a couple of games every year in a different ballpark.

We were at the same hotel the players were in. We saw Al Hrabosky and talked to him. We saw Gene Stechschulte and talked to him for a little bit. We always stay up after the games to watch the players come in 'cause we like to see them. Sometimes they talk to you; it's rare, but sometimes they do. We were just standing there watching them come in and had waited probably about fifteen or twenty minutes to make sure they had gone up to their rooms 'cause we didn't want to bother them on their own time. We didn't want to get in on their personal time when they weren't playing ball and didn't want them to think we were autograph hounds or something like that.

I asked my mom if she was ready to go upstairs, and so we got on the elevator and were standing there chatting. The elevator opened on about the twenty-fourth floor. This guy got on, and I didn't know who he was—maybe an equipment manager or something. Then

Darryl Kile stepped on the elevator with us. I waited for the doors to shut before I said anything to him because I didn't want him getting off. I wanted to talk to him. We had gotten cokes from the bar and they were in bar glasses. I go, "Is that Darryl Kile?" In the elevator there was just myself, my mother, this other guy, and Darryl Kile. He's looking back and forth in the elevator going, "Where? Where?" I go, "I know you're Darryl Kile." He turned around and started talking to us and asked us about our air-brushed shirts. I go, "If I get a shirt made with your face on it, would you autograph it for me?" He said, "Yes, I would."

We rode up one floor with him, and I got off the elevator with him because I was still talking about the shirts. My mom hollered, "Debbie, this isn't our floor," and grabbed the door. So I got back on the elevator and went on up to my floor. I was really embarrassed because I thought he probably thought I was drunk.

About a month after we had been there, we saw him in St. Louis, and I hollered at him to come over, and he signed the shirt. He was kind of reluctant to at first, but I called him Mr. Kile so he paid more attention that way. I asked, "Do you remember me from the elevator in Montreal?" He said, "Yes, I do." I go, "I just wanted to let you know I wasn't drunk." He said, "I don't care." He talked to us and was so nice, just stood there chit-chatting with us like he'd known us for years. He signed the shirt and was just a nice guy.

A few days later, I was watching the Cubs game on TV and could see that something was going on. I could tell it wasn't bad weather, so I thought somebody must have gotten sick. Then my daughter called me and asked, "Did you hear?" I go, "No," because they hadn't said anything on the TV. She told me Darryl Kile had died, and I just lost it. I started screaming and crying and carrying on. My husband came running in from the back and said, "I heard it on the radio." He got after my daughter for telling me 'cause I hadn't heard yet. I just couldn't believe it's Darryl Kile.

Although we'd only been around him a short time, he had talked to me and talked to my mom, and it just made our day. He was a real nice guy.

My husband doesn't care for sports so he doesn't go to the games. My mom and I like to go, and we've been to Cincinnati, Milwaukee, New York, Canada, **Kansas City** and Houston to see them play. On the way home from the Houston game, I was in a pedestrian crosswalk and was hit by a pickup. I have a broken arm, broken leg, and a shattered kneecap so had to cancel plans to go to Kansas City this year.

My mom is eighty-one years old, and she's loves going to the games with me. Matheny is her favorite player. I had a shirt made that has "Gold Glovers" on it. It had Rolen, Matheny, Edmonds, Renteria, and Vina, and Fernando took them down to the dugout and got all the guys to sign it for me. I had a new shirt made of Matheny with his hat on backward, sitting in the dugout, and I got him to sign that when I was down in Houston. He's even talked to mom a couple of times. When we went to Kansas City, he stopped and had a conversation with her about the shirt. When we went to Winter Warm-Up, we went through his line again because I had the shirt with all the faces on it and wanted to get it autographed. He was having a pretty bad day that day and just acted like he didn't want to be there. My mom's pretty religious. We went through the line, and she goes, "Can I tell you something?" He said, "Yeah." She goes, "Smile, 'cause Jesus loves you." He goes, "I know that," and he had the biggest smile on his face. After she said that to him, he smiled a lot and just had a better attitude.

In the 1979 baseball draft, the Kansas City Royals drafted high school baseball standouts Dan Marino and John Elway.

ONE MISSISSIPPI

George McIngvale

George McIngvale, 35, owns DeSoto Title Company in Hernando, __Mississippi__.

(Bob Forsch, left, poses with George McIngvale)

A ll I've ever been is a Cardinal fan. My first Little League and Peewee baseball team I was a Cardinal. My dad and my step-dad weren't baseball fans, but I had a grown cousin who was a Cardinal fan. Before cable, the Cardinals were on the radio and Sunday afternoon away games were on television. I listened to Jay Randolph do the television broadcasts when I was a kid.

June 6, 1978 was the first game I went to in St. Louis. The Cardinals played the Cincinnati Reds. I was ten years old and it was the first time I'd ever been to Busch Stadium. I had a cousin who was older. I hadn't even been to a minor league game, and he said, "I'll take you to a Memphis Chicks game." He and his wife split up, and he said, "Well, I'm not married anymore. Let's just go to St. Louis. Pick a game." I picked the Cincinnati Reds. That was just right at the end of the "Big Red Machine." I wanted to see the Cincinnati Reds because a lot my friends, if they weren't Cardinal fans, were Cincinnati Reds fans with Johnny Bench and those guys so I wanted to go see the Cards play Cincinnati.

It was unbelievable. I can still remember the starting lineup for both teams. I can't remember the batting order, but I can remember who played. I can remember the old victory blue uniforms they used to

> The posted speed limit on the Ole Miss campus in Oxford, Mississippi is 18 mph. So designated because that was Archie Manning's number when he quarterbacked the Rebels in the late 1960s.

wear on the road. They didn't wear them then, but that bright blue can leave a vivid memory. They don't wear uniforms that are bright like that anymore. I know the stadium has changed a lot. They had the cardinal that flew around on the scoreboard, and that's gone. It's all video and advertising now. It's changed a lot. It was easier to get a guy's autograph in those days. The first autograph I ever got was Jerry Morales. I handed my scorecard and my pencil to him in the dugout, and he signed it in pencil. I got him and Mark Littell.

Sometimes I go to Memphis Redbird games, but if I get that close to the bridge, many times I cross the river and go to St. Louis. I go to more Cardinal games. I like to go to Memphis on occasion. If they have a hot prospect, I do what I call a scouting trip. I just like to go up and see the J. D. Drews and the Rick Ankiels that come by. They have a beautiful ballpark and a lot of amenities. It's real nice, but it's still the minor leagues. It's not the big leagues.

I've not seen the Cardinals on the road. I've been to the new stadiums like Atlanta and have been to Texas to see the Yankees play. I don't like them. You go to Atlanta. You can't buy a scorecard and a pencil. I've scored every game I've ever been to. I can open up the scorecard and say, "So and so went two for three this day." And I make notes. I was there when Lee Smith got his three-hundredth career save. He made an appearance in Memphis, and I got him to autograph it for me. Lee Smith was signing baseballs and cards and I brought him something different. He knew he was signing that for me, that I was at the game, that it was something special, and it wasn't just a generic "here you go" thing. I get a lot of comments because I've got a lot of memorabilia signed that might not be worth a lot on eBay, but it's priceless to me. That's priceless to me. I'll trade stuff that's not Cardinal stuff. Once I get a Cardinal piece, it's off the market. I hoard stuff. I'll bet I've got fifty Tom Pagnozzi cards. You couldn't beg, borrow or buy one from me. I don't know why I'm that way. That's just the way I am. Now you might trade me one for something I don't have that's Cardinal memorabilia. I collect no other teams or players. There's just too much stuff out there.

SO SAY YOU ONE,
SO SAY YOU ALL

It was a typical cold and drizzly October evening in the Netherlands. My wife and I had received the rare honor of being invited to dine at the U.S. Ambassador's home in The Hague. Despite the luxury surrounding me, and the magnificent cuisine brought in by waiters in black tie on bone china plates encircled with slender bands of gold, I could think of only one thing that memorable evening of October 19, 1982—the St. Louis Cardinals and the impossible task facing them that day.

It was Game Six of the World Series, and the Cardinals trailed the Milwaukee Brewers three games to two. Worse, in the sixth and probably final game of the Series, a raw rookie with the unprepossessing name of Stuper was set to face the Brewers' best pitcher and future Hall-of-Famer, Don Sutton. When the lavish but interminable evening finally ended, we raced home and I sat in our kitchen with a Heineken and tried to get the game on the Armed Forces Network. Unfortunately, the reception, always unpredictable at best, was terrible. In helpless fury at not knowing the Cardinals' fate, I telephoned the U. S. Embassy. No answer. After perhaps twenty rings of agony, a Marine answered the phone. "Excuse me. "Would you happen to know who won the game today?" I asked with anticipated relief. "What game, sir?" was his stern reply. "The World Series game between the Brewers and the—." "I don't like baseball, sir. My game's football—Auburn Tiger football." "Yes, I understand, but surely someone there at the embassy…?" "Nope." he said, and hung up.

I started to grow desperate, and felt angry that our country could have a Marine on duty who was so indifferent to our national pasttime. Then I remembered my in-laws, back in the U. S. Surely they would know who won? Why not call them right now? But my frustration only increased as, in those days without answering machines, the phone again rang remorselessly. I yelled and punched my defective—but otherwise innocent—radio as hard as I could.

What I did next was so strange and out of character that only a pure baseball addict could possibly comprehend: I began randomly dialing telephone numbers with the St. Louis area code of 314. It took, unbelievably, several calls before I was fortunate enough to find someone at home. "Hello, you don't know me. Hello! I am calling from the Netherlands and I can't find out who won today's Series game...I know it's late, ma'am, but if it's that late there in St; Louis, think how late it is here in Europe...Yes, get your husband." When the kind gentleman told me the score had been 13-1, I refused to believe him. "And Stuper went all the way? Are you sure? With a three-hour rain delay? Really? Hernandez and Porter both homered? Thank you, sir. Goodnight."

Finally, my odyssey was complete. And, after cleaning up what was left of the Magnavox, I went to bed.

————**HENRY I. SCHVEY**, St. Louis

In June 2003, we're going to New York City for the three-game Yankee series. The big sports station in Boston has an auxiliary studio right at Fenway Park. As we were driving down the turnpike, their sports anchor was doing a show from that studio. He said, "Yesterday at this time we had 350-400 Cardinal fans milling around outside our studio. The Houston Astros start a three-game set in Fenway tonight, and I'll give a hundred dollars to the first person who brings me one Astros fan."

————**DICK FOX**, 61, Lost Nation, Iowa

A. Ray Smith had moved the Cardinals AAA team from Tulsa, Oklahoma to Springfield, Illinois, Lampier Field. He announced he was going to have what he called a "Hot Stove League Meeting" in the middle of January at the new Capitol Prairie Convention Center in downtown Springfield. I was a season ticket holder with the major league team, but not with the minor league team. You could only sit down on the main floor if you were a season ticket holder with the minor league team. We drove up there in a blizzard and stayed at the Hilton across the street so we could go over to the building early. I wore my tuxedo so I took my wife and three kids and ushered them down the aisle to the front row, and nobody challenged us. We were sitting there, and we could see through the background of the stage when people were coming in the back door. We saw Lou Brock and Bob Gibson come in and we saw Stan and Lil Musial come in. We saw Cool Papa Bell and Satchel Paige and Bob Feller and all these Hall of Famers coming in.

I grabbed my oldest son Scott who was about seven or eight then. I took him backstage and up to Stan and said, "Stan, would you might autographing a baseball for this young fellow?" He autographed it and we went to some of the others, and Scott ended up getting about fourteen or fifteen Hall-of-Fame ballplayers. The one I'll never forget was Cool Papa Bell because he was real shaky. Scott walked up to him and said, "Mr. Bell, can I have your autograph?" He looked at the ball and said, "Well, son, you've got some pretty good autographs on there now, and I don't want to mess your ball up. I'm so shaky I probably would smear the autograph." Scott just looked at him and said, "Mr. Bell, just make an 'x' and I'll know it was you." He said, "Well, if you want it that bad." So he sat there, and it took him about three or four minutes, but he gave him a perfect autograph.

Then the show starts. I'm sitting on the aisle in the front row. A. Ray Smith comes out and says, "Now for our special mystery guest." So they swing the spotlight around, and it's barely hitting me, but it's aiming on down the aisle. Who comes walking down the center aisle, but Joe D.? I'm pinching myself. I couldn't believe it. There is no way he is going to get by me. I would have tackled him if I would have had to get him to autograph that ball. As he's walking toward me, I get the ball out, and he sees it. He stopped right there and signed it. Boy, when you're in a tuxedo, you carry some weight, I guess. As he's walking toward me, though, my wife is jabbing me on the arm, and she said, "He was Marilyn Monroe's husband." My oldest son was saying, "Dad, that's Mr. Coffee." I'm slapping my head thinking, "Good God, people. He did play center field for the Yankees, but I guess that doesn't count." 'cause now he's Mister Coffee and **Marilyn Monroe's** husband! He just gave me a perfect autograph right on the sweet spot. Nobody tried to stop it. He just signed it, shook my hand, and walked up onto the stage and gave a little talk.

———**GENE SIGLOCK**, East Alton, Illinois

When you walked down the streets in Boston and in New York, we said it was almost like being at home. Everyone had on Cardinal

> To accentuate a wiggle in her walk, Marilyn Monroe would cut a quarter of an inch off one of her heels.... The combination on Monroe's jewelry box was 5-5-5—DiMaggio's uniform number.

stuff. One of the most unusual things was when we went to Arizona two years ago on their Opening Day. We were all excited about it because Opening Day in St. Louis is the biggest thing in the world. In Phoenix, we get up early and go downtown and nothing is going on. We were like, "Well, what do you people do?" They said they didn't do anything for Opening Day. We were like, "No way." One of the radio people noticed us, and they could not believe we were from St. Louis. They wanted us to be on the radio that night, "You came all the way here to see the Cardinals?" "Yeah." "Why?" "It's just what Cardinals fans do. I don't know." They were astonished that anyone would come from St. Louis there to see a game.

It was the first Opening Day I'd ever been to in another city. They had no rallies. They had nothing. We have all these things going on and have giveaways. They had absolutely nothing and were just waiting for the game time.

———**PAULA HOLLEY**, KOA Campground Owner, Barnhart, Missouri

It was a Friday night game with the Mets, about the eighth consecutive game the Cards had lost after Kile passed away. I was feeling really down in the mouth so my husband suggested we go across the street from Busch Stadium to the little bar called Anthony's. We are sitting there and I had asked my husband to get the chips off a nearby table. The bartender, Everett, would not let us take the chips off the table because it was for "special" people, like we weren't special. I had to give Everett a hard time about that. He said, "I'll get you your own chips but don't touch that table. I have it all set up. I have special people coming." I said, "Everett, if you say that one more time we're gonna leave." It wasn't five minutes and here they pull up and it's Tony La Russa and Walt Jocketty and two guys from Anheuser-Busch. We were sitting there having cocktails and I said I wanted to go talk to La Russa. My husband, John, said, "No you can't do that." I said, "I'm gonna be really nice but I want to talk to him." About 1:30 in the morning, Everett is getting antsy because he wants everybody to leave. It's just that table of four and John and I at the bar. Finally, I said, "Okay, I'm gonna go talk to him. I'm really worried about my team. I just want to talk to him." John says, "Okay, if you think you have to do that, you do that. I'm going to the men's room." It was like he couldn't even be there. I waited until he walked out the door, and I

went over and said, "I have waited all night for my husband to go the john so I could come over here and sit with you guys and talk." They all broke out laughing. It was really a good thing. Jocketty, we knew from the cruise, had spoken to us when he came in. He said, "I know you're the lady from Indiana that has season tickets." I said, "Yeah, Tony, I just really wanted to meet you." He hands me the line-up card and says, "Who do you think I should play in right field tomorrow?" Like I would have a clue! I said, "Well, I really think Eddie Perez is who you should play because of the way he played tonight—he almost won that game for us." He said, "Well, gosh I don't know. Are you gonna be really upset with me if I play Drew?" I said, "No I'm not. I like Drew. I met him on the cruise." He said, "Oh, you know Sheigh?" and I said, "Yes, but I'll tell ya what, if you're gonna play him, you need to tell him something. He needs to get his bat off his shoulder and his head out of his butt." He looked at me, and I thought I would die. La Russa said, "I think he needs to get his head out of his wife's butt." Tino wasn't doing any good, and he couldn't give Tino the day off because his boy was going to be bat boy. I saw a real human side to Tony La Russa. We talked a long time. The guys from Anheuser-Busch are trying to ask me what kind of alcohol sells in southern Indiana, and I'm trying to get them off my back. I just wanted to talk to Tony.

——PAM CORRONA, Season Ticket Holder from Vincennes, Indiana

When I was in the left field bleachers in Wrigley Field, it was a hot day. I brought a squirt bottle. Nobody had ever brought a squirt bottle up there. They have a little trough-like where they sell margarites on the ramps going up to left field. I asked the guy if I could fill it up with water and he said, "Yeah." I was squirting these little kids in front of me. I wound up giving them the bottle. I got to talking to the family and said, "If you're ever in St. Louis, give me a call. We'll go to a game, or go out and have dinner or something." Well, they did. The mother and kids came to St. Louis, and the mother called and said, "Could I stay with you a couple of days? I have to leave the hotel." She and her kids came and stayed for twenty-eight days. My husband threatened to leave, and they had to leave—I needed my house back.

She would go out and work during the day. I have no idea what she was doing. It was very strange. The two boys were left here in the house at home during the day. I got scared because I didn't know if she was running from something or what. She would have been in her thirties, the daughter was fifteen, and the one boy was twelve and the other kid was nine. I now don't ask people to come stay with me anymore.

————MAMA LUCY, Busch Bleacher Legend

We went to the Cardinals/Royals World Series in '85 and it amazed me. We got in the ballpark and even Joe Cunningham and some of the Cardinal front office were there, and I was the only person in Royals' Stadium that had Cardinal red and white on. I had, of all things, a Dane Iorg jersey that he had worn in the World Series in '82. My cousin had paid four or five hundred dollars to a collector over in Steeleville, Illinois for the jersey. He let me wear it so I had the white "real" jersey on, and I had a pair of white slacks on and then had the red Cardinal jacket and a cap. We're at game two, and the Cardinals are losing 2-0 in the top of the ninth. There were two outs, and Terry Pendleton comes up with the bases loaded, and he rifles the ball down into the left field corner—three runs scored. And the Royals went down one-two-three, and we won 3-2. I stood up. I had my wife with me, and I thought, "I hope I get out of here alive." I'm walking out, and everybody's patting me on the back and saying, "Oh, man, we're just glad to be in the World Series, and the Cardinals will probably win it in a sweep. We're just glad to be here. We think the Cardinals are great, and the Cardinal fans are great." I was kind of stunned they were so nice. Then we go back for Game Six, and the Royals make that miracle comeback, and of course, who gets the winning hit but Dane Iorg. I go to walk out, and I'm not worried about it, and now they turn on me. They're throwing mustard and ketchup and beer on me, "Cardinal fan, get out of here." I said, "You people are great losers, but you're poor winners."

————GENE SIGLOCK, 59, East Alton, Illinois

In 1964, my cousin Jack McCarthy was the weather guy on a TV station in Peoria, Illinois, where my parents and I lived. Like me, Jack was a big Cardinal fan. The sports guy on that channel was Bob

Chapter Six

There's No Expiration Date on Dreams

Let it be a Pitcher…

Growin' Up with the Redbirds

NIX ON THE CUBS

George McGovern

George McGovern was born in Avon, South Dakota, moved to Canada at the age of three, and later settled in Mitchell, South Dakota. His father played in the Cardinals' minor league system. He has had limited success converting fellow South Dakota friends, Tom Brokaw and Alan Neuharth (USA Today Founder) to the Cardinal Nation.

The current Montana resident chose Missouri Senator, Tom Eagleton, as his initial running mate in his unsuccessful run for the Presidency in 1972.

I listened to the Cardinals on WNAX, out of Yankton, South Dakota. They were a 50,000 watt station, and they picked up the national and regional coverage. I've been a Cardinal fan all my life. I was maybe ten years old when I first latched onto the Cardinals back in the Dizzy Dean era.

My dad would always have the radio on listening to the Cardinals whenever they played. I began developing an interest in them through my father. He followed them all of his life. He played baseball when he was a boy and stayed with it until he decided to become a Methodist minister. In those days, it was quite logical for someone in South Dakota to root for the Cardinals. The Cardinals were such a colorful team in that era. I found them very exciting to listen to. They were usually pennant contenders, if not pennant winners.

In the early days, Joe Medwick was my favorite player. He was sort of the Stan Musial of that team. He could hit and was dependable. I never met any of the Gas House Gang. I had a chance to meet Durocher one time when he was in New York, but I didn't get it done.

I did go to **Sportsman's Park**. I saw my first big league game there. I was just in awe, the size of the stadium, cheers, noise. It was an exciting experience, I don't think I'll ever forget. I was in college at that time. That was a long trip but we were in the area on a speech tournament.

The first thing I look at when I pick up the paper during the baseball season is to see how the Cardinals did. Now I have to watch Houston and Chicago because they are grouped up all there together, and you don't know who is going to be ahead one day to the next. No matter what was going on, whether I was running for President or running for the Senate or whatever, I always looked to see how the Cardinals were doing first.

I went to school in Chicago for four years, so I have kind of a soft spot for the Cubs. A lot of my friends were Cub fans. I never detected the kind of bitter rivalry between the Cubs and the Cardinals that existed between the Dallas Cowboys and the Washington Redskins in football.

Senator Eagleton and I relished in our love for the Cardinals. After the 1972 campaign when we had a brief falling out, it was the Cardinals that helped bring us back together. I called him up one day and said I was coming to St. Louis just for the purpose of seeing the Cardinals, provided he would go to the game. He invited me to stay at his house and took me to the best restaurant in St. Louis. We watched the Cardinals play and that kind of helped. From time to time we talk. The last time we were together was at former Senator Gaylord Nelson's house in Washington...talking Cardinal baseball.

> Joe Garagiola's wife, Audrey, was at one time the organist at Sportsman's Park.

THAT'S THE FIRST TIME THAT'S EVER HAPPENED *AGAIN*

Raymond Warfel, Hong Kong

The years were 1956-1958 and the Cardinal players involved were battery-mates: left-handed pitcher Wilmer "Vinegar Bend" Mizell and catcher Hal Smith. Both were Christian men who regularly attended services with their families at the Florissant Valley Baptist Church. They always attended the early service, which allowed them time to get to the old ballpark, Sportsman's Park at Grand and Dodier, for the usual Sunday doubleheader.

As teenagers and devoted Cardinal fans, my buddies and I would mow lawns during the week—can you believe we got a dollar per lawn, sometimes with a 25-cent tip?—to scrape together three or four dollars, enough to go see our beloved Cardinals play. To get the most value for our hard-earned money, we always went to Sunday doubleheader games, arrived early to see all the pre-game batting practice—long before the McGwire phenomenon—and hung around outside the players' exit from the locker rooms after the games to collect autographs. We usually got in a 10- to 12-hour day of baseball on Sundays and the only drawback was our unreliable transportation to and from Florissant. We depended on a combination of hitchhiking, buses and streetcars, including transfers at Ferguson and Wellston. We frequently got stranded and it took forever to get home, sometimes after midnight.

The players were remarkably friendly and generous to the fans in those days. They always devoted time to signing autographs and the visiting team would chat with fans through the windows of their chartered bus. The hometown Cardinals drove to the park and usually carpooled, which Mizell and Smith always did, sometimes with other players who lived in Florissant, like Wally Moon.

We had autographs from everyone from superstars, Musial, Mays, Koufax, Banks and Aaron, to umpires and even batboys and clubhouse assistants. No player ever refused to sign, at least for a few minutes, and no one ever considered the crazy notion of charging the fans money for an autograph.

After one particularly long Sunday that included an extra-inning game, one of my buddies was scared we would be so late getting home that his parents would punish him. He kept begging us to leave before the game ended but the rest of us wouldn't hear of it. Besides wanting to see the game itself, we had invested 75 cents each in bleacher tickets, crawled behind the shrubs in center field to get into the 90-cent pavilion seats in right field, and scaled a 15-foot fence in full public view to get into the general admission section. By the second game we had worked our way into empty box seats right behind the "on deck" circle, as close to heaven as any of us could imagine. No way were we going to leave before the last out of the game and the autograph ritual. No item on our precious Sunday agenda of baseball was to be sacrificed.

After the game we made our way to the players' exit. Soon Mizell and Smith appeared. In panicked desperation to get home, our frightened friend had the nerve, audacity, or whatever to mention to them that we also lived in Florissant, attended the same church they did, and *could we please have a ride home with them?* To our amazement, they said, "Sure." The next thing we knew we were sitting in the back seat of their car discussing the day's games. Wally Moon was also in the car and he mentioned playing shortstop in the minor leagues. I knew Moon batted left-handed and I asked him how a lefty could play shortstop. He clarified that while he batted left, he threw right-handed. I was mortified not to know this and my friends were silently kicking and poking me to make me shut up and stop embarrassing them with my ignorance about our local hero.

The players insisted on driving out of their way, safely delivering us to our homes instead of dropping us at the nearest major street. Our families and neighbors recognized the players as they dropped us off and waved goodnight. This soon became a regular routine, with Smith and Mizell recognizing us at church on Sunday mornings and looking for us as they left the clubhouse to return home on Sunday nights. They got to know our names and even talked to us about our Little League baseball teams.

Wilmer Mizell passed away on February 21, 1999, at the age of 68. A few months earlier, I spoke via phone with "Vinegar Bend." Mizell, who served as a congressman from his home state of **North Carolina** from 1968 to 1974, had remained active in congressional baseball games, serving as a bench coach. When asked if he could still teach the high leg kick that was his trademark as a pitcher—Willie Mays loved it because he didn't even have to slide when stealing second base—Wilmer laughed and replied, "That's about all that's left." He still remembered giving rides home to us kids more than 40 years ago.

Several years ago, I visited Hal Smith at his home in Texas. Smitty had recently retired from scouting for the Cardinals. He related that the autograph requests he now receives by mail are usually accompanied by a check for $5 or $10. He always returns both his autograph and the uncashed check, believing to this day that fans should not have to pay for autographs.

> Michael Jordan was given his first set of golf clubs by fellow University of North Carolina classmate Davis Love, Davis Love, Davis Love.

WE CHASED THE PHILLIES UNTIL THEY CAUGHT US

Dalton Sullivan, St. Louis

It is impossible to say exactly when I became an adult and no longer a child. There was no magical moment, no date when the baton was passed from adolescence to manhood. I didn't wake up one morning, and suddenly look at the world with a whole new perspective. But I can say, with all certainty, that the summer of 1964 forever changed me. That was when baseball became an everyday part of my life.

That summer, I turned seven years old, and several important things happened. First, I played Little League for the first time. Where? At the ABC fields in St. Ann, Missouri. My first team? The Flyers. I played shortstop, because my favorite player was Dick Groat. Second, I somehow talked my mom and dad into subscribing to **_Sports Illustrated_** for me. My first issue featured Jim Bunning and Chris Short of the Philadelphia Phillies on the front. They were smiling first-place smiles. Later that summer, the smiles would fade. Finally, sometime in June or July, my grandfather had the wisdom and foresight to buy four tickets, one for himself, one for my dad, and one each for my brother and me, to the last game of the regular season: October 4, 1964.

Even though I was only seven, I paid close attention to the pennant race. I listened to KMOX, from which Harry Caray and Jack Buck came into my room every night. I had a pocket-sized transistor radio that I would hold under the covers to listen to the games. I knew the Phillies had a seemingly insurmountable lead as we headed into September, but I also knew that I was going to my first baseball game in just a matter of weeks, with the two men who had instructed me,

When *Sports Illustrated* recently celebrated its 50th anniversary, the magazine still had 8,330 of its charter subscribers.

coached me, and taught me a love and respect for the game that grew stronger every day.

As the day drew closer, something strange was happening. The Phillies couldn't win, and the Cardinals couldn't lose. A 10-game Philadelphia lead vanished in two weeks. As the final weekend arrived, the Cardinals, Phillies and Reds were all within one game of each other. The Phils and Reds were playing each other, while the Cardinals hosted the lowly New York Mets. The final day, Sunday the fourth, saw the Cards one game ahead of the Phillies, and tied with the Reds. If the Cardinals lost for a third straight time to the Mets, and the Phillies beat the Reds, then baseball would have its first-ever three-way tie.

As we walked from our car to Sportsman's Park, I couldn't help but notice that the street we were on was Sullivan Avenue. "Yes," I thought, "This is going to be a good day." As we entered, the cathedral of green spread out before us like an ever-widening horizon. The grass was a deep emerald, the uniforms whiter than white, the red hats stunning in their hue. I know, I was only seven years old, but I was finally at the place where the people I'd listened to, the players I'd imitated, the sights I had imagined, were all laid out before me. There was my favorite player, Dick Groat.

The story of what happened that day is well documented. The Cardinals beat the Mets, the Phillies beat the Reds, and St. Louis won its first pennant in 18 years. One of my memories of that day, after Barney Schultz retired the side in the ninth, is of the fans jumping, leaping and falling out of the outfield stands. My brother and I both wanted to go out on the field as well. I'm sure it was all my grandpa and dad could do to keep the two of us from running out there.

On the wall of my home I have a picture. It is a photograph of the 1964 World Champion St. Louis Cardinals. Beside the picture are four ticket stubs, all bearing the date "October 4, 1964." The section is X, row 17, seats 18, 19, 20 and 21. The cost of each ticket was $2.25. The memory of each ticket is priceless.

I OFTEN REMINISCE
ABOUT THE GOOD OLD DAY

Jim Shucart, St. Louis

I was born in St. Louis, and due to this happy accident, I've been fortunate to be a Cardinals fan all of my life. As a little boy, the only name I knew was "The Man," Stan Musial. When my dad came home at the end of World War II, he elected to stay in the Army, so my mom and I left St. Louis to live on a series of Army bases. I met a lot of terrific men—enlisted men in my dad's unit—who played baseball with me and looked after me. They all knew I was from St. Louis, and they nicknamed me "The Man." I secretly hoped to be like the real "Stan the Man" someday.

After my dad left the Army he went to work for Studebaker on the West Coast, and later transferred to South Bend, Indiana. When Studebaker was bought out, Dad felt the time was right to return to St.. Louis. In 1954, with no job in hand, we came home. I knew nothing of this, though. All I knew was that we were going home to the land of the Cardinals. I hoped I would finally get to see my hero, for I'd never actually seen Stan play ball. I'd only heard stories, and when I was old enough to read, followed his exploits in the newspapers.

By the time we got back to St. Louis, I was 11 years old, and I'd come to accept that bad eyes meant I'd never realize my dream to be just like Stan. However, I still looked up to him as a hero and role model. He was decent, a team player, generous to his fans and the community and, by the way, about the best ballplayer in the game. Finally, we got moved in and I started asking Dad when we could go to a ball game. At age 11, the fact that my dad didn't have a job had no bearing on going to a ball game to see my hero play.

Each time I asked about going, Dad would say, "We'll see." Finally the day came when my dad said, "We're going next week." I was beside myself with excitement. I actually slept with my glove, a Musial model, of course, for the next six nights. I don't remember much of the trip to the park but I recall how *big* it looked when we got there. Sportsman's Park. I remember the sights and sounds as though it were yesterday: the towering stands, the noise, the smell of popcorn, the vendors, the billboards, the flags and the huge scoreboard. "St. Louis Cardinals vs. New York Giants," it read. And not only was I going to see my first major league ball game, and my hero, but this was a doubleheader!

I don't remember much about those games except for what my hero did. Stan hit *five* home runs, and by the end of the second game, I was convinced I'd seen the greatest ballplayer who ever lived. He was more than I'd dreamed he could be. He was magnificent. To my 11-year-old eyes, he was the embodiment of everything good. I can still see the ball arching toward the right field stands; flying high, straight and true. I can still hear the crack of the bat as he struck the ball, and see him trotting around the bases as thousands of us roared our approval. To see him hit one home run was almost more excitement than I could stand, but five home runs in one day! I was hoarse from cheering and my hands were sore from clapping, but I knew I had witnessed history. With a young boy's version of wisdom, I understood that this was something special. A hero who meets the expectations of a little boy is very rare, but on that day in 1954, Stan "The Man" Musial met and surpassed my expectations. It was magic.

On a sunny day in 1963, I was in the stadium again to see a Cardinals game—Stan's last. I was twenty years old. I remember his final at bat: the stance, a funny, coiled crouch, eyes intently staring at the pitcher; the familiar number six on his back; the crack of his bat as he drove the ball for a clean single. I remember him running to first base. I can hear the roar of the crowd as he rounded the bag, then retreated to the base as the throw from the outfield came in to second. Then a pinch runner came out to take his place, and we knew it was over. The crowd cheered. My hero walked slowly toward the dugout, pausing to tip his cap to the crowd. I was that little boy again, cheering for my idol. His gaze passed over me, and in my imagination he was thanking me for being his fan. But no thanks were needed. He would always be "The Man."

SHORT STORIES FROM LONG MEMORIES

In 1985 I was only nine years old, and I lived and died with the Birds on the Bat. My cousin and very close friend, Stuart lived in Kansas City and was a huge Royals fan. We had a childish love for our teams, our cities, and most important, a love for the game. The I-70 battle was built up incredibly on the news. A rivalry was born. Just days before the Series began, my cousin and I were visiting our grandparents in southern Illinois. Our grandfather always had us help him out in the yard, raking leaves, pulling weeds, etc. After we helped him out this particular fall day he gave us each a dollar. One dollar. It was a precious thing to us to receive a whole dollar at that young age. Well, naturally, Stuart and I began talking about the upcoming Cards/Royals Series. I boasted of Ozzie Smith and Willie McGee; he bragged of Bret Saberhagen and George Brett. One thing led to another and we ended up betting our only dollars on the Series. We shook on it like little businessmen. My hope was alive with the boys in red; his was alive with K.C.

We all know what events took place over the course of that Series; I need not explain the details. The team's theme that year was Glen Frey's "The Heat is On," and even in Game 7 when things were pretty ugly for St. Louis, I still hoped the Cards would pull something off and that the "heat" would not die.

When the game ended with the final out, I was in tears. I couldn't take my eyes off of those Royals players celebrating and my Redbirds with broken hearts. But I got up, walked into my room and took the dollar out of my piggy bank. Still crying, I looked at it and stuffed it into an envelope. Writing Stuart's address on that envelope and sealing my dollar inside of it was one of the most difficult things I had ever done. No letter, just the dollar. He knew how much I loved the St. Louis Cardinals—he wouldn't need a note. I asked my mother for a stamp, and I walked out to the mailbox. All of this while the television showed champagne and smiles in the Kansas City locker room. I walked back inside, took one last look at the TV, and went to my bed. I cried myself to sleep that night.

To this day, of all of the money I've ever had pass through my hands, that one precious dollar was the most difficult debt I ever had to pay. I'll never forget it. Because to me, my Cardinals were worth my only dollar.

Fast pay makes fast friends…but Denkinger still owes me a buck.

————**TIM GRAEFF**, 27, St. Louis

I still remember the excitement in Boston with the 1967 World Series. Then, you were into it immediately. There weren't all these play-offs. I remember when they had the red, white, and blue banners all around Fenway. It looked different. It was so great. Just recently I saw a highlight on ESPN of the '67 Series. It was so much fun to see it again. I remember how close Jim Lonborg came to pitching a no-hitter. I remember a cartoon in the paper of a little kid writing on a fence, because Julian Javier got the hit to break up the no-hitter. And he wrote, "Julian Javier is a herk."

————**BILL BRAUDIS**, 46, Dorcester, Mass. from *For Red Sox Fans Only*

When I was a kid, I was a member of the Knothole Gang program. They let the kids in free at Sportsman's Park, knowing they'd be paying customers in the future. The majority of the fans would be in the bleachers while most of the expensive reserved seats remained empty. It became a sport for the Cardinal fans to slowly drift into choice empty seats as the game progressed. I liked to sneak in the seats somewhere behind the third-base line behind the Cardinals' dugout.

There were ads plastered throughout the park. When Bill Veeck sold Sportsman's Park to August Busch, Busch was going to name the stadium Budweiser Stadium, but then he decided on Busch Stadium. They put a million and a half dollars into it, which included a lot of work on the dugouts and the club house and new box seats. Out on the scoreboard, advertisements for Sayman's Soap, Kellogg's Corn Flakes, and Buick cars were removed. I missed the ads that were all over the park. One of the biggest thrills for fans attending a doubleheader was watching the "Star of the Game" sign operated by the *Globe-Democrat* newspaper. After the first game of a doubleheader, fans would consult their scorecards and try to predict what player would get his name placed on the board. There was always great anticipation when a groundskeeper would ride his cart into the outfield to post the name of the new star.

————**NATE WILLIAMS**, Middleton, Wisconsin

When I was in eighth or ninth grade, a friend and I were at my house and we were watching the game when Jack Buck made the call about Ozzie Smith's home run in '85. For some reason the TV was in kitchen. We were sitting there watching as he kept fouling off balls. Then they flashed that statistic up on the screen, "Ozzie Smith has never hit a home run left-handed in two thousand, or whatever number, at-bats." I said to my friend, "I'll eat s— if he hits a home run right now." Well, he did it. That is one of the most played highlights. Everytime, my friend just looks at me and laughs. Fortunately, he didn't make me do it.

——**BRIAN CARR**, 31, Chesterfield, Missouri

Mike Jorgensen played for the Cardinals, managed the Cardinals, and is now the special assistant to the general manager of the Cardinals.

When he was a player, he had a way of doing phantom swings where he sort of gently dropped his bat really low and swung back and forth. When I was about ten, I was doing my phantom Mike Jorgensen swings—really gently, but still, a bat's a lethal weapon—when my dog, Daisy, decided to walk into the path of the bat. She was knocked out cold, and I was sure I had killed her.

I ran to the window and screamed out for my brother who was outside. "Michael, I killed Daisy." My parents had gone to the movies, and my grandparents, who were ostensibly watching me, lived in the apartment below. My older brother came running in, then my grandfather came in. Daisy was still out cold. She had her own little chair and they lifted her and put her in it. My grandmother got some ice for her head. I was beside myself. It was awful.

When I think back on this, the funny thing was that my grandfather, an infinitely practical man, said, in an attempt to make me feel better as I was bawling, "It's okay, Steva, the doga, she gonna be okay." Here, there was a few seconds pause. He'd gotten close to making me feel better, when he said, "And ifa she die, I get you another one." I just burst into tears again.

Now, Mike Jorgensen is probably a really nice guy, but the memories he stirs up make him my least favorite player.

——**STEVE CUNETTA**, Attorney, Seattle, Washington

In the summer of 1964, the Cardinals traded for Lou Brock. Overnight, Lou became a great offensive player and an instant hero in St.

Louis. I believe he batted over .400 in the '64 World Series, which the Cards won. Back then, in my neighborhood, summer meant baseball: watching it, reading about it, playing it, or playing a variation such as Indian Ball, Whiffle ball, Hot Box, or my personal favorite, "three grounders or a fly." But the single-most important thing in life was my baseball card collection—Topps, which were packaged five cards and a piece of that inimitable gum, at a nickel a pack. In the summer of '65, my fellow collectors and I breathlessly awaited the Lou Brock card, as this would be the first time Brock was pictured as a Cardinal, not a Cub.

A few months went by, and the first six checklists, and still the Brock card had not come out. My friend Steve and I were exasperated at this situation. We would wonder aloud what pose Lou was striking in the photo. Bat on shoulder? Follow-through shot? Kneeling as if on deck? Or maybe a glove pose, as if about to catch a fly ball. Sometime in early August, Steve discovered that Paul's Market at 1-70 and Bermuda Road not only sold baseball cards but had the seventh checklist. The seventh checklist! In his quest to be the first guy to have Lou Brock, Steve kept this knowledge to himself, something about which I would later be highly indignant. One afternoon, here came old Steve on his bike down Atherstone Drive, arms in the air, in a state of utter jubilation and triumph, hollering to the heavens at the top of his lungs: "I got Brock! I got Brock!" His bike veered to the curb and Steve took a tumble, resulting in bloodied elbows and knees. My friend was unfazed by his wounds, and had cradled the coveted card against his stomach so that it not be defaced in any way. I rushed to Steve's side, not to offer concern for his condition, but to set eyes on THE CARD. And there was Louis Clark Brock, in a Cardinal uniform, bat over left shoulder. Steve would not allow me to handle THE CARD, but in an uncharacteristic gesture of generosity, he offered me a piece of Topps gum, "compliments of the house."

——TOM HEIDGER, 46, Arnold, Missouri

I was a big Cardinal fan growing up in Moberly, Missouri. One Christmas, I told my mom and dad that all I wanted was cash. I got close to one hundred dollars. Dad had taken me to games once or twice a season, and I thought it was just awesome. So I thought if once or twice a season was awesome, more times would be better. I waited until the Cardinals tickets came on sale in February. I took all the cash and sat down with the Cardinal schedule and picked out close to ten games to go to, spread out through the summer. I kicked in some of my own money. I ordered for about ten games and didn't say anything to mom and dad about it. Finally, one day the mail came and here is this big thick envelope from the St. Louis Cardinals. I thought this was so  cool. I was sitting in the kitchen with all of these tickets for different games, and my dad came home from work. He walks in and says, "What are ya doing?" I said, "Dad, remember that money you and mom gave me for Christmas?" He said, "Yeah, what did you do that that?" "Look, check this out." Dad walked over and said, "Oh, you got some Cardinal tickets. That's great. When we going?" He picks up this pile and says, "April 12, April 24, May 10" and he keeps going and going. Living in Moberly, it's not like living down the road from St. Louis. Most of the games that I had picked were night games. Back then, they used to play a lot more doubleheaders. Twilight doubleheaders were the greatest because you got two games. Every doubleheader they were playing at home was in that envelope, too. Dad could have bailed and said, "This is great. We'll go to half of these," or something like that. But he took me to every one of those games that summer. By the time we would get out of the ballpark and get to the parking garage, we would go to this place called Sambo's because he would want to eat ham and eggs and then drive home. I would sleep on the way home and poor dad had to drive from St. Louis home to Moberly. It would be in the middle of the middle of the night before we got back. He would have to turn around and do it again a couple of weeks later. From Moberly to St. Louis, it's about three hundred miles round trip.

One game Bob Gibson was pitching and dad got a line drive off the bat of Cesar Geronimo with the Reds. He gave it to me.

——STEVE O'BRIAN, 44, Columbia, Missouri

I grew up in Overland, Missouri, just outside St. Louis. In 1960, I played on an all-star Little League team that got to play three innings at old Busch Stadium. They divided the ballpark so there were separate games going on in right field, center field, and left field. These were Little League teams from all across St. Louis, and the idea was to give every boy at least one at bat on the big field. I'll never forget how soft the grass was and how it seemed to go in every direction. Our game was in right field, and my dream was to hit one on the pavilion roof. I had hit one that far in our regular games, but that day I had to settle for a single. Every player has his memories of throwing a no-hitter, or something like that, but this was really special. More than anything else, it opened my eyes to what the major leagues were really like

——**JERRY REUSS**, winner of 220 games in a 22-year career

Although the Cardinals did not win the pennant in 1974, that particular year remains possibly the greatest year of baseball in my life. It is most certainly my favorite.

Together with my best friend, Paul DeBernardi, I went to many games that year and was able to witness two of the greatest moments in Cardinal history: Bob Gibson's 3,000th career strikeout and Lou Brock's 105th stolen base in a single season. We went to numerous games in succession as those two Cardinal stars neared their respective marks. Paul and I wanted to be in attendance for history.

Another fond memory of that season was attending the home opener against Pittsburgh. As we usually did when we went to the ballpark, Paul and I rode the Tower Grove bus from our homes in the Compton Heights neighborhood. Since we were just 15 years old, we thought it easier to ride the bus than to pester a family member for a ride. Besides, it only cost 25 cents one-way apiece for bus fare. Combined with the $1.50 we each needed to buy a general admission ticket, it was pretty enticing to take in a game when ever we wanted.

While we were standing in line to pay our admission, an older man approached us and asked if we needed tickets. After we answered affirmatively, he said his son and daughter-in-law were unable to attend that night and since he didn't want two box seats to go to waste, we could have them for free as long as we didn't mind sitting with him and his wife. We accepted, thanked him for his generosity, and hurried inside. The seats were about a dozen rows up from the field along the first-base line. Imagine our surprise as we saw Stan "The Man" Musial and "Cool Papa" Bell just a few feet from us. They had thrown out the first pitches that night and were now in their seats. It took about four innings for us to work up the courage to approach them for their autographs, but we did.. I treasure the scorecard they signed and I still have it safely packed away. The rest of the game remains a blur, although I recall the Redbirds won despite two home runs from Pirate third baseman Richie Hebner.

———**ED KNIEST**, Jefferson City, Missouri

I babysat for Lindy McDaniel. The McDaniels moved in probably about two blocks from us in Florissant, Missouri. With me being raised with baseball, I knew all about him. I really wanted to babysit for him. It took every bit of courage that I had to go up and knock on the door—I was almost in tears—and ask him if he would like for me to babysit for him. He and his wife thought I was a little bit too young. But after they talked to my mom and knew the background ,they felt pretty comfortable that I could handle it. The first few times I sat, I made sure my mom was home, so if anything happened I could call her. It was very exciting to babysit for him. He included me so much in their activities that I really felt like part of the family.

———**MARY RACKERS**, 54, St. Louis

My father took me to my first game in 1937, a Cardinals-Cubs doubleheader, and I've been a rabid fan since my days as a member of the Knothole Gang. In fact, I still have my Knothole Card, issued in 1942. The Gang was invented by the new Cardinal owners in 1917. It was originally started to reduce juvenile delinquency, but was later enlarged to include many school-age children through the YMCA. Spaces in the left field stands were reserved for us Knotholers. These were a couple of the Knothole Gang rules: "1) I will not at any time miss school to attend a game; 2) I will uphold the principles of clean speech, clean sports, and clean habits, and will stand with the rest of the Gang against cigarettes and profane language in the stands and off the field."

Much in baseball has changed since the 1930s and, '40s. Back then, players could not be free agents and therefore were not paid enormous salaries. More players played "for the love of the game." Players used to leave their gloves on the field, and the bats were on the ground in front of the dugouts. The outfield fences were not as flexible as they are today; poor Pete Reiser had a short career because he kept running into the fences. Baseball games were not broadcast on Sundays.

———**AARON GREENBERG**, St. Louis, Knothole Card Holder

In 1946, my father—then 20 years old—had a ticket for the seventh game of the World Series. His uncle, John "Moon" Mullen—then only about 35 years old, but a much older man than my youthful father—begged my dad for the ticket. My dad did not want to part with it, but Moon insisted that, *since he was* so *old,* he might well die before the Cardinals were ever in another World Series. My dad relented, given this perspective, and gave him the ticket. That was the game when Enos Slaughter scored all the way from first base on a single to win the Series!

By the way, Uncle Moon lived many years, saw many other Cardinal pennant winners, and my dad never never forgot!

———**RICK GEISSAL**, St. Louis, Cardinal Fan

I grew up listening to Harry Caray on the radio. I grew up in the city and nobody had air conditioning back then. Everyone had their windows open in the summer time and we could hear the broadcast, especially if they were in a pennant race. Then, I got a portable radio myself, which in those days was pretty big. It wasn't like what we have now. I couldn't go anywhere without that portable radio. I was, by far, the youngest of seven children, so there basically was nobody to introduce me to baseball. One day I said, I'm gonna go see the game in person. I was a teenager, I was old enough to go by myself. I was not familiar with the different seating areas in the ballpark. I got out there to Sportsman's Park, and I saw this one area where everybody was going into, so I went in there. I thought that was probably the cheapest place to sit. Well, it was what we called the Pavilion. It was right field. It was bleachers but it was all covered over. We really didn't have segregation then, but it seemed like the black people chose to sit there. The seats were inexpensive and yet it was covered over, so there I was in the middle of all of these people. It was really something, because they were doing their gambling, they were betting and some of them had their libations and little brown bags, but they were real nice to me. After that I thought I don't think this is the place I'm supposed to be sitting. Then I found the bleachers the next time I went. As time went on, I was in high school and I found somebody else that liked the ball games and I started going with that person.

My parents were from Europe and they really weren't ball fans at all. I really stumbled across this on my own. It was from listening to Harry Caray and Gabby Street.

——**DELORES DALTON**, Cardinal fan

From where I'm from, it's nothing but cotton fields, sand and mosquitoes. Back in the 1970's the Cardinals were broadcast by KMOX all through the South. It was rare to run into anyone other than Cardinal fans in the 1970's here in this area. That all changed in the 1980's with cable television. I bleed Cardinal red because my family is a generation of Cardinal fans. My grandfather was a Cardinal fan, my dad and my uncle and passed on to me and my children are becoming Cardinal fans. That started back in the 1970's, listening to the Cardinal games. Listening to Lou Brock, he was my childhood hero. During the summer time during my generation, we didn't have summer recreational things. We didn't have a summer swimming pool, we had fishing holes and baseball. I grew up in a community that loves baseball. Baseball was very much a part of the lifestyle back then. It's not as much now because of softball replacing it pretty much in this area.

My first trip to St. Louis was when I was five years old and since then, I have had a love for not only the Cardinals, but also with the city of St. Louis. The sound of those broadcasts that came through, was what kept me in touch and informed and in love with the city that was maybe 4-1/2 hours away. It was a long distance relationship that was for me maintained with that city through the voice of Jack Buck and the radio broadcasts. It would throw my imagination and my thoughts and it would take my mind away from the cotton fields. It would put me somewhere standing on Broadway, walking in towards the stadium. Those moments today when I walk up the streets looking at Busch from the south, looking north and looking over to the east and seeing the Arch, it brings back those moments of walking in the cotton fields and listening to those radio broadcasts back then.

——JOHN CARMICHAEL, Black Oak, Arkansas

Two boys are playing hockey on a pond on the shore of Lake Michigan when one is attacked by a rabid Rottweiler. Thinking quickly, the other boy takes his stick and wedges it down the dog's collar and twists, breaking the dog's neck. A reporter who is strolling by sees the incident and rushes over to interview the boy. "Young Blackhawks Fan Saves Friend from Vicious Animal," he starts writing in his notebook.

"But I'm not a Blackhawks fan," the little hero replied.

"Sorry, since we are in Chicago, I just assumed you were," said the reporter, and he began writing again. "Cub Fan Rescues Friend from Horrific Attack," he continued writing in his notebook.

"I'm not a Cub fan either," the boy said.

"I assumed everyone in Chicago was either for the Blackhawks or the Cubs. What team do you root for?" the reporter asked.

"I'm a St. Louis Cardinal fan," the child said.

The reporter started a new sheet in his notebook and wrote, "Little B——-d from St. Louis Kills Beloved Family Pet."

Chapter Seven

Bleacher Creatures

Where Did the People in Section 500 Go? Try Section 8…

DICK NEN AUTOGRAPHS ARE SELLIN' LIKE HOTCAKES... TWO BUCKS A STACK

Craig Ball

Craig Ball, 34, lives in Maryland Heights, Missouri, where he works at Foot Locker. He was born in Cahokia, Illinois

I love watching the old videos of the '64 games, even though I wasn't born until '69. I remember the first time I saw Lou Brock. I was at the entrance where the players come in and out behind home plate, which is still a popular place for the visitor buses to pick up their players. I'd been hearing him on the radio all the time growing up and we got to stay late after the game one time. The Cardinals were playing the Padres. I'm standing out there, and I'm real little, and I'm just looking around. People are saying, "That's so and so. That's so and so. Brock's on the phone. He's getting ready to come out." I'll never forget—all I had was a little white card or ticket stub or something like that, and one of the Padre players, Randy Jones, comes out, and he autographs my card. This was the same year he won the Cy Young award. I see Lou Brock, but I don't have anything else to get signed. He looks real mysterious to me. I'm watching him walk back and forth inside. He comes out, and I remember getting right up close to him. At the time I was about ten years old and was playing JFL, Little League, football. One of my best friend's parents owned a tee-shirt shop called Custom Graphics. Right next to his store was Lou Brock's Sporting Goods. They worked together and had some kind of sponsorship on a racecar, number 20, "Michelob, Lou Brock and Custom Graphics." Lou Brock came out and somebody walked up to him with a Cardinal tee-shirt and he signed it real big with a marker. I remember looking in his eyes, and his eyes were really bloodshot. I didn't know what to do 'cause I didn't have anything to sign so I said, "Mr. Brock, I know who you got the racecar with." He looked at me and smiled and nodded and patted me on the shoulder and crossed the street, and that was my first brush with Lou Brock. It was just such a strange thing. I'd heard so much about him in the World Series.

We used to live right across the river in Cahokia. I still remember crossing the bridge and seeing the Stadium and just thinking, "Oh this is the greatest thing." We would always sit down the left field line. This was the late seventies, and back then the crowds weren't very big. Every time a foul ball would get hit, as soon as it would get hit down the line into the seats, you'd see everybody from behind the dugout get up and start running down the aisles. It looked like the start of a marathon or a horserace because everybody would come running down the aisles. The banging of their feet made like this loud echo of a drum as they came running down to chase the foul ball. I was pretty little so I would just stand there and watch the crowd get up and see and hear them come running down the aisles. To me that was a real neat thing.

My favorite baseball players are Clemente and Stargell. When I was a kid, I read a story about Roberto Clemente in a book from the Bookmobile. I had a Roberto Clemente tee-shirt. When the Cardinals were playing the Pirates back in '79, Willie Stargell took a gold star off of his hat and stuck it on my batting helmet. I always remember that. So therefore, I always wore number eight. I went to a high school whose colors were black and gold. For some reason the number eight and Clemente and Stargell always were there. The year the Pirates won the World Series, during "We are Family," Stargell used to give out little gold stars to players for doing something good, great play, save, or whatever. If you see any pictures of the Pirates back from the late seventies or early eighties, they've got little gold stars all over their hats. He gave me one of those stars and that was special. I still have it—in a frame with an autographed picture.

Clemente and Stargell are my favorite players, but the Cardinals— it's more I love them all. I have certain favorites over the years, and for some reason I seem to pull for an underdog. Then as I've gotten older, my favorites have changed, and I just like guys that play the game a certain way. In the eighties, I liked Pendleton and Van Slyke, two guys I thought played the game hard. I liked certain things they did, but there were still critics saying, "Oh he's not good enough," or "Van Slyke's a hot dog." I can remember when I'd watch games in public places, people would seem to get more angry if Pendleton or Van Slyke failed. Van Slyke goes on and has a great career in Pittsburgh and Pendleton goes on and is an MVP in Atlanta.

But Ozzie Smith is my one constant, and for so many reasons. He was the first big Cardinal autograph I got. When I was a kid, we didn't often get to stay late after a game. Not being able to drive and get to the games by myself, I couldn't go down early and I couldn't stay late to try and get autographs.

As I've gotten older, I've seen the money thing, and I see how people react to them. I was in Ozzie's Sports Bar out in Westport. I've been going there for about eight years on Sundays for football. There are some regular guys in there that I talk to a lot about baseball. I've seen Ozzie there on many occasions, and I'm so admiring and appreciative of the effort he makes with kids, with people. He was there not too long ago, right after he had his fifteenth-year anniversary. They had a contest where they gave away Super Bowl tickets and he'd just been announced in the Hall of Fame, and Herzog was going to be on the radio at the "Big 550" which is down the hall. Ozzie draws the name for this contest and thanks everybody for coming. He says, "I've got to go down the hall. I'm on the radio with Whitey." No one knew Whitey was there, but there happened to be a lot of people there for this event. There were some kids from some baseball teams. There must have been something going on because they all had their jerseys on, and this was an unusual time of year for them to be there with their jerseys on. Ozzie goes down the hall. We sit there and finish eating and I decided to walk down the hall to see if the radio thing was still going on. The radio thing was over, and Herzog and whoever else had been there had made their way out the back door. All these people are standing out here in the mall area by the escalator. I'm thinking that Ozzie is going to leave, they'll all be disappointed. Ozzie comes out—squeezes his way out of the radio doors—signs autographs for every single kid and person who was there. He could easily have left, he could have disappeared out the back. Hearing some of these kids talk about how thrilled they were and they couldn't wait to tell their mom, or uncle, or call a friend. To me that's what it's all about.

Still to this day, I'll go outside the park some nights and will just watch and start talking to people who are obviously from out of town and help them identify players as they walk out. You talk about good stories, you get some out there. If you're lucky, you'll meet somebody out there who really appreciates and does it for the right reason.

Recently, there was one kid in particular I noticed and he was standing there getting excited and his dad was just standing back smiling. We walked over and started talking to them. Come to find out, they are from Houston and go to the Houston Texan football camps. This kid starts telling me all these stories. He and his father were getting so excited they started talking over each other. We were getting such a kick out of the two of them telling these stories. I made a deal with them. I said, "I want you to know something. I'm gonna put you to work. Apparently you go to a lot of football camps. If you can get me an autograph from David Carr, from the Texans, I'll send you an autographed picture of Ozzie Smith that I have." I told him that I've always been a fan of Ozzie's and have several items autographed by Ozzie. I said, "But here's the deal. You've got to do it. Your dad doesn't do it. Your mom doesn't do it. You've got to do it. You're always there so it's easy for you—I'm not making it too hard on you. And you want Ozzie, and you know you can't get him while you're in town. You do the work. The only reason I'm doing this is I see you appreciate it for the right reason. A lot of kids don't do it for that. They get the stuff and then sell it or they do it for somebody else. You look really excited about it and seem to be a collector. You really seem to like it. I just want you to know that's why I'm doing this for you." That was a little deal we made. We saw them the next day at the game, and they said they were getting ready to head out of town and drive up to Chicago to see a game up there. Just after Labor Day, he sent me Carr's autograph!

WHISTLER'S SISTER

Carri Coffee pictured with Orlando Cepeda.

Carri Coffee

It was the Cardinals' Winter Warm-Up. Carri Coffee was touring the booths with friends when one disbelieving newcomer—when told of the shrillness of Coffee's incredible whistle—said, "It can't be that loud." She whistled for him. The display area came to a complete halt...people were stunned, dogs in Kentucky started heading for St. Louis...Listeners on Cardinal radio broadcasts can clearly hear her whistle even though she sits in the bleachers.

I taught myself to whistle in junior high school. I was walking home one day and started off putting four fingers in my mouth, and I would just practice while I was walking home from school. I figured if the boys could do it, so could I. Eventually, it evolved to a one-handed thumb and forefinger sort of thing. *The Sporting News* one time did a little article, and they dubbed me "The Whistle Lady." They just talked about there being nothing better than a summer evening at Busch Stadium, and what makes it special are the regulars down there. They referred to me as "The Whistle Lady." I get called "The Whistler." I get called "Whistle Girl."

I only whistle when the Cardinals are up to bat. If you go to the ballpark, you hear a lot of people try to imitate me. Nobody does three in a row like I do. Everybody around me knows to hold their ears until there's been three.

If you hear the whistle on the radio, it's so clear and loud, they think I'm sitting right underneath the KMOX booth, but I'm out in left field bleachers.

I was scared to death one time in the eighties. I had some press tickets from my dad that were behind home plate. The ushers walk you down, and they have a little rag, and they wipe down your seat for you. Here I am hauling this backpack with everything I need to be comfortable. We're sitting there, and after they've wiped off our seats and we sit down, I see this blond lady. She's a little bit older and she comes down. She's in a hot-pink satin jumpsuit. She sits down right in front of me. I nudge my girlfriend, Barb, and say to her, "Hey do you think they'd like a taste of the bleachers down here. Get a load of this." And I start to whistle. The lady is turning around, and my life was flashing in slow motion thinking, "I'm going to be kicked out of Busch Stadium. She's gonna get the usher." She turns around and says, "Honey, I wish I could whistle like that." I found out later it was Mary Lou Herzog, Whitey's wife. That made me put a little bit of faith back in people, but that's a different circumstance. It wasn't a regular person. Someone told me that they had watched a World Series game from '85 on ESPN Classic, and said they could hear the whistle. I don't remember when it all started.

As my sister and I got old enough, we would either come down from Webster Groves, about twenty minutes away, on the bus or my mom would drop us off and pick us up. We would just go sit in the bleachers. It wasn't too bad. Then when my sister was old enough to drive, she and I would go down. I was about fifteen when we started sitting out in the bleachers on a regular basis in the late seventies, probably '79. Back then it was general admission so we would always sit in the same section, 589, which is no longer there—it's now the bullpen. When we sat there, somebody would always have a radio so we could listen to the game. Mike Shannon would always say, "Bleacher fans are out in force, especially the 375 Gang." That was us because we would sit out there in left field bleachers in Section 589 and it was the 375 foot marker on the wall to get a home run. So he dubbed us the "375 Gang." We would all wave to Mike when we heard him say this. Sometimes we still call ourselves the 375 Gang, even though we're no longer in that area. But we also call our area "the pit" 'cause we're in the furthest corner of left field. It's hot down there. It's below street level. It's the corner. Right now we're next to the visitors' bullpen so we get to chat with the players and the coaches over there, and that's a lot of fun.

When we were in 589, I had a lot of friends that sat in "the pit." I sat in the same section, but at the other end of the aisle. They would call me "Pit South." There was a whole other group that sat over there. I knew those guys and eventually as people would get married and move away, we all started sitting together in 591. We've been going strong ever since and the World Series in '82 kind of solidified our friendship. We would have to, when we were young, bring our lawn chairs and camp out because it was general admission. For big games, there wasn't anything stopping us from staying a couple of days even. We all knew each other so some people would get up and go to work in the morning. The people that could be there during the day would be there during the day. Then they'd relieve us when they'd get off work, and we'd go home and shower and take a nap. We would just leave our lawn chairs there. That would be for the home opener and all the Cubs' games…plus all the Mets' games 'cause of course the Mets are pond scum. It was a big rivalry and the season closer. So what we would do a lot of times, just our lawn chair would stay out there the whole weekend series for the Cubs. We'd go the day before, and we'd just leave our lawn chair. Sometimes we'd tie it to the fence out there, but that would guarantee our spot in line when the game was over. And, we would just start all over again for the next day. In those days, you couldn't buy bleacher tickets ahead of time. Now you can, since 1997, so I have season tickets down there in the bleachers. They revamped the ballpark in 1996 to put in the grass, painted the walls green instead of royal blue, put the bullpens out there. The bullpen in right field didn't come for a year, but the Cardinals didn't move there for two years. The first two years, the Cardinals were right next to us, and that was just heaven—to have our ballplayers next to us. We loved left field so much, when they moved, we just stayed put. Because, you know, right field sucks. Also, we get to see the replays on the Jumbotron from our viewpoint where we are.

The bullpen went out there in '96. The visitors' bullpen was in the tunnel. The Cardinals were out there in '97 also, but the visitors were in right field. The pitching coach, Dave Duncan, thought it would be great to look across the field from the dugout and see his players, but in actuality the players started complaining 'cause left field's in the sun all the time and right field's in the shade. They said, "Why should we have to sit in the sun? Let's make the visiting teams sit in the sun and let us sit in the shade." Plus, it was closer to the Cardinals' dugout. So then in '98 they moved.

I missed the game last summer—the wonderful play—the unassisted triple play! It's only the eleventh in baseball history. Albert Pujols got one in the College World Series.

The home openers are a big deal. If I'm working, which normally I am, I wouldn't go to the week-day games except for the home opener. Everybody's itching for the new season to start. It's rebirth, and it's spring, and it's all the possibilities, and everybody thinks their team's gonna make it to the World Series. I have a couple of friends who throw parties in the winter—one is in January in Chicago for my Wrigley Field friends. The other is in February in St. Louis—Mama Lucy has that party. It's to get you ready for the season. For those of us who don't get to go spring training, it's just all about rebirth and the possibilities—the goal of the World Series. All winter long you read about them going to spring training. You hear about the new young stars from AAA and all the minors. You can read up what's going on in spring training and that they might bring this player or that player up. It's just always so exciting. I've had friends come from Chicago just to see our opener. It used to be really exciting in the eighties when Gussie Busch was alive. He would come in on the carriage with the Clydesdales and his big red cowboy hat. It's always a big production. We have a big tailgate party on Opening Day. We get out there at 6:00 a.m., and we start barbecuing. It's just wonderful. It's something you look forward to all winter.

We don't even care if the weather's bad. We just move it underneath Highway 40, and we're covered. We're out there in the rain in our ponchos. I carry a backpack. The bottom half is a soft cooler, and the top half is a regular backpack. It just looks like a backpack, but it zips in the middle. For the hot games, I carry six bottles of water, three frozen and three just liquid cold. I carry a Cardinal beach towel to put on the bench 'cause in the bleachers, you've got the bench. Even though my rump is padded, the towel is good. In the wintertime for the home opener, or when we're playing in October—see we're used to playing in October—when it's cold, the towel provides warmth.

Then in the summer days, it's so hot on those benches. If you're sitting, and you go to visit with someone, and you just sit down on that bench, your rump just roasts. It's just amazing how hot it is. So, the towel provides a lot of comfort. That's like the "101" of bleachers—bring your towel, bring your frozen water. I have a bandana for perspiration, but it doubles as my home run hankie so I get to sling that when we get home runs. I bring a squirt bottle. Betty, the beer lady at the top of the steps, lets me dunk it in her ice water. I provide comfort to a lot of people around me. Everybody wants me to spray them when it's hot. I have a little battery-operated fan. And, I bring a radio. I don't always listen to the radio, but I do periodically. I don't want to be rude 'cause it is a social event, too, and we watch the game. If you're listening to the game on the radio, you can't visit as well 'cause you can't hear the conversation.

When you go sit in the box seats, when you think about it, that's the corporate money over there. They get to go back to the office and get to tell their friends that they sat in box seats. They get on the cell phone and wave into the camera when the camera's on them behind home plate. They don't know what's going on in the game. If you come to the bleachers, half the people are keeping score. We're talking about trades that went on. We're talking about plays in games other than ours. Everybody knows what's going on, and if I don't know, I can ask somebody. It's in my blood. My return-address stickers are baseballs. Everything I have is baseballs. I've got a barbecue pit, like a little Weber kettle, that's a baseball. It's just not fun to sit somewhere else. If you get box seats, you will always end up back over in the bleachers. They get razzed a little bit. We say a chant, "Box seats suck. Box seats suck."

We stayed away a little bit with the strike in '94. We have one friend who still won't come back. Between the strike and all the money they're paying and the new ballpark they don't think we need—they were very upset for a long time. We're the working class out there, but we're the true fans, too. Fighting over all that money just doesn't make sense to us when they're making a good living. That was like 2002 when they were talking about going on strike and the strike deadline passed. When the strike was still looming, I get a two thousand dollar invoice for a round of playoff and World Series tickets. They're wanting thousands of dollars from me, and they're threatening to go out on strike. I might get my money back if they go on strike, but they want it, there's a deadline for me to give them my money. There's got to be a better solution. They're just to a point where they're making too much money.

When we won the playoffs, even after September 11, with the strict rules on coming in with bags and stuff, I snuck in two bottles of champagne, and as soon as we clinched it, the corks went on the field. The ushers around us are like family. One of them screamed to another usher on the field, "Throw me that cork. I want a souvenir." We've got pictures swigging the champagne bottle. They're not kicking me out when they see me with glass, 'cause they know I'm going to put it back in my bag and take it with me. I brought thirty Dixie cups and put a sip in all of them so everybody could toast. They know that we're not going to get drunk and rowdy, and we patrol our area. Maybe if we won the World Series, we might jump out on the field. They know I'm going to be responsible even though I'm sneaking something in illegal. They know that it's going to be okay.

In our part of the bleachers, we don't have any fights at all. We like to drink beer out there, but we also like to watch the game. If you get the frat boys out there who are just there to drink and get drunk. We all scream at the bullpen like, if Ray King, of the Braves, is warming up in the bullpen, I say, "Hey, Ray. Boxers or briefs?" It's just playful stuff. It's not talking about your mamma or how bad you do, but it's enough to get their attention and get them a little distracted so they might be off their game a little bit. And you also have a little bit of camaraderie with the other players to the point where we've even asked those guys—like if I wanted to go to Atlanta, I would talk to Ray and give him a business card and say, "Hey, would you put me on the list. Could you get me tickets? I'm coming to Atlanta for the next series." And, they do it. By the way, Ray King's answer was, "Commando." That means—nothing! When they say "Commando," one guy yells back: "Yeah, That's because when you were a kid, your dad told you that if you didn't have a dog, you didn't need a fence." Rod Beck said, "Thong." Sometimes they answer you, sometimes they ignore you.

BUT WILL DAL GO TO MARION, ILLINOIS WHEN THEY RETIRE PETE ROSE'S NUMBER?

Ed "Dal" Wright

Ed Wright was raised in Clayton, Missouri and now lives next door in Brentwood. He is a teacher.

I'm 53, almost 54, so I've been a fan since the '50s. My dad used to take me and then my sisters to the ball games. My first hero was Stan the Man. I went to his last game in 1963 and saw his last base hit go past Pete Rose into right field. Who would have guessed years later that Rose would break his record? Stan Musial and the early Cardinals were just fascinating to me. I loved baseball and followed it during the '60s. My next great hero was Curt Flood. I still consider him a hero.

My dad had played basketball in Army with George Crowe, who was a pinch hitter for the Reds. After a game against the Reds, we waited outside and he introduced me to George Crowe and some of the other players. You could meet the players a lot more easily as they came out of the stadium then. Later, my dad said I looked up at George Crowe, this big guy, and said, "Well, where are all the Reds on the bus?" and he said, "They're not on this bus, buddy."

I started sitting in the left field bleachers during the later career of Lou Brock. You would go out there, and go "Lou," "Lou," "Lou" all the time. A lot of times I would go by myself and I would notice a bunch of people sitting together. I'd kind of creep in close and we would start talking trivia. They always had a trivia question of the game and one night the question was, "Who hit the first grand slam in Canada?" Everybody was going, what? I said "Dal Maxvill," and they just stared at me. The answer was Dal Maxvill. That's why they call me Dal. A lot of them don't really know my real name. We don't always know each other's name but it's like family…It was the late '80s and I was working in property management at the time. It was in September and I got fired that day from a pretty good paying job. I went down to the ballpark by myself just to kind of think, and reflect and have a good time. It had been my birthday about a week earlier and people in the bleachers in our little group had gotten me a birthday card. They had something on the card like "We are sorry we overlooked your birthday, but our best wishes to you. They didn't know I had been fired. That card and just the camaraderie, it really is a family to me down there. It just made me feel good. I looked down and thought, "This is what is important, these kind of people and these kind of relationships." Of course, I survived and went on to a really enjoyable career as a teacher.

A good trivia question would be who pinch hit for McGwire his last game? Kerry Robinson. Who did we trade to get Curt Flood, him being one of my favorite players; and it was Willard Schmidt. They called Schmidt the Cardinal Good Luck Charm, but he was the main player in the trade to Cincinnati when we got Curt Flood. That is a good trivia question. I teach history and one of the things I do every year is I show the ESPN tribute to Curt Flood when he died. I talk about how one person can have such an effect on history. Of course, some people think Flood ruined it by free agency. I say "what do you mean?" because he stood up for being a man instead of a piece of property. Because the owners are stupid enough to pay all of this money, don't blame a man for wanting to have some personal integrity. Most people think that Flood won that lawsuit and, in reality, he didn't. I always say he would have been in the Hall of Fame, as he had a tremendous career and he gave it up.

The night of Bob Forsch's second no hitter in 1983, W.P. Kinsella, the author of *Shoeless Joe* was in the press box. He was in St. Louis for autograph signing and book tour and he was there that night and many of us thought he brought some magic to the stadium that night. It was very cool.

I remember when Lonnie Smith came back from rehab. He played and they took him out in the sixth inning and he came and he sat in the left field bleachers for the rest of the game, after he took a shower. Suddenly we look up and there is Lonnie Smith sitting in the bleachers. We were all glad to see him but it was kind of strange to see him there.

In 1982, I ran out on the field when the Series ended, it was one of those moments that was so hard to describe, the thrill. It was like things were in slow motion and I ran to the infield and scooped up some dirt and put it in my pocket. I somehow got some Astroturf. I don't know if people were tearing it up and distributing it or what, but I got some Astroturf, which I still have. All of the sudden I looked around and the police were out there and they had some dogs. That was such a thrill to be there.

In 1999, I'm in Columbia, Missouri at an education conference. Mark McGwire hit 499 the night before and I said, "You know, I have to go to Busch Stadium in case he hits number 500." I left the meeting. It was a big social hour night and people looked at me like, "What is wrong with you?" I ended up paying about $75 on the street to a scalper for a ticket. McGwire ended up hitting number 500 that night. I drove back to Columbia after the game and arrived about one a.m. People were coming out of the bar and they said, "Where were ya?" I said, "I was at Busch Stadium." They said I was crazy but it was worth it.

Mark McGwire waves at the bleachers.

THE CARDINALS FILL THE POTHOLES IN HER SOUL

Barb Davis

Barb Davis, 53, is retired from working for the city of St. Louis.

In the old days in the bleachers we just had so much fun talking with the players; because the bullpen bench was right in front of us. We had all the pitchers and catchers from the bullpen and Dave Ricketts, when he was the bullpen coach, and occasionally other players would come out. George Hendrick, between half innings, would come over and sit on the bench, which he wasn't supposed to do. We used to have so much fun there. We laughed so hard. Sometimes we missed plays in the game. It was the dirt field before they put in the Astroturf, when the tractor would come out in the fifth inning and drag the base paths, the guys on the bullpen bench would take aim at the driver with baseballs to see who could get closest to the tractor driver, or hit the tractor driver. They made sure that they didn't get him, except for the Fourth of July one year. We had a game the Fourth of July, and they took a baseball, and they put firecrackers on the baseball. When he came out, they let fly with the firecracker baseball. They were throwing it so it wouldn't get anywhere near him or near the tractor. Unfortunately, they threw it a little too hard. It did hit the tractor and the firecrackers went off. So the driver swore revenge on the bullpen. He came out one day, and he just jumped off the tractor when they threw. Of course, the tractor wasn't going very fast, and he stopped it right away. The bullpen denizens were told to stop that. The last day of the season the whole bullpen bench—they hadn't done it for a couple of months now because they had been warned about doing it—the whole bullpen bench waited until the driver got just in front of them, just as he was going around second base, and all of them let fly. There must have been twenty baseballs flying at him. That was the day that they got him. They didn't hurt him. I was told at the beginning of the next season that he got his revenge. I said, "What did he do?" They said, "We can't tell you." I have no idea what he did, but he got even with all of them.

One time, there was a color guard on the field. The color guard had guns, but they were wooden guns and they didn't have a chamber or anything on them. They looked like a rifle, a silhouette of a rifle. Before the game, one of the Cardinal players, Butch Metzger, comes running out of the dugout screaming as they were doing their warm-ups. He came running toward the bullpen screaming and hollering, "No, no, leave me alone, leave me alone." Then a second player, Mike Wallace, comes running out of the dugout with a gun. He stops and he takes aim. He shoots Butch Metzger. Of course, this gun isn't shooting. Metzger dropped like he was dead. Mike Wallace comes over, and he stands over him, and he puts his foot on his chest like he is gonna shoot him again, and he aims the rifle. You can see it's this piece of wood, but this lady up in the stands lets out this war hoop and goes, "My God! He shot him!" We were laughing so hard we fell off the seats.

I do remember one time when Mark Littell was pitching for the Cardinals and Mark was deaf in one ear. Not too many people knew that. When he didn't want to listen to what people were saying to him, he would turn the deaf ear to them. He was sitting on the bullpen bench and he had his head on his hand and his eyes were closed. I think he was just resting his head. One of the other guys put a baseball on top of his head. He sat there the whole rest of the inning and halfway through the next inning with the baseball on his head. He is completely oblivious to this baseball sitting on his head. I guess he was asleep…and he couldn't hear the players' snickers.

Rick Bosetti stapled Al Hrabosky's glove to the bench. Al always came out to the bullpen in the fifth inning to rev up the baseball and get everything ready. That was a routine with him, just like his Mad Hungarian routine. Bosetti was a utility player at that point for the Cardinals. They had been fixing the Astroturf. A piece of the Astroturf would come loose and the groundskeeper would come out with a staple gun and staple it back down. He forgot to take the staple gun with him. Rick sees the staple gun and he knew what glove was Al's sitting on the bullpen bench. He stapled it to the bench. Here comes Al and all of the guys on the bench moved down to the other end. They used to have three benches together out there for the bullpen. This is before they put them where they are now. They were down on the field then. It was our end actually that the glove was stapled to the bench right in front of us, so they all moved down to the other two benches. They weren't gonna be anywhere near there. Al comes out and he goes to pick up his glove and of course, he can't because it's stapled to the bench. He just turned around and goes "Bosetti!!!" He knew exactly who did it. He got mad.

I knew Teddy Simmons pretty well when he was here. He introduced me to Gussie Busch. It was awesome. The Cards had a promotional type of thing, like a booster club. It was like a precursor to Cardinals Care, only it wasn't so much involved in the community as Cardinals Care is. They would look to do philanthropic things and volunteer work throughout the community. It sounded like a pretty good deal, and it was through the Cardinals. Ted suggested to me—"Why don't you come to the meeting on such and such a night," and so I did. It was held at the Stadium. Ted said my name to Mr. Busch, when I was introduced to him, and Gussie says, in that really gruff way, "I understand you are one of the greatest Cardinal fans in the city of St. Louis." I said, "Where did you hear that?" and he says, "Oh, I have my sources." He was a very nice man. I met his wife Margaret once and she helped me out on a problem I had at the stadium because she was vice president of the club at that point and she took care of some things for me. Mr. Busch invited me out to his home. He said "We're having a barbeque Saturday, why don't you come out?" like I had known him all my life. I had just met the man. I didn't go. I was a little awestruck.

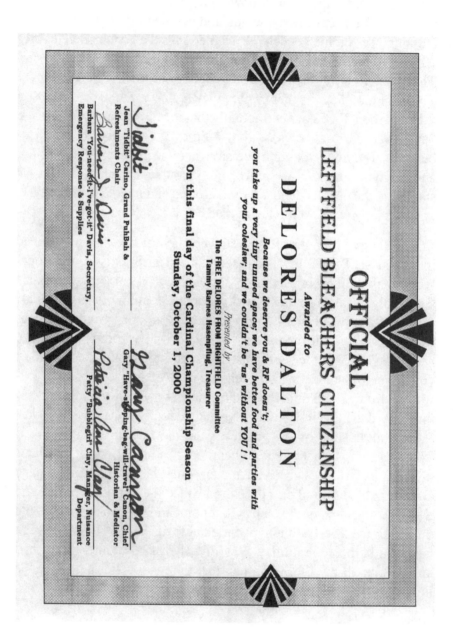

OFFICIAL

LEFTFIELD BLEACHERS CITIZENSHIP

Awarded to

DELORES DALTON

Because we deserve you & RF doesn't;
you take up a very tiny unused space; we have better food and parties with
your coleslaw; and we couldn't be "us" without YOU ! !

Presented by

The FREE DELORES FROM RIGHTFIELD Committee
Tammy Barnes Hasenpflug, Treasurer

On this final day of the Cardinal Championship Season
Sunday, October 1, 2000

Tidbit

Jean "Tidbit" Carino, Grand PuhBah &
Refreshments Chair

Barbara S. Davis

Barbara "You-need-it-I've-got-it" Davis, Secretary,
Emergency Response & Supplies

Gary Cannon

Gary "Have-sleeping-bag-will-travel" Canon, Chief
Historian & Mediator

Patricia Ann Clay

Patty "Bubblegirl" Clay, Manager, Nuisance
Department

Chapter Eight

Busch Stadium

The Sweet Spot

WHY CAN'T SUGAR BE AS SWEET AS AL HRABOSKY?

John W. Maher, St. Peters, Missouri

T he baseball Cardinals and St. Louis have always been tied together in ways no one outside our city could understand. It's a form of magic I've experienced nowhere else in any sport, and it exists despite whatever the Cardinals' record is in a given year. This is a love affair passed on from generation to generation.

To be raised here was to barbecue to the sounds of Jack Buck, as he painted a picture of the day's game so clear you could see it with both eyes closed. It was going to Sportsman's Park as a Cub Scout to see Stan Musial play. It was watching Lou Brock, the original and true "Base Burglar," wearing a Brock-a-brella as he shagged balls in the outfield. It was Bob Gibson's scowl, and knowing he would not allow the beloved Cardinals to lose on that day. It was Willie and the '82 Series. It's sitting in Big Mac Land with the kids and their "Straight A" tickets. And it's so much more.

For something magical seems to happen to players when they put on the jersey with the Birds on the Bat. They seem to become once again the children we all are at heart, and the true love of the game returns. They are free to play as they did growing up, before the sport was clouded with canceled series, strikes, agents and walkouts. Here we play base-ball as, to quote, "Like it oughta be." And that tradition exists generation after generation in St. Louis. Two incidents in my life some 20 years apart illustrate this special respect between St. Louis fans and players.

While in high school, my friend Bryce and I were able to secure jobs selling souvenirs at Busch Stadium. Being the mid-'70s, these were not our most impressive years statistically. Gibby was gone. Whitey was years away. There was little to care about if winning was all one sought, as Cincinnati and Pittsburgh ruled the National League. Yet, people still came to town to see the Cardinals. More fans, in fact, than Pittsburgh enjoyed as they won.

Each day after setting up, and while awaiting the opening of the gates, we wandered down to the edge of the field and watched the Cardinal players work out. Being young businessmen, we were quick to retrieve any balls hit into the stands to later sell, never suspecting this would one day be an industry in itself.

During the '70s the Cardinals had a unique personality on their pitching staff. His funny facial hair and incredible act that seemed to break hitters' concentration endeared him to St. Louis at a time when we needed a new hero. Al Hrabosky was St. Louis' "Mad Hungarian," and we loved him.

Though we were just kids, Al was great to us. We got to see him before the games, before he put on the angry stare he used on hitters. And we knew; No player ever enjoyed playing ball more than Al did back then. Two days in a row, he sat along the wall watching others throw in the Cardinals' bullpen, we would go over and ask him to sign the balls we had retrieved in the stands. He never refused as stars so often do today.

Al asked us what we were doing with the balls he signed. We told him we sold them at our stand for big bucks to out-of-towners seeking the great souvenir to take home and show their friends. After laughing for a moment, he signed our baseballs, then took one of the finest balls and asked a favor in return. This one, he told us, was to go for free to a youngster who appeared to be a great fan but didn't have any money. And he trusted us at our word it would be done as he had asked.

That day a young boy about seven years old lingered at our stand several times. It wasn't hard to see that he didn't have money enough for even a pencil with the Cardinal emblem. In our rush to sell merchandise, we dropped a ten-dollar bill, which he saw and retrieved. He gave us our money back when we didn't even know it had fallen. To him went the magical ball, as Al had asked. The boy's father came back with him a few minutes later to return the ball, thinking it had been obtained in some wrong manner or was a mistake. But, after we explained the story, I thought for a moment I saw tears in that dad's eyes as he and his son walked off hand in hand, the child's grin bigger than the Cheshire Cat's. I think often of that ball sitting somewhere and that boy showing it to the world—a gift to him, from the Mad Hungarian.

BEER: MORE THAN
A BREAKFAST DRINK

Russell Phillips

Russell The Beerman has been a beer vendor at Cardinals and Rams games for 25 years. Russell, 54, is a teacher in the off-season.

It's fun. You get to interact with the fans. You get to "feel the ball game." When you're really busy, you don't get to see it. I got to see McGwire hitting his sixty-two home runs and Pujols doing what he's doing now. You're right there—part of the action—'cause we're out there in the seats.

For about the last ten years, I've been selling Bud Light. I had sold Budweiser for about fifteen years before that. In a regular day, we sell about five cases of beer. We get a commission on the case, or by the bottle or can. You get twelve percent of the case, which costs one hundred thirty-eight dollars. That's sixteen and some change. If you have some extra cans that you sold, you get paid by the can, too. We don't get a wage, it's strictly commission on what we sell. "Cold days are bad days." "If it's extremely hot, it slows me down, and the fans slow down, too." The '82 World Series was when I sold the most—about thirty-one cases, and made $500 that day plus tips. Those were twelve-ounce bottles. We sold about five cases before the game got started. That's an extraordinary crowd. It's the same way when the Cubs come to town. It picks up with that same kind of intensity where you get maybe two cases an inning.

Way back, a long, long time ago, people would try to steal beer from me, but not anymore. There's a very nice crowd nowadays. In the '82 World Series, I was watching a fight, I got excited. I looked up and a six-pack was gone. Sometimes, they'd try to just sneak one out when I wasn't looking. They don't do that anymore. I can leave a case of beer and go get some change—just leave it there—tell someone, "Hey, watch this for me for a minute."

They open the doors for us two hours before game time. We have up until about half an hour before game time to get checked in. If you checked in later than that, chances are you wouldn't get the product or the assignment—just the leftovers. They might not even give you a beer assignment, you might have to sell popcorn. Beer sales are steady for the most part so most vendors like to see that. Most everything at the ballpark sells pretty good if you hustle.

I'm a teacher by profession. When I was younger, I was off all summer so I would go to a lot of Cardinal games. Back in 1979, I was just sitting there one day watching the game, and watching the vendors, and noticed an article in the paper about vendors doing their things. I was thinking that would be a good summer job for me. I went on down and put in an application that next season. I pretty much work the bleachers all the time.

I've known some of the same people for ten, even twenty years. A beer costs five seventy-five a can, a sixteen-ounce can. Most people do tip. Some just let you keep the quarter, and some give you a dollar and a quarter—they just give you seven. A good day at the ballpark would be about six cases of beer, which runs you around ninety nine in commission and multiply that with the tips, probably I would make about eighty-five in tips along with that. That would be a good day. Now, I'm not making that lately.

Twenty-four cans in a case, the tips vary—some nights I might average twelve dollars a case. Some nights I might only average eight. Some nights I might average twenty dollars. It depends on the crowd, the team playing. Some teams draw better drinkers and tippers than others. My tips are better when the Cardinals are winning—better drinking and better tipping.

Last season Pujols hit two home run balls right through me. They were saying I was a magnet so they told me, "Go down there while Pujols is up at bat so he can hit another home run." I couldn't even catch it. It went right through my hands. If I get it, I would have to give it away. The Cardinals don't want the people who work there keep foul or homerun balls.

The weirdest thing I've ever seen at the ballpark? I've seen people propose marriage. I've seen a wedding party—they came to the game on a Saturday afternoon still in their wedding clothes. I saw a bachelor party, where all of a sudden the guy started crawling around. I said, "What's going on?" And there was a stripper who had put a boom box on the bench and did her thing—before the guards came over. There was a period of time, I think back in the eighties, when people used to "moon" people. That was weird. There was this one guy who would leave the bleacher section and go to another section up above and then moon down to the bleachers. He was kind of a regular there, but I haven't seen him in a long time.

After the baseball strike we had a down couple of years. The crowd seemed to change. Before the strike, the rivalries were stronger. The place was noisier, crazier. Now I think we've got more educated people, yuppie types. It's just not as wild as it used to be. It's really kind of calm. It's sort of like a hangout. There's die-hard fans. But there's also a lot of fans with their cell phones. It's like a meeting place. It's quieter. People aren't as much into the game as they used to be. We used to have police officers out in the bleachers, but now we don't have any. Back then, there would be fights breaking out. It would depend on a certain rivalry. Somebody would have a sign or a stuffed animal and burn it in effigy and the crowd would get mad. They'd get on each other's nerves. Now they don't have that—they're friendly. Even the Chicago Cubs and the Cardinal rivalry at Busch Stadium is friendly. The fans of both teams go out and drink together and they buy each other beers at the ballpark. They show them around the town. And, vice versa when they go to Chicago. I've been there, too. It's a friendly rivalry nowadays. Back then, it was a lot wilder.

The coldest I've been at a baseball game, a temperature of around fifty-three at the start of the game and maybe hit forty-nine by the time the game's over with. I know on July 4, 1980, the temperature was about a hundred and one. I passed out that day from the heat. That was when they had the AstroTurf. I wasn't working the bleachers. I was working the box seats. They're moveable stands, and they're on top of metal. The metal floor and Astroturf made it around a hundred and thirty-forty on the field at that level. The heat just emanated from all that.

A SMILE IN EVERY AISLE

Carrie Moschino

When Carrie Moschino left Decatur, Illinois, a dozen years ago to attend Patricia Stevens College in St. Louis, she had no idea how much the Cardinals would influence her life. Carrie lives in Mt. Vernon, Illinois with her husband, Mike. She met him while ushering at Busch Stadium.

B eing an usher for the Cardinals was the most exciting ten years of my life. Every night was new and exciting. It wasn't like it was, "Oh, I have to go to the ballpark again." I met so many different people who have become my friends. Our job of being an usher, and the organization will tell you the same thing, is to make sure people have a good time when they walk into the stadium.

The top of the list of things—was the McGwire home run race. Going to work every night was like a dream. I couldn't wait to get out of my full-time job to go over there to see what would transpire that evening. As McGwire was close to setting the record, the feeling in the ballpark was just electric. When he was in the on-deck circle, you could just feel it. It was something I'd never, ever felt before with a particular player coming to bat. There was just something totally different and so unique about this man who did this. He was just unbelievable. Just the lightning, the excitement, people getting on their feet when they saw him go in the on-deck circle. Just the way the crowd reacted when he would hit a home run out. It was magical.

We would always have problems with people trying to sneak into the section. But when the McGwire race started, people would come from miles around to see Mark and wanted to get an autograph. If they didn't have seats in these boxes, they had no chance. So the organization became more lenient and agreed to open the gates two hours before the game. If people wanted to come down to this area from the upper seats, they were allowed to do it. Then our job, once we came on duty a half hour before the game started, we'd have to tell the people standing that they had to head back to their seats. Most people were fine, but you'd have some that would move away from that wall, and then go sit in a seat. As the game went on, we'd see people hopping from seat to seat to seat.

The best "story" from a fan was when somebody told me that these were their company seats. They had seats up in terrace, but looked down and saw nobody sitting in the company seats so they came down. Or they'll say, "My buddy's getting a beer, and he's got the ticket." Then some people will try to fly by me and not show me their ticket. I'd have to say, "Excuse me." They'd say something like, "Oh my son's down here. I have to go pick him up." We'd get all kinds of excuses.

One scary time was the game when McGwire was ejected after the first inning when he was arguing balls and strikes. We had the con-tour plastic bottles coming at us. Usually something of that magnitude, we have to go down on the field. It's not like we're going to be able to stop fifty thousand people from rushing the field, but just for us to have a presence there. That day was definitely scary.

People were just upset. People had been driving in from places like North Dakota, or coming in front Atlanta. They would just feel like, "I drove all this way, and the person I came to see got thrown out in the first inning. That's not acceptable." Everybody had the same thought process going through their heads. We had objects coming at us from everywhere. That's why I'm glad there are no glass bottles sold in the stadium.

Most of my St. Louis friends work for the Cardinals. My bridesmaids and my maid of honor at our wedding all worked there in the stadium. I made a lot of friends there. That was mainly the reason why I took that job. I was eighteen when I moved to St. Louis. I didn't know a soul. I wanted to be able to meet people in this new area. When I was a kid, my dad would take me to Cardinal games. When I was about six years old, we went down for a game. I saw the ushers there show-ing people to their seats and looking like they were having a good time. I told my dad, "I want to be one of those some day." So, when I moved to St. Louis and was going to school, I needed a part-time job to give me something to do and give me some extra play money. I went over to the Cardinal offices and said, "I would like to work for the Cardinal organization." They told me to come back in January because that's when they do their hiring. So I did. They interviewed me and said, "Well, we'll be in touch." At the time there was a waiting list.

Tips aren't expected. That would never be a reason why I took the job. Sometimes if there's a rain-delay, and the seats would be wet, the ushers would take towels and wipe them off. Occasionally someone would give us a tip, anywhere from a dollar to two dollars—one time I got five dollars. The biggest tip I got was ten dollars, but it was never expected.

Sometimes people would try to bribe me to sit in my section. The ushers got new uniforms several years ago. A lot of people took a liking to our jackets, really nice lightweight windbreakers that we'd wear when the weather was chilly. I had people say, "I'll give you fifty dollars for your jacket, if you'll let me sit down in the field boxes." Every year they'd give us a new lapel or stickpin to wear on our uniforms. They gave us all a "70 McGwire" pin to wear. Some people remarked, "I can't find that pin anywhere." We'd tell them it was a pin made exclusively for the ushers. Sometimes people would offer us twenty bucks for the pin "if you let me do whatever—sit in the section—go down and try to get an autograph during the game," which was a big no-no.

I had a couple of instances where somebody was sitting really close to the field and didn't even see a foul ball coming—it was just a line drive shot. We tell people when we seat them down there to be alert for balls and objects thrown into the stands. Sometimes your reflexes can't be that quick. It wasn't like the person wasn't paying attention, it just came so fast you didn't have time to put your hands up over your head or face. One person got hit on the side of the forehead in the temple area. When that happens, the person usually cannot walk out on their own. Then we call for first aid and they're there very quickly. They take them up to the first aid room and make sure they're okay.

The supervisors have walkie-talkies, but the ushers have access to house phones located around the stadium. We just tell them what we needed and the location: need first aid if somebody got hit by a ball; need clean-up, somebody spilled their soda, need a mop.

One thing we had to deal with regularly was intoxicated fans. One time we asked one person to leave the stadium. Of course his friends all had to leave with him because he needed someone to drive him because he couldn't drive. We'd have instances where the friend didn't want to leave, even though this guy kind of screwed up their day. Sometimes people would get a little irate, "Why are you kicking him out? He's our ride home." Those were the people I didn't like to deal with, but I knew I had to, those who had way too much to drink and were making a spectacle of themselves or using profanity, which is a no-no there.

We wanted to make the ballpark a family-friendly place for people. People aren't going to return if they have a bad time or if the person behind them is using profanity. I find myself going to other places, like the Cubs games, and watching the ushers and comparing the fans. When the Cubs would come into town, some fans would be rambunctious—because that's our big series. I just went to San Francisco in July when the Cardinals were there. I was really watching their ushers. I was asking one usher, "Where can I get a cup of Ghiradelli San Francisco chocolate?" He said, "Ma'am, I'm sorry, but I don't know." At Busch Stadium, we didn't use the words, "I don't know." We'd have handbooks in our back pocket. We could pull that out and that would tell you where the food items were in the stadium or whatever you needed to know about the stadium. I would still have to pull mine out, even after working there for ten years, because I didn't know everything around the stadium. We would say, "I'm sorry I don't know the answer to that, but I will find out for you. Tell me your seat number, and I will come back and tell you." But this usher at San Francisco just told me he didn't know and then dropped it. That was it.

We always had to go down to the front of our section when there were two outs in the final inning, no matter which team was ahead. Then, once the game ended, we had to turn and face the crowd as people were exiting just basically to see if anybody needed assistance in getting out of the stadium, to see if people were intoxicated and couldn't get out of the stadium. Our sections had to be cleared out. If people were still sitting in their seats, we'd say, "You need to head for the exits." "Well, we're letting the traffic die down." We'd tell them they needed to do that up in the concourse because we had to clear out the area so the clean-up crews could come in. If there was a long game at night and there was a day game the next day, the place had to cleaned up after every game. We would politely tell people that we needed to clear out the area.

We were paid by the event. I worked one game that went eighteen innings—it was a late game, very late game. By the time I got out of there, it was a short night. If it was on a weekend, I didn't mind it, but if it was during the week when I had to get up the next morning, sometimes I'd be dragging. If the games were starting to go into extra innings, they'd usually ask us if we wanted to leave. Usually, I wouldn't. I'd say, "No, I'm here. I'll stay on." If it got as late as two in the morning, I'd be ready to go if they were releasing us to go.

It was always exciting if it was somebody's first baseball game there. If there was a little kid, and it was their first game, I would go up to guest relations. We had some extra giveaway items like baseballs we gave out the week before or baseball hats. I'd go up and say, "I have a little boy or person in my section, and it's their first trip to the stadium. Do you have a little something I can give to them?" The youngster will remember that. It will totally make their baseball experience to know that somebody took the time to go get something and bring it back to them. It will help them to remember the game. If there was ever any way I could get my hands on a baseball, I'd hand it to a kid. That makes them want to come back—people remember that.

My boss, Mike Ball, was great. He's still there. He's wonderful. He was always one you could go talk to if you ever had a problem or a concern, or got into a situation. He was our main boss, and then we had the usher chiefs. They would oversee the supervisors as well. I loved every minute there!

QUICK HITS AND INTERESTING BITS FROM THE LAND OF AHS

On June 18, 1974, the Cardinals beat San Francisco and Lou Brock swiped a pair of bases. Brock was celebrating his 35th birthday that day and his play during the game belied the fact that he was closer to age 40 than he was to 25.

After the game, my friend, Paul, and I were stationed near the players' exit, along with other autograph seekers. We had decided to head for home after about an hour or so when we noticed someone leaving from the press gate, about 30 yards away. Even though there was not much light, we quickly recognized it was Lou Brock.

We, along with a couple of other teenage stragglers, rushed toward him, shouting, "Lou! Lou! Wait up! Can we have your autograph, please?" Thankfully, he was kind enough to stop.

Lou was with his wife, and he had his hands full with gifts from his teammates. He said, "I'll be glad to sign for all of you but can we walk to my car so I can put these things in the trunk?" A chance to talk and walk along with a Cardinal great? Sure thing, Lou!

As we walked along the Seventh Street overpass to the Stadium Garage West, Lou made conversation with the four or five of us who followed in his wake. Did we like the game? Where did we go to school?

About then, Paul noticed the roar of the last Tower Grove bus pulling out from the bus stop. "Oh, no!" he cried. "There goes the last bus." Lou asked if we were without a ride home, but I said we could call one of our moms to come pick us up. *Besides,* I thought, *I'll walk home if it means I get to talk with one of my favorite players.*

Seeing a chance to ask a question, I spoke up. "Lou," I said, "Tell the truth. You gonna break Maury Wills' record of 104 stolen bases this year?"

Lou hemmed and hawed a bit, saying, "I don't know. That's an awful lot of bases and Maury was a pretty good player."

I brushed aside such modesty and exclaimed, "C'mon, Lou. You *know* you're gonna do it. Maury's only a Dodger."

At this remark, Brock chuckled softly and smiled. "Well, maybe you're right," he said. "We'll have to see." Noting the sparkle in his eye, I knew he was seriously planning to set the mark.

By this time, we'd reached his car and, true to his word, Brock stood there and signed for us. After thanking him once again for signing, we all watched as he and his wife got into his car and drove off. The high from that encounter lasted a long time for Paul and me. In fact, it still brings a chill to me to this day when I think about it. Paul passed away seven years ago but when I remember the fun and excitement of the 1974 season, it brings him alive for me once more. Thanks again, Lou, for that brief period of time almost 30 years ago, when you made the whole summer for a couple of kids from South St. Louis.

——**ED KNIEST**, Jefferson City, Missouri

My sister Judy started working for the Cardinals in 1967, and became administrative assistant to several general managers. The one who hired her, Bing Devine, helped move the outfield fences in the 1970s. It made the distances shorter, but created a gap between the wall and the bleachers. One day he asked me, "What do you think?" I said, "I don't like how it separates the fan from the field." The next year the temporary fences were removed. Ushers never want to keep fans away.

Even then, you had to be at least sixteen to be an usher. I couldn't wait: It's still the best way to learn baseball. It also drew my future. One of my locations was level 4 in deep center, where a ramp between the scoreboards circles the stadium. In one place you can lean against the rail and see home plate. Ushers were told to patrol it and keep the aisles clear—of other people and ourselves. Here's the kicker: When nobody was looking, *I'd* lean on the rail, fix on the batter, and see from about 500 feet the difference between a fastball and change-up. I began doing play-by-play *for* myself, *to* myself. Nobody'd confuse me with Jack Buck. Still, I got to thinking: I can do this.

One day I was sitting past the Cardinal dugout when Ron Fairly hit a foul ball right at me. I dove straight ahead and fell on my face. The ball hit where my head would have been. Those fans are tough: They booed me for bailing out. But for memory, I love the time Jerry Reuss was pitching for the Redbirds. The Expos' Bill Stoneman hit our Richie Allen. Allen walked to the mound, both benches emptied,

and from my location I glimpsed into our dugout and saw Reuss—the only player who didn't go on the field. I said to a photographer, "Look at that!" The guy snapped the picture, whereupon next morning page one of the *Globe Democrat* shows two photos—the brawl, and Reuss sitting it out!

Fast-forward twenty years later. I'm working with Reuss on an ESPN telecast. I tell him the story, and he's flabbergasted. *"You're* the guy who caused that picture. Some usher. I've been waiting to deck you." Next time we worked together, he brought in his scrapbok and there they were— the brawl and Mr. Reuss. That's the thing about ushering. Full circle. Full life.

——**BOB CARPENTER**, Tulsa, former Cardinal and ESPN announcer on
his ushering days at Busch Stadium

When I was sixteen, I would sneak down to the ballpark. My mom would say to be in at eleven o'clock, and I would push it closer to twelve. After the game, I'd try to get some autographs. When Jack Buck would come out to the stadium, he would come out the players' exit, too. But fans who were looking for players wouldn't pay much attention to him. As a kid, I used to collect money for cystic fibrosis. Mr. Buck was a chairperson with cystic fibrosis. I just felt like that was a good thing I could say something to him about so I'd walk up to him and would walk with him from the glass doors down the street to his car parked in the lower level of the garage. I told him one time, "Mr. Buck, I collect money for cystic fibrosis. I saw your name on the letter I give to everybody for their donations." He thought that was real nice. He asked me where I worked at, and I told him I worked at a grocery store—I bagged groceries for Kroger. He said that was his first job, too, that he used to bag groceries. I thought that was really neat. Every night he'd come out, and I'd say hello to him and shake his hand, and he'd say, "Good game tonight, huh?" I'd comment on a great play or my favorite catch. Just hearing his voice live and not on the radio, it sounded even more imposing. I thought that was a really neat thing. We'd talk about the game a little bit, he'd get in his car, and he's say, "See you tomorrow, Craig."

——CRAIG BALL, 34, Cardinal Fan

In the World Series in '82, I had a megaphone there. A lot of people don't know how to use a megaphone. If you want to use a megaphone at a sporting event, you don't turn it up to "ten" and blast everybody's ears around you. They are directional, and you can stand up and point the megaphone at the person you want to get a message to and turn the volume way down to one or two and just speak in a regular tone. He can be a hundred-two hundred feet away from you and it sounds like it's somebody right next to him talking to him. I had more fun knowing how to use that megaphone. Our seats were actually inside the dugout because they moved the dugout down a little bit, but back then we were just on the inside edge of the dugout. Mike Caldwell of the Brewers was shutting us out. It ended up being a 10-0 game. It was about the sixth inning. Caldwell's up at bat, and he's going to *bunt* with this big lead. Being around the players, I know how they would holler at another player or the umpire, so he squares around to bunt and holds the bat out there, and the ball comes over, and the pitch was high. He didn't move the bat. I stood up and had the megaphone and pointed it right at the umpire and said, "Come on ump. Get in the game. He offered at that pitch." Man, the mask comes off, and he goes charging over to the Cardinal dugout. Gene Tenace and Hub Kittle were in the corner of the dugout. I saw them step up on the top step and turn around and point at me. The umpire looked up, and I held the megaphone up. I didn't use any profanity or anything. He just stood there and glared at me for about thirty seconds and everybody sitting around me was just laughing their fannies off. He thought somebody in the Cardinal dugout was getting on his case.

——GENE SIGLOCK, "Megaphone" Cardinal fan

PLAYIN' FAVORITES

My first contact with Cardinal players came when I was about 10. We had great seats on the first-base side of Busch Stadium, where the Cardinal bullpen was at the time. Greg Mathews had just finished playing catch with Tommy Herr and started signing autographs. I'd brought an old rubber baseball that had a large "X" marked on it. It was all that I had for players to sign. When I handed it to Greg, he took a long look at it, handed it back to me, reached into his glove and pulled out the ball with which he and Tommy had been playing catch. He signed it, "To Derek—Best wishes, Greg Mathews" and gave it to me. Wow! That made my day. I was also able to get Vince Coleman's and Ray Soff's autographs on that ball the same afternoon.

I cherished the ball so much that when we went out of town, I would take it with me, and I'm glad I did. One weekend we went camping and, before we left, I forgot to turn off my electric blanket. It malfunctioned, caught on fire, and burned my entire room to the ground. Thank God, I had the ball with me. It is one of a few things from my childhood that did not burn. Now I keep it in a fireproof safe. I don't ever want to lose that ball.

——**DEREK ADAMS**, St. Ann, Missouri

Steve Kline was very upset the first year he was at Winter Warm-Up because he said they had promised him that his autographs would be free. He said his idea is that the player should never charge for an autograph. That's part of the business. That's part of what you should be there for. Even though they explained to him it was for charity, he still felt like some of the fans would think he was getting some money out of it.

He's the epitome of what every player should be. He loves the fans. He goes out there. We go on a lot of the road trips. He doesn't try to hide from the people. He'll be right out in the middle of everybody visiting and shaking hands. Almost every game you go to, he will stay out and sign autographs until they make him come in. A lot of them aren't going to do that. He's out there goofing around with the grounds crew and with the real people. He loves it, you can tell.

——PAULA HOLLEY, Cardinal Fan

It was Albert Pujols' first year, right after he won Rookie of the Year. His autograph was quite expensive at Winter Warm-Up. I know it's a fund raiser. At the end, he stopped over with some kids who couldn't pay and was signing an autograph for them. One of the ushers tried to stop him, and he argued with the guy and said, "I don't do this for the money. I do it for the kids." He almost had to threaten the guy to get him to leave him alone because the guy was trying to stop him from signing autographs for these kids. I was really proud of him that day. You could tell that those little kids could probably barely pay their way to get in to the event and certainly couldn't pay what it took to get his autograph. He stayed and talked to him and treated them really nice.

——DIANA CAMREN, 30, Cardinal Fan

One day I was replacing glass for a customer, and I had to make a trip to Schnarr's True Value Hardware on Clayton Road. As I was waiting for the glass to be cut, I browsed around the store. There was a customer checking out, and I thought to myself, "That guy looks so familiar." But I couldn't place him. Then I heard the cashier call him "Stan." *Click!* "Could that be Stan Musial?" I wondered. I went out to my van, just in case, and grabbed a piece of scrap paper. As l came back in, he was leaving. I asked the cashier, "Who was that man?"

She replied, "Stan Musial." Out the door I went. "Excuse me, Mr. Musial?" I asked. He turned around.

"Uh, sir, I know you probably get bothered for this all the time, but I thought I would ask anyway. Could I get your autograph for my son?" I held out the ratty piece of paper, along with a pen. Stan said sure, and he walked to his car and opened the trunk. He asked me what my son's name was, and I told him "Joe." He dug in his trunk and came out with a card with a picture of himself alongside his stats. He personalized it to my son, and signed it. Great! But he didn't stop there. He then dug a baseball out of his trunk, and went on to personalize it to Joe, and signed it also.

I thanked him, and as I drove away on cloud nine, I thought to myself, "If I'd known I was going to get a baseball out of this, I would have told him my son's name was Alan!"

——ALAN STOBIE, St. Louis

In the late seventies or early eighties, at the Baseball Writers' Dinner, it was still at the Gold Room in the Sheraton Jefferson, and Jack Buck was the master of ceremonies. Nancy, my wife, got the tickets late so we were sitting in the very back of the room. They had all the players up on the stage. On each side of the stage, there were these real narrow steps, about eight steps that went up one side and came down the other. We're sitting there at a table of ten. This one father had brought his ten-year-old son along. The boy had a baseball and wanted to get some autographs. There was a rookie outfielder by the name of Duke Carmel who was with the Dodgers sitting at the left end of the stage at the head table. Next to him was Willie Mays. Next to Willie was Hank Aaron. Next to Hank Aaron was Bob Gibson. They'd all gotten awards. That's how they got them to come—they'd give them an award. The father wouldn't go up there with him so I told the boy, "Come on, I'll take you up there 'cause I've got a ball I want to get autographed, too." So we walked up to the edge of the stage. I said, "Hey Duke, Duke." I got his attention, and I held the ball up. He cupped both his hands so I tossed the baseballs up there, and he signed them. I thought he was going to toss them back down to me, but he didn't. I walked up and since I was there, I couldn't miss the chance, so I go and get Willie's and Hank's and Bob Gibson's autograph, too. I just got Gibson's autograph and started to walk down the steps on the other side of the stage and Gibson grabbed me by the arm and nearly jerked my arm out of socket. I said, "What's wrong?" He said, "Look what you started, buddy." I looked around and everybody in the room was lined up behind us to try to come up the steps. So the little boy and I just got down the steps and then Jack came on the P.A. system and told everybody to go sit down because they were going to start serving the food. Then we went to the back of the room, and here Steve Carlton came in and sat at the table next to us so we got his autograph, too.

Bob Burnes was the sports editor of the old *Globe-Democrat* and was head of the Baseball Writers' Dinner every year. In 1981, he got upset because some of the young players were demanding an appearance fee to come in for the awards they were going to give away at the

Baseball Writers' Dinner. Bob got so upset that he canceled the dinner in 1981. That's the only year, I think since World War II that there hasn't been a Baseball Writers' Dinner in St. Louis.

——GENE SIGLOCK, East Alton Illinois

I'm at a Safeway Supermarket in Tempe, Arizona a few years ago when this big guy rounds the corner pushing a cart. I looked closer and realized it was Diamondbacks pitcher, Andy Benes. As we approached each other, I looked at him and said, "Get thyself back to St. Louis, young man." He just looked my way and smiled and said, "I love St. Louis."

——ANDY PONCRACZ, Chandler, Arizona

I think Pujols is my favorite player—I'm a girl so I have to go with the good looking ones. But, he's good, too. I'd have to almost change up and say Matheny is gorgeous, and I love his attitude, and I love his devotion. I have so much respect for the fact that he's a strong Christian guy. I love when he gets up to bat, and they play the song called, *Dive*. It's one of my favorite songs. The song is written by a man by the name of Stephen Curtis Chapman, and it was written when he was up in the mountains with his buddies. They were engulfed with tons of fish in the river, and the people on the shore were watching him and his buddies in the water with their waders on. They're catching these huge fish in the river. Everybody on the shore was screaming at them thinking it was so cool. It was like the analogy that made him write the song because he was saying, "I'll bet those people on the shore who could see us in the water with the fish were just ecstatic, but to be in the water with the fish, there was nothing in the world like that that would compare. In life, so many times we get on the shoreline and we stand back and we watch and we celebrate what's going on. But you know what, God wants us to dive in—to be a part of life and to be a part of the world and to be a part of what's going on and what's happening and not just sit on the sideline and watch." So the song is: "I'm diving in. I'm going deep in over my head. I want to be caught in the flow, caught in the rush...." It's awesome when you really listen to the words and the beat. I think Matheny probably made the choice of having that song played when he goes up to bat. Maybe it gives him that rush.

——HEIDI DINAN, Mrs. Missouri 2004

Dizzy would pitch nine innings, and then the next day if they needed an out in the ninth inning, he would go in and relieve. A guy brought me in a soft-cover book about four years ago. He told me it was a true story about Dizzy Dean. He told me he'd had a hard time finding it and getting it so he told me to be careful with it. When I finished reading the book, I told him, "I'll give you forty dollars for this book that's all beat up." But he wouldn't sell it to me. I think the name was either "Dizzy" or "Dizzy Dean." It was back when he was with the Cardinals and he started going with this girl, Pat. The owner, when he thought the romance was getting serious, called Dizzy into his office. They didn't want him to get married. They told him, "Diz, we hear you're thinking of getting married." Diz said, "That's right." Then the owner told him they didn't want him to marry this girl because we think it would be hard for your career. Dizzy said, "Well, whatever you say doesn't make any difference, 'cause I'm gonna marry Pat." Then the guy dropped the bomb. He said, "I'm going to tell you something. You know that Pat has slept with every Cardinal on the ball club besides you." Dizzy said, "Yeah, I know. That's why I'm going to marry her."

———DON SAFOREK, 79, Barber—still active

My favorite player is Willie McGee, but I don't think he could be a super star in any other city. The type of fans the Cardinals have, the core fan, there's a combination of effort and humility that just resonates with the type of people that are in St. Louis. I haven't seen it displayed quite in that same fashion in other cities. He seems like a shy guy, who just puts his head down, a little bit unorthodox—his playing style isn't your typical "smooth, flawless, Andruw Jones' outfield." I think that's why Bo Hart plays well. When Joe McEwing first came up, he was playing well with the Cardinals. I think it's not coincidental that when he went to the Mets he just didn't keep up that level of production. Certain types of guys are able to tap in and feed off of that.

———BRIAN CARR, 31, Chesterfield, Missouri

Hands down, without a doubt, Lou Brock was my favorite player. He played as I was growing up and started knowing the game. He was just one of the first people I got to see play when I was a kid, and we always sat in the bleachers. There was a baseball card collectors convention down at the Holiday Inn at Lindbergh and I-270. I was in high school, and Vince Coleman was going to be signing. I went down just to get his autograph. I had a bunch of cards. In fact, I had a Tom Seaver rookie card that I remember selling there, for like $60. It was bent up a little bit. As I'm waiting in line for Vince Coleman's autograph, he took a break so they let us get out of line. I went in to play a video game and there were these two little kids in there. They seemed a little young to be off by themselves. These two kids started playing the game with me, the three of us, kind of took turns on one game. Somebody walks in behind me. I didn't see the person, and they said, "Daddy!!! This is our new friend." I turned around and it was Lou Brock. Apparently, they had a babysitter with them that had walked away for a minute. I remember him coming up and thanking me for playing with them. He said, "Is there anything I can do for you?" I said, "No." He ended up buying me a picture of himself and signing it and giving it to me. That was absolutely wonderful.

One time, a classmate and I were arguing about who our favorite player was. It turned out both of our favorite players was Lou Brock. My friend is black, and I'm white, so she was arguing how she had to be a bigger fan because she was the same color.

My dad said, "Lou's good, but you should have seen Stan the Man play." I said, "Well, Keith Hernandez, he's gotta be the best left-handed hitter ever. He sprays the ball, he hits for average and my dad says, "You should have seen Stan the Man play." We would go through the same thing with multiple people—"Willie McGee, boy, he's so great and the fans just love him." And he says, "You should have seen Stan the Man." Everybody worshipped him. As far as my dad was concerned, Stan Musial was Mr. Cardinal.

——**MICHELLE DITTON**, St. Louis

I have had quite a number of favorite players over the years. Some of them are friends. Dave Ricketts as a player and then later as a coach. He is really nice. I know Dave, I know his wife Barbara. Throughout the years he has been a very, very nice man. His family is nice. The game was over and they would go to their cars. If there were 50 kids standing outside waiting for his autograph, he would stay until he signed every one of the 50 autographs. Pete Vuckovich would do that, too!

——**BARB DAVIS**, Bleacher Creature

Probably Stan Musial is my favorite player over the years because of the way he is, and the way he played the game and the way he is when he's not in the game. He's so accessible to everybody. People laugh and say his signature isn't worth much 'cause he signs everything you ever ask him to sign. He's very down to earth.

Kay Hoenig with Tom Pagnozzi.

When we were on a 2000 tour at spring training, we went to bed on Saturday night after having gone to a pre-season game, all was well with the world. We got up on Sunday morning and found out that Walt Jocketty traded Joe McEwing, another very favorite, for Jesse Orosco. I have never let him live that down. Every year we see him at spring training, we bring it up again. He said for us not to feel bad, his son didn't talk to him for two weeks.

——**KAY HOENIG**, Matched-up Cardinal Fan

Just prior to spring training in 1986 or '87, Ozzie Smith and his brother were shopping in a department store at one end of a large mall in St. Louis County. I was head of security for the store, and had stationed a couple of officers in the area, in case people approached Smith and started to bother him while he shopped. I stayed with Ozzie and his brother.

Soon, an older lady in her late 60s or early 70s recognized the Cardinal shortstop and ran up to him. "Are you *really* Ozzie Smith?" she asked. He acknowledged her with a smile and said, "Yes." She then told him that it was her grandson's birthday, and he was sitting in her car in the parking lot. She asked if Ozzie would go out and tell this little boy "Happy Birthday," assuring him it would take only a couple of minutes.

Ozzie turned to his brother, handed him the various sweatsuit items he was carrying, and said he would be right back. Then he left the sporting goods department with the lady.

Ozzie returned…about 20 minutes later. He smiled and said, "The lady was parked at the *other* end of the mall." He'd had to walk past hundreds of shoppers.

Ozzie's brother asked, "What did the kid say when you wished him Happy Birthday?"

Ozzie laughed and said, "Nothing. He just sat there in shock."

I told Smith that even though the visit took 20 minutes of his time and the little boy was speechless, he will forever be telling his children and grandchildren about the time when he was a kid and Ozzie Smith wished him a happy birthday. I know I won't forget Ozzie's act of kindness.

——**JIM KEITH**, Sulpher Springs, Missouri

Willie McGee is my favorite all-time Cardinal. I love Willie McGee. He went out every day and gave the one hundred and ten percent. He was so humble and he never wanted to be in the limelight. He just gave his all, and he's a good man and a good person. When Bud Smith came up, he wanted number 52, and there was such an uproar with the Cardinal Nation—they didn't necessarily retire Willie's number, but they put it on hold and said no one could take it. That's when Bud went from fifty-two to fifty-one.

——**CARRI COFFEE**, The Whistle Lady from the 375 Gang

My favorite Cardinal player over the years probably is Ozzie Smith. He handled himself so well. The reason it's Ozzie is because he, basically at his height, not being a very tall person, played shortstop so good. He was so awesome on Opening Days for St. Louis. We'd sell out because we'd come to watch him do backflips when he went out to field his position on Opening Days. He really was the franchise. I think the whole city of St. Louis knew that. We knew he was never going to leave, and that's the way we felt. I really liked him.

During my younger days, there were a lot of players who stood out. There was one player that I really hated to see go, Andy Van Slyke. He played left field really good. It killed me when he went to Pittsburgh. Everybody always told me I looked like Andy.

——**KENNY WALLACE**, NASCAR Driver

In '61, I was in Washington with the Peace Corps, and Sargent Shriver had a party. There were cabinet officers there, Robert McNamara, Stewart Udall, and that crowd. Suddenly everybody is starting to move over to the front door because somebody is coming in. My wife said to me, "Who is that?" I looked and said, "Oh my

God. No wonder they're all moving over. It's Stan Musial." She said, "Who's he?" She went over to get his autograph, and she said, "Make it out to Frank." He said, "Okay. How old is your little boy?" She said, "Thirty-seven." I met him that night and reminded him that I had seen him play at the L.A. Coliseum. I had seen him thrown out of the game—the only time. He'd made the remark that he'd never been thrown out of a major league park, and I reminded him of that, and he said, "Well, it wasn't a major league park." What happened was he objected to a call at the plate. I have no idea what he said, but he protested vigorously and they ejected him.

——**FRANK MANKIEWICZ**, Former presidential campaign manager for Bobby Kennedy and George McGovern

My favorite player has got to be Dizzy Dean. That was my first hero. When I was a kid, Dizzy and Paul Dean were on the cover of the Grape Nuts box, and I told my mother and grandmother, "We've got to have Grape Nuts." There was also a sport shirt which was Dizzy and Paul, "Me and Paul." This phrase came from when Dizzy was interviewed at the beginning of the '34 season, "I'm gonna win about thirty games and Paul will win about twenty something." So "me and Paul" became the slogan for that year. He did win thirty. Dizzy could deliver, and he was colorful. You looked forward to seeing him

——**VICTOR GOLD**, Nationally Syndicated Columnist

I hate to name a favorite player because every time I had one, he got traded. Ray Lankford, of the recent Cardinals, was my favorite. The very first Cardinal cruise we went on, he was there and he just treated me like the guy next door. They say he was real hard to get at the stadium, but if he saw me, he'd come over. I could bring my kids over and he'd sign a card. I don't want the Barry Bonds of the world. I'd rather have a Ray Lankford or somebody who wants to sign for the fans. To me that's worth ten times as much as a Barry Bonds autograph. I like Joe McGrane, and I don't know why. He was a Cardinal. When I was a young kid, I liked Keith Hernandez. I guess that was because I lived in Hernando, Mississippi, and that's the only tie I can think of it.

It's gotten a lot easier over the Internet for me to acquire different pieces of memorabilia. My favorite picture is a picture of me and Stan The Man, that he signed. That's one of the few times I've ever been tongue-tied. What do you say to Stan Musial? I'm not Catholic, but to me that's probably like meeting the Pope or something. For the Cardinal Nation, that's the top guy. He was Mr. Cardinal. He asked me where I was from and talked to me, and I just was tongue-tied. I didn't know what to say. That was only two or three years ago at a Winter Warm-Up.

———GEORGE McINGVALE, 34, Title Company Owner

I'd say probably Bob Gibson is my favorite Cardinal because of his work attitude and the way he played the game. He was a very intimidating individual and a hard worker. I particularly liked it when he broke his leg and wore the sign around his neck to answer all the questions the media was asking him.

After he had broken his leg, he came into the clubhouse, and people were asking him questions, and kept repeating the same types of questions. So he just cut out a piece of paper or cardboard and hung it around his neck with: "Yes, it hurts. No, I don't know how long it'll be."

———EDNA TETLEY, Cardinal fan

I started collecting bats when McGwire hit his five hundredth home run. The bat when he hit sixty-two. The fifty-fifty-fifty club bat. I have this shrine in my home basement. I've also got a lot of sports paraphernalia in my bar. I've got a Mark McGwire shrine with all sorts of different pictures of his accomplishments. I even had two cars of mine—I got the first and last Cardinal license plates. I got two for home and two for here. One of them was "SVNT" and one was "7T"—they are on both my vehicles.

———RON DEMPSEY, Owner, Playboy Club, St. Louis

As a kid I was a major Cardinal fan. I went to school at St. Gabriel's with Dickie Musial, and every now and then his father would come to pick him up, and we were all excited about it. Stan Musial was the greatest thing ever to hit St. Louis. It's kind of interesting the impact that Mark McGwire had was very similar to Musial's impact when I was growing up. At the end of the day, you would get questions like, "What did Musial do?" first, and then "Did the Cardinals win?" When McGwire played for the Cardinals, the first question people asked was, "What did McGwire do?" and then "How did the Cardinals do?" People who didn't know anything about baseball would always ask about McGwire or Musial. They didn't know how many balls it took to get to first base, but they wanted to know what Musial did. The same thing, they wanted to know what McGwire did.

—————DON MARQUESS, Card Maven, St. Louis

In 1998, I pulled into the gas station near my house around 7:30 P.M. I had the radio tuned to the baseball game, and I paid attention as the Cardinals put the first two batters on in the fifth inning. I hopped out of the van, but left the radio on loud enough to hear as I started pumping gas.

Nearby, I heard the thumpa-thumpa of loud rap music as an old truck rumbled to a stop at an adjacent gas pump. Annoyed, I turned the radio up louder. Ray Lankford was the third batter in the inning. He walked on four pitches. Now the bases were loaded and nobody was out. Next up…Mark McGwire.

As I strained to hear, the rap music suddenly stopped. A second later, the truck had also tuned in the ball game. On a hot, steamy summer night in St. Louis, I wondered how many people stopped what they were doing to see, or hear, what McGwire would do.

He struck out. I looked over at the "rap" truck and a young man looked at me. He threw up his hands and laughed. "Maybe next time," he yelled.

When writers or movie-makers get sentimental about baseball, I usually don't like it. I never sat through Ken Burns' nine-hour PBS documentary and I couldn't finish Roger Kahn's *The Boys of Summer.* I did like *Field of Dreams*, but thought the father-son plot was too syrupy. However, like it or not, I realize that I have marked key events of my own life with baseball

—————JEFFREY FISTER, St. Louis, Cardinal Fan

Chapter Nine

Cardinalpalooza

SHE'S SO BEAUTIFUL—SHE'D BRING A TEAR TO A GLASS EYE!

Heidi Dinan

Native Californian and O'Fallon (Missouri) resident, Heidi Dinan is the reigning Mrs. Missouri.

Several years ago, I was working for Michelin Tire in Greenville, South Carolina. One of my many customers was Jeff Dinan of Friends Tire Company in St. Louis. He would tell me all about the Cardinals and Jack Buck. I didn't even have a clue who Jack Buck was. I really didn't care. I was raised in California. But even out there, we lived in a different area than Los Angeles so we never went to a baseball game. I was into ballet. I had nothing to do with baseball.

I was in accounts receivable, and Jeff would call in to place orders, and also I would apply their checks from his tire company. We'd talk about that on occasion, just different business transactions. While I'd be working on a project on the computer, he'd say, "Are you almost done?" "Yeah, I'm almost done. Hold on just a second." While he was holding, he'd tell me what the Cardinals were doing and tell me I had to watch the game that night.

When I started talking to Jeff, he was so excited about baseball, about the Cardinals, and he loved St. Louis. I think the reason he loved St. Louis is just because the Cardinals were part of it. He'd send me faxes all the time with the latest Cardinal scores. He mailed me a Cardinal hat one time, and I kept it up at work at Michelin. When I kind of started liking Jeff a little bit more than just as a customer, I would wear red every Tuesday. I don't know why I picked Tuesday, but I would red every single week on Tuesday for the Cardinals. He'd ask me on Tuesdays, "Are you wearing red?" I'd never met him.

Jeff kept telling me I had to come to St. Louis. I thought, "I am not coming to St. Louis for some tire guy." I had never even seen what he looked like so I thought "absolutely not." It was right after September 11, 2001, when he went out to South Carolina to meet me, just as friends. The season was over by then so for the whole winter the Cardinals were all we talked about.

My very first Cardinal game was Opening Day of the season the next year. We were just dating then. Just to look around and see all the people in red, and people standing on the street just sporting their jerseys and yelling "Yea Cardinals." You know how the crowd can be down there. I was so in awe. To be down with everybody, with the Arch in the background, to see the fans and the enthusiasm, and the ball caps—it was beautiful.

Then we went to just about every game that year. For one game, he had on-the-field batting practice tickets from KMOX from one of his buddies, so Jeff, my daughter from a previous marriage who was six years old then, and I went down on the field. We were just standing there. Jeff had planned this with my daughter, Kelsi, and I didn't know anything about it. Jeff pulls out of his bag a baseball and hands it to my daughter. It's the Cardinal ball. His friend from KMOX was there with the camera and said, "Let me get a picture of Heidi and Kelsi." Then he told Jeff to get in the picture, too. We had the team behind us batting. We're standing there and Jeff said, "Okay, honey, look at the ball." I said, "Okay, it says Cardinals." I held the ball up to the camera so they could read it. He said, "No, read the ball." "I did, sweetheart, it says Cardinals." And we're smiling for this picture. "No. Read the ball, honey." So I

looked at it, and he had written on the ball, "Heidi, will you marry me? I love you." I was so excited. I think my smile was so big that he couldn't read my lips when I said, "Of course." So he asked, "Honey will you marry me?" So we were hugging and kissing and my daughter is rolling her eyes like "Okay, can we please get on with things here?"

A JEWEL OF A GUY

Bob Beumer

Bob Beumer owns Hamilton Jewelers in St. Louis, a long-time sponsor of Cardinal baseball, even before Beumer bought the store from Dorian Magwitz in 1987.

Bob Beumer and Whitey Herzog

Hamilton Jewelers have done various things with the Cardinals over the years. We do the Cardinal Rookie of the Year award. Now we give out gift certificates to the ball players for before the game Buck at Bat that we sponsor. Jack Buck gave us a lot of good sponsorship and fond memories and good PR for many, many years. Dorian Magwitz is kind of an interesting name, and Buck would always say Magawitz —he always put the "A" in the middle. It's amazing how much business we have gotten out of southern Illinois and Indiana. We are a big Rolex dealer. We have always done Rolex ads and people come in because of Cardinal baseball. It's always been interesting the relationships you form. Gary Carter is going into the Hall of Fame this year. I got to meet Gary with his $100 gift certificate the first time and then he bought many, many things for his wife and girls as he came into town.

Andre Dawson, when he played for the Cubs, was having a big anniversary and Diane DiPino, Frank's wife (the left-handed pitcher that had come from the Cubs to the Cardinals), and I got to be good friends. She knew Dawson's wife well so she picks up a pretty good sized bracelet, very easily 5 figures. She tells Andre that this is what his wife wants for her anniversary. Well, Andre, as a good husband does, takes a look at it and says, "Yeah, that would be great. Can I use this $100 gift certificate I got last night?" He applied it to the $18,000 purchase.

Jersey Joe Cunningham is my favorite player over the years. He is a good friend of mine. He could have probably been rated very heavily except for the one guy who played in front of him, Stan Musial. Ozzie Smith has always been a favorite of mine because he has always been a gentleman in my store. He was a real neat guy and he would talk with people. Whitey Herzog is always a stitch. He comes in the store and you can say "How's the weather, Whitey?" About 45 minutes later, he would kind of wrap up the story. One of my favorite moments was about a week before Christmas, we had Ozzie and Whitey in the store at the same time. Whitey literally held court. This was the week before Christmas when we were wall-to-wall people. Whitey had his arm around Ozzie and he's just telling stories. It was like being in the locker room.

Before the $100 gift certificates, we used to give watches. In the middle '80s Dorian Magwitz would get a deal with Bulova or Wittenauer and he would give everybody the same watch. The guys would say, "I don't want this watch, I want a watch for my wife." Pretty soon we had about 100 watches, all the same, that we couldn't do anything with. Now these guys come in and they can get something for themselves, they can get something for their wives. We get players, we get managers, we get coaches. I had a neat experience with Bobby Valentine when he was coaching the Mets. He came in and it was his anniversary the next day and we bailed him out.

My second year in spring training at St. Petersburg and Dorian calls me and says, "Don't tell anybody, but Willie McGee is going to get married and he needs rings down here to take a look at." I went down there and brought all these things down. We go in the clubhouse and here is Willie McGee picking out his engagement ring sitting on one of the Cardinal trunks in the locker room. Don't tell his wife.

QUICK HITS AND INTERESTING BITS

George Will spent a lot of time here in Washington sneering about how he was a Cub fan, and the Cub fans had this Emil Verban Society, which was irony. They named it that because they knew Verban was a failure. The fact is he's got a pretty good line. He played for the Cardinals for a while. Vic Gold was a big Republican writer and politician. He and I are different parties, but we agreed that we were surely united on the Cardinals. We decided we would start a small Cardinal club. We thought maybe we'd get ten—twelve guys every six months or so and have lunch and talk about the team. Somebody heard about it and put a little item in the Washington Post. We had like a hundred and fifty members at the first meeting, and we have well over three hundred now. It probably got started about fifteen years ago. The Stan Musial Society has only one bylaw: "We will meet occasionally!"

You can hear the Cardinal games here in D.C. on KMOX if you drive up by the Cathedral at night because it's the highest place in the city. You have to sit in your car. I went up there one night in August and noticed three or four other cars are parked. That's where the fans are gathered.

I only get to go to St. Louis and see a game one weekend a year.
——**FRANK MANKIEWICZ**, Former presidential campaign manager for
Bobby Kennedy and George McGovern

The Cubs fans are very loyal to their team but it is a different thing. It's almost like it's a long suffering thing that they wear as a badge of honor, the fact that they keep coming to the games and they lose every year. They are turning it around and they have a real chance now and in the future. With Cardinal fans, we take pride in the fact that we are Midwestern, that a lot of the ballplayers like living here because comparatively we don't bug them as much as other people would and we don't get down on them as fast. Sometimes I see that in a negative light though because it's almost like you can be mediocre here and get away with it better than you can some other places.
——**GARY CANNON**, Cardinal fan

Cardinal fans know about the game, we understand how it works. We understand why we have a squeeze bunt, why you would walk somebody. The history of the Cardinals in St. Louis, the great players that have come through here. The players stay even though they can get more money somewhere else. It's an absolute love affair between the players and the fans and you just don't get that anywhere else. A true Cardinal fan would never throw a home run ball back on the field because that is something to treasure, to keep.

——CATHY LEONARD, Bleacher Season Ticket Holder

Meeting Stan the Man was neat. My father took me out of school in 5th grade in the Washington area. The principal asked why I was leaving, and I said, "I have to go meet Stan the Man." I didn't necessarily understand the concept of that. I said to my father when we were meeting him, "Like, isn't he supposed to be playing the harmonica or something? It was really cool. He was in this sort of maroon jacket. He was older. I said, "This is a guy is who supposed to be one of the greatest baseball players of all-time?" It was very hard for me to sort of wrap my head around it. My dad was super excited. He was like a little kid. It was then that I knew that it was baseball and academics that had to be a priority.

I think any ballplayer would agree that the Cardinal fans are the best fans there are. If you go anywhere, and you see another Cardinal fan, it's like a club—always there to support each other. We have met people at games that my dad has kept in touch with, he has helped them out, they have helped him out. It's a community unto itself. I feel very lucky to be a Cardinal fan. I couldn't imagine being a fan of any other team.

——DANIELLE CHERRICK, 21, Rockville, Maryland;
Barnard College Senior, majoring in Neuroscience

I was seven years old when I saw my first Cardinals game in 1964. The Cards were something like 13 games out in August and beat the first-place Phillies the day we went. We lived several hours from St. Louis. After the game, I begged my dad to bring me to another game that year. As he told the story, he looked down at me and somehow just couldn't say no, although he really didn't want to do it. So, he had a bright idea. He told me he'd bring me to another game that year *if* the Cardinals got into first place (of course thinking he was totally safe since they were well out of it late in the season and were trailing several teams). Well, as fate had it, the Phillies collapsed and the Cardinals got hot and went into a tie for first with three or four games left. I woke him up at 4:30 A.M. the next morning and said, "Let's go." He tried to bribe me, but it was no use. He got up, we drove to St. Louis, and the Cards went on to win the World Series. That was many years ago. I have a family of my own now, and I took them to the August 13, 1997, game at Busch Stadium. The Cards were playing the New York Mets, and when they stuck us with three runs in the first I found myself thinking, "Oh, no. Not one of *those* games." But then Mark McGwire came up to bat in the bottom of the inning with a man on base. My son Adam's eyes came alive. After Mac swung and missed, I told Adam to remember that no ballplayer gets a hit every time. He looked at me in disbelief and said, "Dad, he's gonna hit a homer. No doubt." I turned to watch another pitch and BOOM-upper deck! We went wild.

McGwire had another home run and a single that night. Unfortunately, he struck out in the 10th and the Mets won the game. Afterwards, we were waiting for my wife to return from the ladies' room. As the crowd streamed by, I looked down and noticed that Adam was crying, although he was trying to hide it. When I asked him what was wrong, he said, "I hate the Mets." I told him teams have players from everywhere, that the Mets even have a player from St. Louis, and all the teams are just trying to do their best. That's what makes baseball so much fun. He said he didn't care; they should have let McGwire hit another homer anyway. Looking down at him, the tears in his eyes under a shiny new red batting helmet, I found myself getting a little misty as well. I remember a few years ago another boy was at the ballpark with his dad, saying much the same thing. Now my dad is gone, but these bittersweet baseball memories will never leave me.

——MIKE RAY, Branson, Missouri

The Cardinal fans are great fans. They stick behind their team whether they're winning or losing. In the late-seventies, and there were very many good teams around then, the Cardinals were not very good, but that's when I first became a fan. My mom and my grandma were big Cardinal fans. I guess it was just that their baseball games were always on and I learned to appreciate it from them. I have scorebooks that I had when I was a kid that I used to keep score of games that were on TV and

the radio. I have every scorecard from every game I've been to from 1976 through the present. They're all put away in little file boxes, all in order. Over the years, I've seen players, and we'd be talking about a certain game or something, and I'd get the score-cards out to look at. I'd remember thinking I might have been at that game so I look through the cards and sure enough.

I still collect baseball cards. As a child I collected the Topps cards, the packs. I had a few hundred then but never got the complete sets. But in the last fifteen years or so, I buy the complete Topps set every year.

——**KAREN DONTON**, Anheuser-Busch Executive

Some people would be smoking in the seating area and would try to hide that. I've seen them try to hide it down by the side of their seats, and turn their wrists where you can't really see it. I'll see them look back at me to see if I'm looking at them and they'll take a puff. I can smell that a mile away. I'll go down and say, "Sir, you need to put out your cigarette." They'll say, "I don't have one." I'll say, "What's in your other hand?"

Smoking was allowed until '93, but if we received a complaint from another guest saying the smoke was starting to bother them, then we would go down and tell them they needed to go upstairs to the concourse to smoke. To this day, that's where the smoking area is. Then they began changing that rule all throughout Major League baseball. In the beginning, when they first implemented it, people said that since it was an open-air facility, they could smoke. At first, a lot of people were a little bit upset about it, but for the most part, as time went on, and as they realized more and more that a lot of places were becoming "no smoking" areas so they resigned themselves to the fact that's what they had to do. I don't think many people decided they weren't going to come to the game since they couldn't smoke, maybe a few, but I never encountered that.

——**CARRIE MOSCHINO**, former Cardinal usher, Mt. Vernon, Illinois

If everybody could be Willie McGee, what a great sport baseball would be. He knew he could play but he was very humble and never, never came across as arrogant. Pete Rose is a sad situation. He was one of the best selling points for baseball when he was playing there has ever been. He hustled. He never threw away times at bat either. That's why he has the record. It didn't matter what the score was, he wanted to bat that fifth time and get another hit. He truly had that in his mind from the time he started, he had that drive. In 1989, Pete Rose signed an agreement that allows him to keep telling a lie; that was part of the agreement; he can keep denying that he did something that he knows he did. They tried to frame a guilty man.

——GARY CANNON, 60, Bethalto, Illinois

I moved to St. Louis in 1974. The first year I lived in St. Louis, I went to all eighty-one home games—that was my goal in life. That's when you could buy a bleacher ticket for a buck. I loved it. You had a lot of regulars out there. Still some of the best fans at the ballpark are in the bleachers.

There was a gentleman from the East Side they called the Mayor of the Bleachers. He had gone to every ball game back to World War II. He used to sit in the pavilion in right field at the old ballpark. He passed away a few years ago but there is a plaque where he used to sit with his radio every night. They put a plaque up when he died, just like a plaque for Jack Buck in the press box. I sat there with him on several occasions.

——NORM RICHARDS, Canton, Missouri Native

About a dozen years ago, I was in a bar called Good Times in Lowden, Iowa when a local came in and said, "Oh, Mr. Cardinal Fan is back in the area." So I said, "How are you doin'." He said, "I'm doin' great. My Cubbies scored 22 runs this afternoon." I waited a few minutes and then yelled down at him, "Hey Shawn. Did the Cubs win today?" The place cracked up because most of the people remembered that about a dozen years before the Phillies beat the Cubs 23-22.

——DICK FOX, Retired Cardinal Fan

My wife and I started dating during the 1982 World Series, Cardinals and Brewers. I was doing a lot of surgery at that time. Pam was a nurse at the hospital. I had done surgery on a patient. Later, I called back up to the hospital to see how the patient was doing. Pam said, "Oh, she's doing fine." I asked, "Did you have to give her any pain medication?" She said, "Yes." I said, "When did you have to do it?" She said, "About the bottom of the fifth." I knew right then and there that was the girl for me to marry.

——DR. BILL HAYES, Herrin, Illinois

JACK BUCK WAS GOD'S WAY OF BEING NICE TO CARDINAL FANS

(You didn't really think we were going to omit Jack Buck from this book, did you? The following was featured in the author's *Remembering Jack Buck* book of 2002.)

Susan O'Leary

Susan O'Leary of St. Louis is the mother of John O'Leary who was badly burned in a home accident in 1987. Many people credit Jack Buck with inspiring young John to fight for his life.

Our son John, who is soon going to be twenty-six, was badly burned on January 17, 1987. It was about nine o'clock on a Saturday morning, and there was a fire burning in our fireplace in the family room. John, at age nine, had the curiosity as to what would happen if you took some paper and lit it and poured gasoline on it. He went out into the garage, poured gasoline on this piece of lit paper, the Saturday comic strip. Of course, before the gasoline even hit the paper, the fumes ignited and just exploded spewing gasoline all over John. Immediately he was inflamed completely. He ran into the house, screaming, and our son Jim threw him down on the rug and burned his own hands trying to put the flames out on John. John was at that time burned on a hundred percent of his body, eighty-five percent were third-degree burns, and fifteen percent were second degree burns, so he was burned all over. They didn't expect John to survive the two-minute ambulance ride from our house to St. John's Hospital.

That night there was some kind of big sports dinner. A friend of mine, Colleen, who is Red Schoendienst's daughter, told her mother about it that day. That night Mary Schoendienst told Jack what had happened. Then on Monday or Tuesday, Jack appeared at John's room in the burn unit at St. John's. At that time you had to put on a mask, and hat, and gloves, and booties just to come into the room. He came in, and John had swollen to about twice his usual size. The only thing that could be seen on John were his eyelids and his lips. He was on a respirator so he couldn't talk—he was not in a coma. But Jack came in, and just talked to him, "John, you know when you get yourself out of here, and you're feeling up to it, I want you to come down to the ballpark, and I want you and your dad to come up, and I want you to sit next to me in the broadcast booth." We found out years later, that when he left John's little cubicle, he walked up to the main station, and said to the nurse, "That kid's not gonna make it. He's really messed up, isn't he?" The nurse said, "Yeah. John is going to die. He's not going to make it." Jack just grabbed a towel and put his head down on it and sobbed, not knowing us, not knowing John, just having driven out there. He came out another two or three times to the hospital. He brought Ozzie Smith. He brought Larry Stallings of the football Cardinals. His wife Carole came out a couple of times to deliver a tee shirt to John or something else from Jack.

Before John was able to go down to one of the games, he started getting baseballs in the mail. We knew they were from Jack Buck; although he claims he didn't send them. We knew that Jack was doing it. He would say to John, "All you have to do is write a thank-you note to the person who sent you the ball, and you'll get another one." The burns were terrible, and John lost all of his fingers, but he would write those thank-you notes and three or four days later, he would get another autographed ball.

We took him down to the ball field, and the first night he just was there in the booth. Then there were other occasions when he went down early with his dad. He and his dad and Jack Buck and Red Schoendienst, and maybe Ozzie Smith, sat and watched batting practice, just the five of them. John periodically would go up and visit in the booth throughout the years, just say "hi" to him.

At Jack's induction into the Hall of Fame, Jack said something to the effect that "I have been called a hero. But I'm not a hero. The real hero is John O'Leary who's back in St. Louis and encountered massive burns and is overcoming them." Can you believe that Jack Buck made reference to John at his induction into the Hall of Fame? When John graduated from St. Louis University, three years ago, Jack and

Carole were invited to a dinner for John at Busch's Grove restaurant, which they couldn't attend because he was broadcasting a game that night. When we got to the little hut at Busch's Grove, there was this present on the table. The maitre'd said, "Mrs. Buck brought this over about an hour ago for John." When John opened it later, he found that Jack had given him the Waterford cut-glass baseball that he received when he was inducted into the Hall of Fame. It was incredible. He's just an absolutely incredible, amazing person. There is no doubt in my mind. I just wrote his wife a note and told her that it had been a privilege and a joy and a thrill and a blessing to have had the relationship we had with her husband, and that there was no doubt in my mind that Jack was most definitely a part of John's mastering his comeback from a terrible, terrible accident with the incredible burns. John is the most seriously burned patient that has ever survived at St. John's Hospital. They've got that in his record. I have talked to people, and they have said that there is no one else. A doctor said there may have been two since who have come back but that neither of them have the mobility and have the life that John has. I told Carole that there's no doubt in my mind that Jack's goodness and his interest in John was one of those parts of the puzzle that helped John come through and ultimately live the life he is living right now. John was in the hospital four months and Jack was very faithful to him throughout that time, whether it was a phone call or coming out, by himself or bringing someone else with him, to visit John.

In a local story recently, John simply said that Jack Buck had been to him like a grandparent who lived out of town, who you loved very much, but didn't get to see. When he died, it really hurt. John said what Jack Buck really did, "he visited me, and he sent me balls, but his interest in me changed so many things in my life and made me realize what I could do for other people." After John's party that Jack couldn't attend, the next day we were having Sunday brunch in our house, and the phone rang. It was Jack and he wanted to know how John's party was, if you can imagine.

All of us, like all of St. Louis and so much of the world, has just been saddened and so touched by the passing of this man who was so good to people he had never met before. That was the amazing thing—his compassion for people that he had never even known before.

There is no doubt that we all feel like he's a part of our family. We would talk about how unusual it was for someone to have an interest in someone they didn't even know. I remember saying to John's doctor, "Why are you letting somebody come in here?" We had found out right before he got there that he was coming in. I said, "How can you let Jack Buck come in here when you're telling me that John might die. Any little germ could cause the end of him in hours. How can you let someone else come in?" Doctor Vatche Ayvazian, Burn Specialist, said, "You never know when just that one moment, that one visit, that one person, is going to add a spark that will just contribute to someone's ability and their decision to keep fighting." Really we feel so strongly that he did that for John. We were "family from afar." There's no doubt about it. They were certainly always in our hearts.

I'm thankful that my son is the person that he is, and to just be able to attribute a great portion of that to the encouragement and the interest that Jack took in John. He had him on the radio his first time when he sat by his side. It was the summer after the accident and he and his dad sat in the booth. We were in the Anheuser-Busch booth looking over there constantly. It went fifteen innings, and John was by Jack Buck's side the whole time. He was on the radio talking about his dad saying that he had beaten him in a footrace a week before. I can remember John saying, "We did have a footrace, and I won." So for a little boy nine years old who had been through all that, Jack Buck was very perceptive and like in everything else, he was able to get into the heart of where John was and say something pertinent like that. John would go down and visit him periodically in the booth after he was out of the hospital. Jack would mention John, "My friend, John O'Leary, back in St. Louis," or "I wonder if my friend, John O'Leary, is listening to this game." So he was just very sweet with him all the way through. That was fifteen years ago.

It's almost like Jack Buck was an angel.

TO BE CONTINUED!

We hope you have enjoyed the first annual *For Cardinals Fans Only*. You can be in next year's edition if you have a neat story. You can email it to printedpage@cox.net (put "Cardinals Fan" in the Subject line) or call the author directly at 602-738-5889.

For information on ordering more copies of *For Cardinal Fans Only,* as well as any of the author's other best-selling books, go to www.fandemonium.net.

The fine art baseball photographs in this book were provided by Don Marquess of Marquess Gallery at Union Station in St. Louis.

(314) 973-1440
www.baseballfineart.com
www.marquessgallery.com